THE ROAD TO RUIN

Niki Savva is one of the most senior correspondents in the Canberra Press Gallery. She was twice political correspondent on *The Australian*, and headed up the Canberra bureaus of both the *Herald Sun* and *The Age*. When family tragedy forced a career change, she became Peter Costello's press secretary for six years and was then on John Howard's staff for three. Her work has brought her into intimate contact with the major political players of the last 35 years. She is now a regular columnist for *The Australian*, and often appears on ABC TV's *Insiders* as well as on political panels on Sky News.

The Road to Ruin

HOW TONY ABBOTT AND PETA CREDLIN DESTROYED THEIR OWN GOVERNMENT

Niki Savva

SCRIBE

Melbourne • London

Scribe Publications Pty Ltd
18–20 Edward St, Brunswick, Victoria 3056, Australia

Scribe Publications UK Ltd
2 John St, Clerkenwell, London, WC1N 2ES, United Kingdom

First published by Scribe 2016
Reprinted 2016 (twice)

Typeset in 12/17pt Adobe Garamond Pro by the publishers

Printed and bound in Australia by Griffin Press

The paper this book is printed on is certified against the Forest
Stewardship Council® Standards. Griffin Press holds FSC chain of
custody certification SGS-COC-005088. FSC promotes
environmentally responsible, socially beneficial and economically
viable management of the world's forests.

Scribe Publications is committed to the sustainable use of natural resources and
the use of paper products made responsibly from those resources.

9781925321401 (paperback)
9781925307542 (e-book)

A CiP entry for this title is available from the National Library of Australia

scribepublications.com.au
scribepublications.co.uk

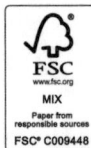

For Andreas and Elpiniki,
whose courage made everything possible

Contents

Prologue

On the night of 15 July 2014, *The Australian* marked its 50th birthday with a star-studded celebration (is there any other kind?) at Sydney's Hordern Pavilion.

The prime minister, Tony Abbott, was standing near my seat at my designated table, talking to *The Australian*'s editor-at-large, Paul Kelly. As I approached him, the prime minister called out cheerily: 'Niki, how are you?'

Instantly, my protective radar went up. The last time I had seen him, a few months before, at a drinks function in the cabinet anteroom for women in the media, he could barely bring himself to speak to me. I found out later that my invitation, and that of fellow columnist Grace Collier, had been prompted by Sophie Mirabella over drinks, after a dinner in Mirabella's honour a few nights before.

As I was standing near the entrance to the anteroom with the ABC's Alex Kirk, Abbott hadn't been able to avoid me, but it was like trying to talk to a block of wood. His face was smothered in thick orange-coloured pancake make-up, his hair coloured and glued into place with hairspray. He looked like he had walked out of Madame Tussauds, which was apt, given what he had been and what he had become. He was not the Tony Abbott many of us knew — the larrikin, unkempt, undisciplined politician, the man known for his many acts of kindness, including to myself when my mother, Elpiniki, was ill. He had become someone, or something, else. It was Tony Abbott acting as prime minister.

He stood side-on to me, directing all his remarks to Alex, speaking to me only when I interposed. He moved on quickly to another group, after making small talk with Alex about her recent long holiday overseas.

After he moved on, the *Sunday Telegraph*'s political correspondent, the irrepressible Samantha Maiden, plonked herself beside me because she said she wanted to see the fireworks when his chief of staff, Peta Credlin, entered the room. Maiden was friendly with Credlin, but, like any good journo, had a healthy streak of mischief. 'There won't be any fireworks, Sam,' I said. There weren't. When she arrived, the three of us talked about shopping on the internet for clothes, then a bit later Credlin spoke to the gathering about the record number of women chiefs of staff in the Coalition government. There was no mention of the record low number of women in cabinet. Oops.

So this night in July, a few months later at *The Australian*'s celebration, I was on my guard as I stretched out my hand to shake Abbott's. In the middle of the handshake, with no preamble, he said, 'Now, Niki, can you please stop criticising my chief of staff?'

'Why?' I asked.

'Because,' he said, 'sometimes, when ministers tell you things, they are not true.'

'You know what, Tony,' I said, 'sometimes they are.'

I was set to launch into a lecture about the way they were running the government, what they were doing wrong, but bit my tongue, saying instead: 'Anyway, Tony, this is a conversation for another time. We are here to celebrate a great occasion. Now, when did you start working for *The Australian*?' Nineteen eighty-nine, he said. Well, I said, I began there in 1970.

At my table, I had a terse exchange with Bill Shorten over Clive Palmer, who was then doing what he does best—causing mayhem. I told Shorten that Palmer was a bully and that Labor was being cowardly by not taking him on. Shorten tried to suggest that the only reason I was being critical of Palmer was because he was making life uncomfortable for the government. After what had just happened with Abbott, I was in no mood to cop any BS from BS or anyone else, so I made him retract in front of everyone at the table, which included the *Daily Telegraph*'s then editor, Paul 'Boris' Whittaker.

The guest speaker, Noel Pearson, had made a brilliant speech that night. As per usual. Everyone was, rightly, fawning over him. I was preparing to do a bit of fawning myself when Pearson walked over, said hello, then volunteered how much he enjoyed reading my columns. Wow. I did not even think he knew or remembered who I was. Others said similarly kind things. I was on a high, very pleased with myself after having put down both the prime minister and the opposition leader. I even made up with an old adversary, Paul Keating. Keating was in the distance talking to someone, so I went up, tapped him on the back, and told him I was going to say hello even if he yelled at me. The last time I had seen him was on a plane when I was with Peter Costello. Keating had cut me dead that time as he shook hands with Peter.

This night, at the Hordern Pavilion, he was pleased to see me. 'Hello, love,' Keating said, 'I was going to drop you a note.' I assumed this was after a column running off Kerry O'Brien's interviews for the ABC, where Keating had held up my front-page story in the *Sun News Pictorial* from the 1987 election, declaring,

'Howard: My Sums Wrong'. Along with so much else that went wrong—like having no health policy, all precipitated by the madness of the Joh-for-PM campaign—the double-counting in the tax policy, which Keating discovered, helped kill Howard's chances in that campaign. Keating said in the O'Brien interview that it was his favourite front page of all time, so I had recounted how it came about, in a longish piece for *The Australian*. Or perhaps Keating's better humour with me was because in my book, *So Greek,* I had recounted a dinner party at Kerry Packer's home where Packer 'commissioned' Paul Lyneham to do a *60 Minutes* special on Keating's piggery. That story confirmed all Keating's conspiracy theories. All my other sins had been erased—for the time being, at least.

I should have known it would go a bit pear-shaped. Clutching a half-full glass of white wine, I went to speak to my friend and mentor over many decades, Laurie Oakes, who was chatting to Peter van Onselen, the MC for the night. In the middle of a sentence, my glass slid out of my hand and smashed loudly on the concrete floor, sending glass and grog everywhere. 'Boy,' said van Onselen, 'I'm glad I'm not drinking.' I had a choice: to cop to the drunkenness charge, or plead arthritis—I could own up to being either infirm or inebriated. 'It's my one and only glass all night,' I protested. It had been. Like most young journos of my day, I used to binge drink, but thankfully grew out of it, encouraged on the path to near-teetotalism by massive migraines. Laurie said, helpfully, that if I had drunk more it wouldn't have happened. This was similar to a quip Laurie once made after I complained to him that evil tweeters were accusing me of having a drinking problem. 'Your problem is, you don't drink enough,' he said.

Although this was mortifying, it did not completely mar what was an otherwise splendid night, but hubris never goes punished.

Thanks to a prime minister acting like a raging bull and full of it, my days as a columnist could have ended early, if not for the support of the paper's then editor-in-chief, Chris Mitchell, who endured regular expletive-laden complaints about my contributions from the prime minister, including one a matter of days after that event.

That night provided me with two important insights. The first was that Abbott took more offence at criticism of Credlin than of himself; the second, that he took her word above that of his colleagues. They lied; she told the truth.

This was an untenable dynamic. The combination of the two of them, so successful in opposition, proved to be deadly in government. Together, they masterminded their own downfall.

After that night in July, I also recalled that the last time I had shaken hands with Abbott was when he was opposition leader.

I had visited him in his office for a cup of tea. During our conversation, I suggested he needed to soften up a bit, to turn the aggression and the negativity down a couple of notches. He dismissed my comment, saying that when you had 'your boot on their throat,' you kept it there.

That one sentence summed up his approach as opposition leader, which unfortunately carried over into his prime ministership. Anyway, he was very complimentary about my columns at the time, urging me to keep them up, no matter what. As I was leaving, I stretched out my hand to shake his and thank him for the cuppa. To my surprise, he grabbed my hand, pulled me in, and planted a big kiss on my cheek. Back then, I was the darling of the conservatives. It wasn't long before I became the she-devil. Like I keep saying, nothing lasts forever.

CHAPTER ONE

Sowing the Seeds

A month before he was toppled by Malcolm Turnbull, Tony Abbott received an alert from an unusual quarter. The deputy leader of the National Party, Barnaby Joyce, left the early-morning leadership group meeting that was held every sitting day in the prime minister's office to walk with Abbott to a function in the Great Hall. As they made their way, Joyce told the prime minister he would face a challenge from Turnbull around the time of the Canning by-election.

It was August 2015. Like others, Joyce could see the signs: unusual groupings at dinner, which Joyce later likened to springing people out and about with their mistresses; a few embarrassed looks; odd expressions here and there. As an old boy of St Ignatius' College, Riverview, Joyce was still well-plugged into the Sydney scene, picking up on the vibe and gossip about Abbott. He was also hearing things from contacts close to New South Wales federal Liberals. Joyce could read the polls, too, and as he would later say, you didn't have to be Sigmund Freud to understand their deeper meaning. Abbott's leadership was terminal.

Joyce had been very close to Abbott, but there had been a serious falling-out, triggered by a number of factors. Joyce had quietly stood aside as shadow finance minister when Abbott as opposition leader came under pressure to dump him. When the Nationals' leader, Warren Truss, fell seriously ill towards the end of 2014, Joyce read reports that the prime minister wanted Truss to stay on, because he feared instability would engulf the Coalition if Joyce were to become leader. Joyce was infuriated by those reports, but stayed silent publicly. He was convinced they were sourced from deep inside the prime minister's office. Joyce made no secret of his displeasure at Abbott's delegation of power to his chief of staff, Peta Credlin. In his typically wildly funny, wildly politically incorrect, irreverent way, he would joke privately about the eunuchs being in charge. Pretty soon, Joyce could find little to laugh about. In July 2015, when the government approved the $1.2 billion Shenhua coal mine on the Liverpool Plains in his electorate, Joyce snapped, declaring the world had gone mad.

Not long after that, Joyce concluded Abbott would not recover and that the prime minister should think seriously about stepping down. Nevertheless, when he suspected there were moves afoot to unseat the prime minister, he thought he owed it to him — because Joyce had always seen Abbott as an incredibly kind man, even though his first duty was to protect his own leader, Warren Truss — to warn him. Abbott neither responded to Joyce's warning nor engaged with him about it. He simply changed the subject.

Despite that, Joyce felt good about having done what he thought was the right thing.

There was something else Joyce was girding himself to do if Christmas came around and Abbott was still limping along in the job, with the opinion polls where he expected them to be. He was going to tell Abbott he should do the decent thing and step down as prime minister. Unlike Abbott's Liberal cabinet colleagues, Joyce firmly believed that, in these circumstances, Abbott would accept it was beyond him to recover and that he would quit. He did not think Abbott was the kind of man who would stay on to drive them all over a cliff, which is what they thought would inevitably happen if Abbott remained in the job.

Joyce would have had the guts to do it, too. He thought that would have been a more fitting end to Abbott's rule than to be voted out by his colleagues. Whether Joyce's confidence in what Abbott would do was well placed was another matter entirely.

There were so many warnings, so much advice from so many people to Abbott, at so many different times, on so many different issues. He ignored them all. He did not listen to Julie Bishop, Joe Hockey, and Christopher Pyne when they told him immediately after the election to appoint more women to cabinet. He did not listen to Peter Dutton when he told him to kill off the Medicare co-payment, nor later when he urged him to remove Hockey from Treasury so he could appoint Malcolm Turnbull to the job. He did not listen to John Howard when he told him not to reintroduce knights and dames, when he warned him about delegating too much of his authority to his chief of staff, and similarly when he advised him to appoint Turnbull as treasurer. In fact, Abbott ignored every significant piece of advice that Howard gave him. All these matters, and others—all of which contributed to his downfall—are explored more fully in succeeding chapters.

Abbott particularly refused to take the advice regarding his chief of staff, including from his friends, people who had been through the wars with him, who believed his relationship with Peta Credlin was destroying his prime ministership.

Connie Fierravanti-Wells had always been able to speak frankly with Abbott. They went back a long way, having first met in 1990 when they were both staffers in opposition. She also ran against Abbott as a candidate for preselection for Warringah in 1994, but still thinks that Abbott was the best candidate on the day. She was there when he rang his wife, Margie, to tell her he had won endorsement, urging her to come down and bring the girls with her.

Connie remained true to the leader, but she was not blind to his faults. In early 2015, she could see the damage that was being inflicted on Abbott inside the parliamentary party. Even her own loyalty had been severely tested. There was briefing going on against her before the 2013 election, which she sourced back to Abbott's office. After the election, she did not make it into the ministry; rather, she was appointed parliamentary secretary to the minister for social services, despite her hard work on aged-care and mental-health policy, and despite the fact there was a crying need for more women in the cabinet — especially after fellow conservative Sophie Mirabella was defeated. She was disappointed she didn't make it.

Nevertheless she didn't make a fuss, and worked hard, hoping for promotion later. As the senior conservative from New South Wales, she represented the views of many of Abbott's base who did not want to see him ousted. Late on the night before the spill motion against him in February 2015, she visited him in his office, a bit after 10.00 pm. She was brutally frank with him, raising something few people would dare broach, but which only a woman who had known him a long time could, while hoping he would appreciate she had his best interests at heart.

She believed he needed to hear, unfiltered, exactly what his colleagues were really thinking. In their view, he had to remove his chief of staff, because they blamed her for many of the government's problems, and they resented her treatment of them. This was not only about the abuse she heaped on them, but the fact he had closed himself off from them — a separation they blamed on Credlin. Connie told him, without mincing words, that they were prepared to take it out on him, because they did not like her.

She told him it was important that he get rid of her, because politics was not only about what was real.

'Politics is about perceptions,' she told him. 'Rightly or wrongly, the perception is that you are sleeping with your chief of staff. That's the perception, and you need to deal with it.'

She told him she was speaking on behalf of many people in the New South Wales division who cared for him, who did not want him to lose his prime ministership. She warned him that if he did not move her on, he would lose his prime ministership.

'I am here because I care about you, and I care about your family, and I feel I need to tell you the truth, the brutal truth. This is what your colleagues really think,' she said to him.

Abbott told her he wasn't going to move Credlin on. He said the rumours they were having an affair were not true. Abbott did not get angry when Connie confronted him about this most sensitive of matters. He did not remonstrate, or raise his voice. He simply, calmly, denied it.

Within two days after she had spoken to Abbott, after the vote that mortally wounded the prime minister, Credlin visited Connie in her office, a typical backbencher's room made warmly personal by the display of family knickknacks, including beautifully intricate doilies handmade by her Italian grandmother. They talked for an hour and a half. Connie was equally frank with Credlin, telling her she had to go.

She also told Credlin about the rumours—that colleagues believed she and Abbott were having an affair. Credlin also denied it, saying it wasn't true, that they were not having a relationship.

Connie told Credlin that, for Abbott's sake, she should go. Credlin said she believed that she was vitally important to Tony, that without her he would not be able to do his job. She believed

Tony's enemies were trying to get to him through her. Credlin gave no hint that she had even thought about going, not even for a moment. Connie was troubled, because she remained convinced that this would result in an extremely unhappy ending for Abbott. She tried to make Credlin see the consequences for herself as well.

'One day, Tony will be sitting on a park bench in Manly feeding the pigeons, and he will blame you,' she told her.

Connie had dared to ask each of them directly the one question that so many people inside the government whispered to each other, which they thought might help explain what they otherwise found inexplicable about this most complex relationship, which they believed was having such a detrimental impact on their lives, on their ability to do their jobs, and on the standing of the government.

One long-time Coalition staffer, searching for historical comparisons to capture the ultimately destructive and self-destructive nature of the relationship between the prime minister and his chief of staff, landed on one, saying: 'She was his Wallis Simpson.' This was not meant to imply an affair; it was meant to describe the depth of the dependence, the consuming obsession, and what Abbott was prepared to sacrifice for it. Like King Edward VIII, who gave up his throne because he could not do the job without Wallis by his side, Abbott had convinced himself he could not do without Credlin. Ultimately, it cost him the highest office in the land.

There were so many people trying to come up with the least harmful resolution to what was a diabolical problem. Abbott had been a brilliant opposition leader. Unfortunately, he was failing as a prime minister. Joyce was not the only one around that time who was contemplating ways of convincing Abbott to do the right thing by the Liberal Party and by his government. Could his wife,

Margie, be prevailed upon to speak to him? Would a petition of elders or businesspeople do it? Could John Howard be persuaded to tell him that time was up? There was growing desperation.

Their motives were simple. They wanted the government to be re-elected, yet they were convinced that with Abbott as leader they would get smashed. They could not find the means to separate the two people at the helm, held in bonds so tight that no one else could penetrate them. They were not only destroying one other; they were destroying the government, too.

Cabinet ministers as well as backbenchers had also lost confidence in Hockey, despite the benign second budget he'd delivered. They had doubts about his work ethic, they thought he was ill-disciplined, not up to the job, incapable of taking advice, had spent what little capital he had, could not recover in that most important of all portfolios, and was more than likely to falter as treasurer under the extreme pressure of an election campaign, especially if the government went into it with a tax-reform package. So they wanted him gone, too.

Abbott and Credlin had been on a war footing every day for four years before they got into government. Their four-year war was brilliant, brutal, and extremely effective. The problem was that, once they got there, they couldn't stop campaigning. Like soldiers or war correspondents hooked on adrenaline, their expertise and their passion was all about the fighting and the crushing of enemies, real or imagined, rather than on governing.

A year before the 2013 election, there had been a gathering of former Howard staffers at the Rugby Union Club, a popular watering hole a stone's throw from the elegant red-brick building in Barton that houses the federal Liberal Party secretariat. Credlin's speech that night set off alarm bells.

One former staffer remembered her saying that she wanted to

fill the executive corridors with warriors. Another recalled that she complained about the dominance of the public service by Labor types. Those present were people fully committed to the Liberal Party, but they were professionals in every sense of the word, driven by a desire to resume good government after the waste of the Labor years under Kevin Rudd and Julia Gillard.

Yes, they liked making hits on their opponents, but for many of them this was not what being in office was all about. They had a different concept of the way public service should be conducted, as well as the way public servants should be used.

What they heard filled them with dread, just as it did whenever Abbott called Credlin 'the fiercest political warrior' he had ever known, which was often. He said it in his victory speech on the night of 7 September 2013. After he thanked his colleagues, and his party, he singled her out: 'I thank my personal staff led by Peta Credlin, who is the smartest and fiercest political warrior I have ever worked with.'

He kept repeating it, including in June 2015 to a group of high-powered women in senior executive or government positions who had been invited to the prime minister's residence in Kirribilli, supposedly to celebrate their achievements, only to hear a celebration of the talents of Credlin. So effusive was the prime minister in his praise of his chief of staff that many of them cringed. They felt embarrassed for him. The other thing they felt that night was the absence of his wife, Margie. They wondered why, regretting her absence because they liked what they had seen of her — which was not very much — so they'd been looking forward to seeing more of her, or perhaps speaking to her.

The two women were seldom seen together, and by the end, not at all.

Abbott luxuriated in delivering admiring paeans to Credlin's ferocity when he wasn't bending over backwards to appease her. She insisted on it, and he was happy to oblige. He had been a warrior himself in his university days, so he had a special appreciation of that quality in her.

For others, it showed a disturbing lack of insight into what was required to run a successful government.

The other thing that worried them that night at the Rugby Union club, about their conversations with Credlin, and her husband, the party's federal director, Brian Loughnane, was the lack of commitment to policy or reform. They recall in conversations, especially with Loughnane, the belief that all of that reform stuff could be sorted once they got there—the most important thing was getting there. Which, in one way, it was, at least as far as Loughnane was concerned. It was his job to get them there, which he did very well. As it turned out, it seemed to be all that mattered to Abbott and Credlin, too, to their eventual cost.

Credlin had begun her political career as a junior staffer in the Howard government. Few remember her as a policy wonk. She was a striking figure: tall, attractive, especially in amongst all the suits. Even with other women, she got noticed. She worked in the office of the then leader of the government in the Senate, Richard Alston, where she impressed co-workers with her ability to get across the arcane detail of the operations of the upper house. She was described to me by some as efficient, effective, unexceptional; by others, as 'brilliant but impulsive'.

People only really began paying attention when she married Loughnane, for which Kay Patterson, the health minister under Howard, takes credit. The story goes that Patterson, a bright, engaging woman, who remained a staunch public defender of Credlin's, pinned a photo of Loughnane to Credlin's computer, telling her he was the man she should marry. Patterson relied heavily on advice from Credlin on everything from staffing to her wardrobe. Co-workers from back then describe Credlin as 'ferociously ambitious'. There's that other F-word again.

There were many colleagues who met Credlin in her early days in Parliament House who had initially formed positive impressions of her. Staff from other offices who became friendly with her remember her as a sweet young thing who would bake cakes (she was said to be a good cook) to bring into the office to celebrate birthdays. Many of them, initially counted as friends, would revise their opinions after experiencing closer or more prolonged contact with her, wondering what had happened.

For some, it was traumatic. She was Helen Coonan's chief of staff when the high-flying senator was minister for communications. It was a complicated area, which Credlin got across well, but she had little patience with those she thought could not keep up, or with those who tried to present the minister with advice that differed from hers, or who had the temerity to openly disagree with her.

Her management style was apparent even then. Staff were kept working until the early hours of the morning, or at weekends, sometimes on minor matters. Long-serving staff were slowly stripped of responsibilities, as she made herself indispensable to Coonan. After the departure of experienced Coonan advisers, she called a staff meeting, where she broke down and cried about her increased workload because of the loss of corporate memory. Her tears elicited no sympathy from staff who believed she had brought it on herself.

She would brief journalists on impending announcements without telling the press secretaries. They only found out when journalists rang them, seeking additional information. If staff raised this with her, she would not take it well. The fact that the journalists came to her was the staff's fault, not hers, she would argue; in reality, her colleagues believed, it was she who initiated the contact.

Shane Evans had worked for Amanda Vanstone when she was justice minister, then later when she was immigration minister, so he knew what it was like to be in a high-pressure environment.

In late 2006, after applying for the vacancy, he was appointed policy adviser on information technology in Coonan's office. Credlin began by trying to make a connection with Evans by saying to him: 'I love you gay guys—you gay guys are so much fun.' He thought this an inappropriate comment for a chief of staff to make to an adviser, but he went with it.

It didn't take long to go from that to what Evans later described as hysterical outbursts, accusing him of mismanagement and incompetence, expressed at the top of her voice, replete with swear words.

'The day after, she could be warm and charming, and behave as if nothing had happened. But if it wasn't you in the firing line, there was an unnerving awareness that someone else probably was,' he recalls.

'The volatility and lack of respect were defining characteristics of the office under Credlin.'

Evans remembers a staff dinner in Sydney's Chinatown, where he and a female colleague decided to leave at the end of the meal.

'Others looked like settling in, but it was late, and we got up to leave. Peta, obviously wanting to continue holding court, openly challenged us about leaving, in front of everyone who was there.'

To his colleague's response that she was 'tired', Credlin replied: 'I've seen your phone bill, and I know you stay out much later than this.'

Evans says now: 'It was a minor incident, but telling about her willingness to cross lines and obsess over the details of her staff, right down to the minutiae of trawling through their phone bills to see who was communicating with who and when.'

Evans said that the performance of the office suffered because of Credlin's outbursts and often highly emotional dressing-down of staff members.

'Many felt vulnerable, and the extreme shifts in behaviour generated a constant sense of unease. The unpredictability was all-consuming at times, because the shouting — often accompanied by scattergun and hysterical demands — was driven by how she was feeling, rather than what was needed to get the job done,' he says.

'I inherited a policy of free Internet filters for families, which the government was planning to fund to the tune of $80 million, but she was insisting they had to be "100 per cent effective". There was no such thing, and I told her so.'

Evans says Credlin was unwilling to engage in discussion, or consider the advice on the subject. 'What Peta wanted to be the facts were the facts,' he says.

'Because I was not prepared to divorce myself from reality, I was cut out of the loop and no longer had visibility over critical decisions.

'She did not seem to have the capacity to consider evidence or information that did not fit her worldview. Her behaviour became imperious, particularly when challenged around things she clearly didn't fully understand.

'In her mind she was right, even though she was soon proven to be wrong.

'When the Internet filtering scheme launched, and the filters were circumvented by a 16-year-old kid, I was the one in the firing line. It was as if I was the one who had guaranteed they would be 100 per cent effective.'

With the story set to run in the news that weekend, Evans and

Credlin agreed on how to manage the fallout of the story; but by Monday, Credlin was on the phone, accusing him of a 'fucking bullshit, do-nothing' approach.

'Political offices don't function effectively if advisers can't do their jobs without fear of abuse or retribution,' he said.

'And there was retribution. Advisers, senior departmental officials, and even the minister's own appointments to statutory bodies would be deemed "hopeless" or "incompetent" by Credlin. It mattered, because Credlin had created an environment where the minister was increasingly isolated and reliant on Credlin's advice and counsel.'

Then there was Fiona Telford, who had years of experience working for conservative politicians, and had been press secretary to the Victorian shadow racing minister, so had had some dealings with Credlin when she was director of communications for Racing Victoria in 2001.

'My dealings with her were always pleasant, and as a result I looked up to her and admired her tremendously,' Fiona told me. 'I went for the job as press sec with Helen Coonan because I thought working with Peta would be a great opportunity. Boy, was I wrong about that!'

Fiona began working in the Coonan office in 2007. The belittling, the intimidation, began early, with name-calling and finger-pointing in front of colleagues. It built up to intolerable levels. Telford had to get across a huge amount of technical detail in a very short space of time, but it was clearly not fast enough for Credlin.

There was months of denigration, some of it witnessed by co-workers. Colleagues in other offices saw the after-effects. To this day, some of them cannot forgive Credlin for the way she treated people. The final straw for Fiona came on the evening of the annual

Press Gallery Ball, in June, which was one of the really bright spots on the calendar for hard-working staffers. Fiona recalls Credlin calling her into her office around 6.00 pm to tell her she had been speaking to several journos from the press gallery and had been told they did not think she could brief them properly. Assuming there had indeed been such feedback, a degree of scepticism might have been in order, given that it is not beyond journalists to tell the odd fib to get around press secretaries to a higher source (the minister or the chief of staff). Whatever the truth of the claim, rather than counsel a younger, junior co-worker new in the job, Credlin dealt with it in a particularly threatening manner.

Fiona remembers Credlin in the office that evening in full flight, finger pointing, yelling at Fiona, calling her 'a fucking useless bitch', telling her 'you don't fucking know anything'. She went home in tears. Fiona, who had done well in her previous jobs, was shattered.

When she arrived at work at 7.00 am the next day, Fiona called her parents in Melbourne, crying down the phone, saying she could not continue because she felt she had let down the government and was no good at her job. Her parents, understandably upset, told her to leave straight away and come home.

Instead, believing she could still contribute to the government in what was an election year, she went to see Tony Nutt, then principal private secretary to John Howard. Anxious not to lose a good worker, Nutt found her another job with the minister for justice and customs, David Johnston, where she began the long task of rebuilding her confidence.

'Fearing more retribution and ridicule from Peta, I was loath to speak to her about this again, and to Helen Coonan's credit, she dealt with my departure with respect and appreciation for my reasons to leave,' Fiona says now.

'Unfortunately, the damage by Peta was done. I had little confidence in my ability, but thanks to David Johnston and his kind staff, I was able to do my work with him as minister until the election. The election loss, however, was the tipping point, and following this I fell heavily into a state of anxiety and depression on my return to Melbourne, which would last over three years.'

Fiona wanted her story told. It has taken courage for her to speak out; however, she was anxious for others to know the impact such behaviour in the workplace can have on people. She was no whingeing staffer unable to cope with a few swear words thrown her way. She had been around political offices for years.

'I'm a strong person, and tried to battle Peta and her bullying the whole four months with Helen Coonan. But she got to me, and it's taken me near on nine years to finally speak out about it, as I am with you right now,' she said.

Credlin in full flight—the combination of the hair, the height, the vocabulary—was something to behold. In fact, we have beheld it. The shots of Credlin shouting, lecturing, wagging her finger at Liberal frontbencher Stuart Robert in front of the cameras a week out from the 2013 election gives an idea of what this was like, if not the full flavour. There was no audio accompanying that footage. If there had been, we would have heard her dropping the F-bomb repeatedly at Abbott's frontbencher.

He was happy to relate the incident for this book. As the shadow minister for defence science and personnel, Robert was attending an event at Holsworthy with the then opposition leader. He says that as he and Abbott were getting their hair and make-up done, they had a bit of a giggle about the ridiculousness of it all. Credlin snapped at them both to get their heads straight and to stop goofing off. Robert then asked Credlin if Abbott could do a fundraiser for him wearing a red-and-black tie—which Robert had brought along especially — after the event. Robert wanted Abbott to take off his famous blue tie, then pose for a picture wearing the other one. Robert wanted to auction off the red-and-black tie with the photo of Abbott wearing it. She said no, they would get to it after the election — there was no time before then.

Robert accepted that. After the event finished, he and Abbott hung around in the foyer, waiting for Credlin to join them. Seeing that they were hanging around waiting anyway, Robert seized the opportunity to ask Abbott directly if he would pose with the other tie. Abbott was only too happy to oblige. Robert took the shot on his mobile phone. Credlin came along at the critical moment, saw what had happened, and, according to Robert, 'did her nut'. There was a bit of back and forth, inside, then it stopped. As they walked out the door, she started up again, shouting, F-bombing him, wagging her finger in his face, all of it in front of a television camera. Robert, who says he gave as good as he got, accepts he shouldn't have asked Abbott, and later apologised to her.

He could get past that, especially as the notoriety created by the incident and a picture of Abbott wearing a tie that wasn't blue raised several thousand dollars from the auction, which was spread across key marginal seats. Robert is coy about how much he raised, except to say, 'More than you could imagine'. What he could not get past, in government, when he was the assistant minister for defence, was reading about decisions in his portfolio in the newspaper, or watching the prime minister announce them with Kevin Andrews after David Johnston was dumped from the portfolio. What he couldn't get past, he says, was the briefing against colleagues, for which he held her responsible.

If these were isolated incidents, they would be bad enough. They were not.

This reminded me of two lectures from Peter Costello. The first was delivered before I began working for him, when he told me the rules of my engagement, one of which was never to criticise or undermine any of his colleagues.

The second was after Tony Smith, who had been a senior member of his staff for almost a decade, won the Victorian seat of Casey. Costello gathered all the staff in his office to tell us that we had to treat Tony with respect because he had done something none of us had, which was to stand for election. We didn't really need to be told that, but he wanted to make the point. It was a good one.

Credlin had come close to leaving politics a couple of times. After the Howard government lost the 2007 election, she was employed in the office of the then opposition leader, Brendan Nelson. The first time she threatened to resign there, his chief of staff, Peter Hendy, talked her out of it. Hendy was an experienced operator with a serious policy bent. He began working life as a cadet in Treasury, was Peter Reith's chief of staff during the Howard years, became chief executive of the Australian Chamber of Commerce and Industry, then left to join Nelson. His rule for dealing with staff in these situations was to counsel them, then, if they threatened to resign again, he would let them go. He explained his approach to Nelson, asking him to back him if it happened again because he would let her go. Nelson refused. He had told Hendy when he signed up as his chief of staff that he had hired Credlin because she was Loughnane's wife. He could not allow Hendy to remove her, for the same reason, and told him so.

There were others there who spoke well of Credlin at the time, saying that she mentored some of the younger female staffers.

When Malcolm Turnbull wrested the opposition leadership from Nelson, she remained in his office, sidelined. It was an extremely unhappy time. She would cry, literally and figuratively, on the shoulders of colleagues.

Not all of them remember her with animosity, but even those who got along well with her in that office believe her judgement on the three vital Ps—policy, process, and politics—was flawed even then. In despair at the way her political career was going, she was about to quit to pursue studies when Turnbull was sacked by his colleagues.

When Abbott appointed her as his chief of staff, she was effectively the last woman standing. It was meant to be.

The tenor of their working relationship was set early. Unusually for a chief of staff, she accompanied him almost everywhere. Normally, chiefs of staff stayed back in the office, ensuring that policy formulation was proceeding. Political and press staff usually formed the travel corps.

The reason, according to one former senior staffer, was simple. She did not trust him out on his own. Nor could anybody else be trusted to make sure he stayed disciplined and on message.

As a minister in the Howard years, across his range of portfolios, he ran a good office, even though—as recounted in *So Greek*—he showed no interest in matters economic. There were never stories of waste or incompetence. People would get exasperated when he goofed off, but otherwise there was nothing to suggest that, once in office, there would not at the very least be an efficient administration. It was the one thing after the six-year soap opera of Kevin Rudd and Julia Gillard that everybody thought was a given.

Abbott had also always employed lots of women in his office. Maxine Sells—quiet, competent, devoted—was his chief of staff in the Howard years. A former bureaucrat, she had been around for decades, working with John Howard in opposition. But when Credlin took over, Maxine was demoted. She was appointed to look after the opposition's policy-formulation committee. Often she would not even be told when meetings were being held. Credlin would go. In government, Maxine was assigned to look after correspondence in a back office.

Maxine's isolation, a technique of Credlin's to force people—especially staff who had been close to Abbott—into positions where they had no choice but to resign, infuriated her former colleagues.

Another technique was to 'restructure' the office. Credlin knew that one sure-fire way to control the boss was to get control of his diary. The way she did this, within six months of his ascension to the leadership, was to remove the person doing it.

Suzanne Kasprzak had worked for politicians since 1985. After the 1998 election, Peter Costello set up a dedicated tax unit to oversee the implementation of the GST, which was headed up by Phil Gaetjens, Costello's chief of staff. Gaetjens chose Kasprzak to work as his executive assistant. Gaetjens couldn't speak highly enough of her. She then went to work for Tony Nutt in the prime minister's office, and handled John Howard's diary for five long years. She was a stalwart and absolute professional, renowned for her hard work and efficient manner. She was in Malcolm Turnbull's office when Abbott won the leadership. Most of Turnbull's staff, including Credlin, who was then deputy chief of staff, stayed on.

Pretty soon, Credlin decided she was unhappy with Suzanne's work. She would go into Suzanne's office, close the door, and start yelling at her. It happened time and again, with Credlin shouting at her that she was moody, she was inefficient, people were complaining about her. On it went.

After a few months, Credlin insisted that all diary requests had to go through her. She would put a red line through every request she disapproved, including those from backbenchers.

Howard as prime minister had a system whereby backbenchers

were given time to speak directly to him on whatever issue they liked, whether it was personal or whether they were seeking money for their electorates. Suzanne would block out ten minutes or more for this, depending on the circumstances. It kept everybody happy. In Abbott's office, Credlin told Suzanne to stop doing it.

Suzanne would continue to sneak in the odd request. Then, six months into Abbott's leadership, Credlin 'restructured' the office. Abbott called Suzanne in, thanked her for her work, told her he had never been better served by anybody, but in the new restructure there was no job for her. He gave her a bunch of flowers, which she threw in the bin as she walked out of the office. She left feeling fragile, her confidence wounded.

In 2015, when Tony Nutt was appointed to handle Turnbull's transition to the prime ministership, he got Suzanne back to help with the diary.

Terry Barnes, who worked as an adviser to Abbott when he was health minister, has a theory that Abbott liked to be surrounded by 'strong, charismatic' women. His former press secretaries, Claire Kimball and Simone Holzapfel, and the head of his department, Jane Halton, fitted that bill. When it was suggested by Howard and Arthur Sinodinos that Abbott should loosen his ties with Halton, he refused that advice, too.

The other strong, charismatic, female figure he became attached to was the former member for Lindsay, Jackie Kelly. He was devastated when he learned she was quitting politics.

However, there had never been anyone quite like Peta Credlin. 'Tony had a fatal flaw which she exploited,' Barnes told me. 'She was his Lady Macbeth.'

When one senior member of Abbott's staff resigned before the 2013 election, he gave Abbott some well-intentioned advice. He told him he needed another senior person in the office whom he trusted, to make calls on his behalf and liaise with his backbench. He suggested a former MP for this job. There was little response.

The former staffer confirmed to me what others had said about the pattern being set early. Everything had to go through Credlin. Given what oppositions can be like — usually rabble-like — her maintenance of discipline was a considerable achievement. While her colleagues described her as 'reasonably astute', they did not put her in the camp of the political genii. Her level of influence, the extent of her power, just kept growing to the point where, in the words of one colleague, 'megalomania kicked in'.

'I would have had no problem if she had been principal private secretary, where she could weigh in on key issues and stay out of the weeds. Instead she had to be in the weeds on everything,' he said.

Her former colleagues affirm she could usually get Abbott to do — or not do — everything she wanted. They were sceptical about suggestions she was ignorant of issues, or incapable of preventing him from stumbling on them, whether it was Prince Philip or Bronwyn Bishop. Either she was complicit, or her judgement was as flawed as his.

Abbott's inner larrikin would sometimes break free, but not often.

They said one example of her level of control surfaced years ago, when she convinced Abbott not to vote for Peter Reith for the Liberal Party's federal presidency, even though Abbott had already committed himself to supporting Reith.

Abbott had encouraged Reith to run against the then president, Alan Stockdale. Howard had suggested to Abbott that he needed someone in the federal presidency who was a national figure, whom the MPs as well as business could respect, who could bulk up the Liberal Party. He told Abbott that Reith would do a good job.

Abbott agreed. In fact, he told at least one of his MPs around that time that he thought Reith would make a good federal president. Nevertheless, at one point, a few weeks out from the federal conference when the vote was scheduled, Reith had a feeling that there might have been a change of heart, so he spoke to Abbott, seeking an assurance that he still had his support. He pressed Abbott to make sure he was still OK with his candidacy. Abbott told him, without equivocation, that he supported him and wanted him to run.

The conference was held in a Canberra hotel around the end of June 2011. On the day, Abbott, who was sitting on the stage in full view of the room, with television cameras rolling, ostentatiously filled out his ballot paper, and then, in front of everyone, showed it to Stockdale. Howard was angered by Reith's public humiliation. Other party elders, even those who supported Stockdale, such as David Kemp, were appalled by Abbott's behaviour.

'Show and tell' might have been considered best practice in Labor caucus ballots, but it was definitely not the Liberal way.

Reith spoke to Abbott after the vote to ask him why he'd done it, why he hadn't told him beforehand that he either didn't want him to run or was going to vote against him. At least then, Reith reckons he could have made a strategic withdrawal. 'Ah, mate,' was as much as Abbott could muster. There was no explanation. Nor was there the next day, when Abbott rang Reith to appeal to him not to do any media on the subject. As if.

A disappointed Reith told the ABC: 'He (Abbott) certainly asked me [to run], and he didn't just ask me, he asked people around him to join in my campaign.'

Abbott refused to go into it at the time, saying he didn't want to talk about who said what to whom, but denied having given Reith 'false hope'. Recalling the episode for this book, Reith summed up this claim of Abbott's with two words: 'He lied.'

People familiar with the backroom plays back then say that Credlin was instrumental in getting Abbott to switch, because she thought Reith was too risky. Reith was high profile. He was an advocate for workplace reform, which Abbott desperately wanted to keep dead, buried, and cremated, so the worry was that he would cut across the leader. Others believed that Reith was determined to clean up the federal secretariat to make it more accountable to the executive and the party, so Abbott, fearing anything that might threaten Loughnane and, by extension, Credlin, decided to play it safe.

So, rather than tell Reith in advance he had lost his support—at which point, Reith would have withdrawn—Abbott killed Reith in front of the cameras.

It confirmed for many what they had suspected. This was that Abbott was not a creature of the Liberal Party. The National Civic Council connection with BA Santamaria made them suspicious, too. Abbott had never had deep wells of support within the party, except in its most conservative parts. He did not have rusted-on supporters across the broad sweep of the party, like Howard did.

A number of people described him as a 'loner'. While he socialised with fellow liberals, particularly Christopher Pyne, with whom he shared regular dinners, there was no one they could say with confidence would have taken a bullet for him.

He seemed susceptible to a firm hand, particularly from women.

Credlin made herself indispensable to him. She would do his make-up, fix his hair, feed him food off her plate, let him sip wine out of her glass, bake him biscuits (especially if another female staffer had made some for him, too), then stand where she could eyeball him as he performed. He would look to her for approval, so he would know when he was doing as required or not.

He lost his cool occasionally, usually during political discourse with colleagues; she often did her block lashing out at staff or MPs. According to one co-worker, when she was in a 'fit of rage' she would take it out on the person next to her. It didn't matter who it was, whether it was Abbott or another staffer. There were no accounts of her losing her cool with her previous bosses. When James Boyce was still in Abbott's office, he would occasionally fight back; Abbott never would.

'He would concede on the spot to calm the situation down, figuring whatever the problem was, it could be sorted later,' one former staffer said.

'He gave her a lot of credit for a lot of things. He didn't understand why her weaknesses were so damaging to him. He didn't see it would become a problem. I said to people quietly before I left, she would be his downfall. It really, really, worried me that he allowed it to happen.

'He worshipped her.

'He came to see her as the person who kept him in line. She was the disciplinarian. Absolutely the disciplinarian. When the cheeky Tony wanted to come out, or the conservative warrior, she had to pull him back into line. She had to keep him focussed and stay on message. He got used to it. He couldn't trust himself without her.

'All this stuff about him being a misogynist is BS. He needs a strong woman around to bash him into line.'

Often, it was the way she did it that would leave his friends embarrassed for him. At the funeral of his close friend Christopher Pearson, she got in a huff over something—they were not sure over what or why, assuming she'd been put out because Abbott had offered lifts to friends—so she deliberately dallied, talking to people, keeping Abbott and his friends waiting, even after one of them went to tell her politely they were waiting on her to leave.

Later, they confessed their disappointment at her behaviour—and their bemusement at his tolerance of it.

But her strict discipline of him, to make sure he did as she directed, did help get him there—especially when you consider where Abbott was at the end of 2007. In many ways, it was the reverse of *Pygmalion*. She turned him into a statue with limited movements, like the made-up street artists who perform outside department stores.

The 2007 campaign had been a disaster for Abbott. He was late for the National Press Club debate against his Labor shadow, Nicola Roxon, then swore at her while the camera mikes were on. He took exception to something that asbestos campaigner Bernie Banton said, and ended up looking like he was beating up on a terminally ill man. When Jackie Kelly went on radio during the 2007 campaign to dismiss as a 'Chaser prank' racist pamphleteering concocted by her husband and others that had purportedly come from the Labor Party, John Howard—about to give his final speech as prime minister to the National Press Club—had to slap her down. It was Abbott who had suggested the line to her.

His was a lively intellect. He was engaging, and prone to saying what he thought, which often got him into trouble. It made him real, but also, in the eyes of many, unelectable. She helped change all that when he became leader by accident in 2009.

So, while keeping him in check helped deliver government, so did everything else that goes towards making a campaign successful—including the hardworking local candidates, the advertising, the messaging, the overall strategy. Above all, unity was the key. MPs set aside their doubts and hunkered down behind him.

Yet Abbott convinced himself—a view she both encouraged and shared—that the victory belonged to her. In 2014, when

Julie Bishop did what deputies do, and raised with him backbench concerns about the operations of his office, including Credlin's behaviour, Abbott told her that without Credlin she would not be where she was. First, he was dismissive of the concerns, then he was dismissive of the messenger herself. He could not see what an insult this was to a woman who had made it there by dint of her own performance.

Abbott's relentless focus on the flaws of both Kevin Rudd and Julia Gillard helped bring them down. Yet while their combined incompetence helped make Abbott electable, it did not make him acceptable.

He never immersed himself in the economy. This was another major failing, given the doubts that arose during opposition about Joe Hockey's suitability in the job, which were only to be magnified and exposed in government.

Abbott refused to acknowledge for a long time that he had broken any election promises, then, when he finally did 'fess up, it was more like an aside. He convinced himself he hadn't broken any, and if he was challenged on it, he exploded. A case could have been made for going back on promises; however, refusing to concede only made it look like he was lying about lying. This was a particular blind spot that frustrated MPs no end.

Although Abbott and Credlin's tactics in opposition had worked superbly, they were never going to be sustainable in government. For a government to work well, different talents from many different people are required— whether in ministries, ministerial offices, the public service, or the party organisation.

In my weekly column for *The Australian* on 6 June 2013, a few months before the election, I offered what I believed was constructive advice about what was needed for Abbott to succeed in government.

I said he had the potential to be either a bad or brilliant prime minister if he got there, but in order to succeed he had to do the opposite of what then prime minister Julia Gillard was doing.

Gillard is accused of not listening to people, or not listening to the right people, and not seeking enough advice from a wider circle and of ignoring proper processes. Policies are sprung haphazardly. Even if they are good, they get wrecked by ham-fisted politics or tactics, all of which has brought her to where she is today.

One complaint about Abbott is that his inner circle too often comprises only two people — him and his chief of staff Peta Credlin, a one woman Praetorian Guard who is married to the party's federal director Brian Loughnane, which adds another layer of complication and potential conflict.

Abbott described Credlin recently as 'outstanding'. Considering where they all began, it is hard to argue with that. Nevertheless, no matter how outstanding, one individual cannot assume all the policy, political and media responsibilities in a prime minister's office, where every issue eventually lands.

It is critical to consult while trusting experts to do their jobs in accordance with established procedures because what gets you there won't necessarily keep you there.

That morning, his most senior staffer after Credlin, Andrew Hirst, rang to tell me I had got some things wrong. Earlier, however, I had received a text from his boss: 'Niki, enjoyed today's piece and got a good chuckle from the cartoon. Cheers Tony.'

That 'cartoon' was a magnificent illustration by Eric Lobbecke, showing Credlin as a sword-wielding Amazon with Abbott peeking out from behind her, fingers demurely intertwined. John Lyons saw the illustration hanging on Credlin's office wall when he interviewed her for *The Australian*, for a piece published on 21 February 2015. He was taken aback when he saw it displayed so prominently, because of what it said about their relationship.

Whatever message Abbott took from that column, it wasn't the right one. The same goes for Credlin. All the seeds were sown then. All he had to do was make a few adjustments. He never did.

Both of them had the potential to be wonderful role-models. He was the most community-minded prime minister we have ever had. His fire-fighting, his surf live-saving, his many acts of kindness should have made people warm to him. But almost every time it looked like people were prepared to approve of his behavioiur, or at least stay benign about it, he would do or say something silly or injudicious. His language was too brutal, his tone too threatening, and he indulged in extended culture wars, particularly against the ABC.

She was an attractive woman from country Victoria, intelligent, well educated, well respected in her school days, who had worked hard to become one of the most powerful women in the country.

He probably never would have made it without her, and there was probably no other politician she could have worked for who would have got there. They had a lot in common, apart from their religion. She controlled him. He relied on her to the exclusion of all others. It worked magnificently for a time, but neither could make the changes necessary to keep it working. It was inevitable it would end the way it did. Everybody except the two of them could see it coming.

The discontent grew rapidly, deepened, and persisted. There were a number of pivotal moments on their road to ruin. The first ministry, the first budget, the running sore of broken promises, the resentment by colleagues of their exclusion, their belief she undermined them, and the extent of her influence, as well as her interference, all fired the hostility. His final, humiliating, captain's call on Australia Day 2015 of the knighthood for Prince Philip, coupled with the loss of government in Queensland by Campbell Newman, triggered the shambolic spill motion against him in February 2015—a bare eighteen months into his term, with demands from cabinet ministers as well as backbenchers that he sack or move Credlin and Hockey.

It was a grim warning that left him shattered, but not shattered enough to make the changes his party demanded.

When Bronwyn Bishop's helicopter crashed into the political landscape and stayed there for eighteen days before the wreckage was cleared, MPs lost hope that Abbott's position was recoverable. The cabinet debate over citizenship confirmed it was impossible, and then his handling of the same-sex issue, which many of his MPs branded as a breach of trust with them, sealed his fate. They had wanted him to come good; they had given him seven months, a month more than he had asked for in February. In their bones, they knew he did not have it in him to recover.

The worst Labor leader since Arthur Calwell looked set to become prime minister, but a large chunk of the Liberal Party was not prepared to sit back and allow Bill Shorten to win government. Abbott should have been wiping the floor with him. Yet Labor had remained ahead in thirty consecutive Newspolls, and in many of them Shorten was the preferred prime minister.

A core group of eight—James McGrath, Peter Hendy, Arthur Sinodinos, Mitch Fifield, Scott Ryan, Mal Brough, Wyatt Roy, and Simon Birmingham—the G8 plus one, Malcolm Turnbull, came together in that winter of discontent. Others soon joined.

Kevin Rudd was given no warning, but even he lasted longer than Abbott. Julia Gillard had plenty of warnings, but even she lasted longer than Abbott.

Abbott ignored all the warnings, from beginning to end — the public ones, the private ones, from his friends, his colleagues, the media.

His colleagues were not being disloyal. They did not feel they had betrayed him; they believed he had betrayed them. Their motives were honourable. They didn't want him to fail; they wanted the government to succeed, and they wanted the Coalition re-elected.

Abbott and Credlin had played it harder and rougher than anybody else to get where they wanted to be. But they proved incapable of managing their own office, much less the government. Then, when it was over, when it was crystal-clear to everyone that they had failed, when everyone else could see why they had failed, she played the gender card while he played the victim, accusing Malcolm Turnbull, Julie Bishop, and Scott Morrison of treachery.

CHAPTER TWO

The Peta Principal

If I was a guy I wouldn't be bossy, I'd be strong. If I was a guy I wouldn't be a micromanager, I'd be across my brief, or across the detail. If I wasn't strong, determined, controlling, and got them into government from opposition, I might add, then I would be weak and not up to it and should have to go and could be replaced.
— Peta Credlin, *Australian Women's Weekly* The Women of the Future Awards, 22 September 2015

Tony Abbott's overwhelming preoccupation was the wellbeing of his chief of staff, Peta Credlin. His concern for her happiness, his extreme protectiveness of her, his deferral to her, the transfer of his power to her — which allowed her to employ it ruthlessly — alienated his colleagues from cabinet ministers down, lost him the respect of business people who witnessed it, and forced the departure of experienced staff with expertise in policy, media, and office administration.

He diminished himself as he allowed his office to be degraded, from top to bottom. His wife, Margie, a woman of warmth and dignity with the potential to be his greatest asset, was put in a chiller. He was either oblivious to this or complicit in it. He either simply tolerated it or he incited it. Either way, as he subsequently acknowledged, he was ultimately responsible for all of it. It was one of the biggest single factors in his loss of the prime ministership, wreaking on him the humiliation he feared most: dismissal at the hands of his own colleagues.

The fact he could not see it coming, could not see how bizarre his behaviour appeared to others, or what effect it had on their opinion of him and his fitness for the job, was a most worrying aspect of it. It was pitiful to watch. In every encounter, he accepted Credlin's word above the word of others. In almost every conflict, she was the one he sought to placate. There was a pattern. She would have a meltdown, storm out, and he would feel compelled to go after her to mollify her or make sure she was all right. She never had to apologise for her behaviour, while others — from cabinet ministers down — were counselled to seek her forgiveness.

As they walked out the door, long-serving staff warned him of what would happen. Claire Kimball, who had worked for him off and on, paid as well as unpaid, between 2004 and 2011, always believed he could be a good prime minister. She grew frustrated, not only because she believed Credlin was leading him down the wrong road, but also because he was so willing to be led. When she left, she told him he would end up 'friendless, policy-less, a national joke, but Peta Credlin still hanging off you'.

It took a while for the stories to begin to emerge. Even now, there are people reluctant to talk about it. They feel either loyal to Abbott, or loyal to the cause, or they have been convinced to keep quiet to protect the legacy. Or, years later, they are still frightened. There are a number of reasons why such unacceptable behaviour went unchallenged for so long. People who are mistreated at the workplace are sometimes too scared or too embarrassed to talk about it. Perpetrators are often in positions of power, so people fear retribution.

Before publication of this book, Abbott contacted former staff to ask if they had spoken to me, pleading with them not to say anything that was critical of the office or to diminish all the good things that had been achieved.

But there were many willing to say what they witnessed, what they heard, what happened — former staff, ministers, friends — because they wanted the complete story to be told. They do not want a sanitised version of history to be created. The anecdotes related here are based on primary sources — that is, they were related to me by people who saw or heard or participated in what transpired.

There is so much of the behaviour of two adults who had the privilege of occupying the most powerful, most prestigious offices in the country that left those who encountered them uncomfortable, or bruised, or incredulous, or outraged. The most common description of the relationship: weird.

Consider this. At a meeting of cabinet ministers in his office, one of them told an off-colour joke about submarines. Credlin stood up and stormed out of the room. A distressed Abbott took off after her. She walked back in a few minutes later, with Abbott following closely behind her.

The prime minister addressed his bemused colleagues, saying: 'I think we owe Peta an apology.'

He turned to the towering inferno beside him. 'Sorry, Peta,' he said. A couple of them, including Joe Hockey, chimed in: 'Sorry, Peta.'

Credlin then launched into an angry lecture, telling them they were the reason the government was doing so badly among women. Forget the first frontbench, which she and Abbott had concocted between them, with only one woman in the cabinet when there were others ready, willing, and able to serve, and against the explicit advice of his most senior colleagues to appoint at least another two. Forget Abbott's strongarming, replete with F-bombs, of Danielle Blain to withdraw from the race for the federal presidency to give Richard Alston a clear run. Forget the fact that all appointments to any board or service, whatever gender, whatever status, had to be cleared by the prime minister's office (that is, by Credlin), with a standing rule (until after the February spill) that no appointments were to be renewed, unless no other candidate was available, in which case they should only be reappointed for a year or so, by which time a replacement would be found.

Tales of displays of Credlin's volatile temperament, where Abbott was also sprayed by not-so-friendly fire, were legendary. There were two famous incidents that played out in Abbott's offices in Sydney in front of all his staff.

One involved his then senior press secretary, James Boyce. After the 2103 election, Boyce, Credlin, and Abbott had attended an event that had gone well. They walked back into the office, laughing and joking. As they got out of the lift, Credlin asked Boyce a question. He didn't know the answer offhand, so he told her he would get it for her in a minute. It seemed innocuous enough, but for some reason she lost her temper. She began yelling at Boyce, telling him he was incompetent and that he wasn't up to his job. He tried to tell her to calm down, that he would get her what she wanted. She got angrier still, and continued yelling. As he walked into his office and slammed the door, he told her to fuck off.

Abbott followed Boyce into his office. He told Boyce he knew Peta could be hard. He said that while he was no expert on women, he had a wife and three daughters. He said he always found it was best not to fight back. It was much better to accept what they were saying, apologise, then deal with the issue when things were calmer. Boyce thought this was ridiculous, telling his boss he would not cop that kind of behaviour.

Around a dozen staff in the office could see or hear what was happening. Credlin was hanging around outside Boyce's office, trying to listen in to the conversation. Finally, she burst in, screaming at Abbott that she would not have him fighting her fucking battles. Boyce couldn't believe it. 'For fuck's sake,' he yelled, so everyone could hear, 'he was trying to defend you.' She took off, then Abbott took off after her, calling out to her, 'Peta, Peta.' Boyce almost quit that day. His departure followed not long after. When they could laugh about it later, that episode became known among staff as the Phillip St massacre.

The other memorable incident had occurred earlier, towards the end of 2012, involving one of Abbott's most devoted long-time staffers, Murray Cranston.

Cranston was the bravest person in the room at a full staff meeting held in the Sydney office, when they were all asked for their thoughts on how the office could work better. Addressing Credlin directly, because he had become concerned about the treatment of junior staff, Cranston volunteered that 'the elephant in the room' was her temperament. Cranston pointed out that her mood swings had a dramatic effect on the morale of the office, particularly on junior staff who had been yelled at or sworn at by Credlin.

Credlin fled the room in tears, closely followed by you know who. Abbott's advancer, Richard Dowdy, later told his fellow staffers that he saw the prime minister-in-waiting sitting outside on the kerb of a busy Sydney street, trying to calm down his inconsolable chief of staff. Rather than look into the complaints of the treatment of junior staff, Abbott instead counselled Cranston, who had been with him in the Howard years, to buy Credlin a bunch of flowers by way of apology. Cranston did so. They cost him $100. When he presented them to Credlin, she tossed them aside.

Cranston could laugh about it later, when he told workmates that Credlin thought better of throwing them out, and regifted them to Margie Abbott, along with a note in appreciation of her support during the year. What he did not find so amusing was his old boss, speaking from the ignominy of the backbench, when it was all over, asking rhetorically what it was that Credlin had done that was so wrong.

In the lead-up to the 2013 election, Cranston was in the back of a Commonwealth car, with senior press secretary Tony O'Leary, on the way to Perth airport. Abbott, who was in the front seat, was on the phone to Credlin, who had not travelled with him on this occasion. The conversation got heated. Cranston and O'Leary could hear her shouting at him to fuck off. Abbott said little.

A number of times, in typical fashion, she would yell at Abbott that without her he would not have gotten where he was, or that he would be nothing without her. Those who witnessed it said she was in his face, wagging her finger. Those who heard it—well, they could hear loud and clear. The truly sad part was that he believed it.

Credlin did not always have to yell at Abbott, although she often did. There were other ways of showing her displeasure, or making a point that kept him distracted or on edge.

Jane McMillan, the director of his press office during the first year of government, recalls another Credlin meltdown, this time at the scene of a critical meeting between prime minister Abbott and the then Indonesian president, Susilo Bambang Yudhoyono.

The meeting to restore the bilateral relationship after the spying scandal and boat turnbacks took place in early June at Batam. Credlin always insisted on sitting close to Abbott at official gatherings (a strategy that led to a conflict with Joe Hockey at Brisbane's G20, but that's another story), but in the bilateral meeting there was only room for Australia's ambassador to Indonesia and a note-taker. Abbott decided that his national security adviser, Andrew Shearer, should sit in as note-taker.

Credlin, already fragile over an attack on her from Clive Palmer in parliament, where he stated that Abbott's paid parental-leave scheme was designed for her benefit, took off in a huff.

When the meeting ended, Credlin was conspicuously absent from the briefing before the release of the leaders' joint press statement. Those who were there say Abbott was completely distracted from the job at hand, because he was so concerned about Credlin and whether she was OK.

'The tone of the press statement was going to be dissected for days, and determine whether Australian/Indonesian relations were considered "back on track",' McMillan recalled for this book.

'It was day one of a lengthy international tour that was taking in D-Day in France, Canada, and our first visit to the White House via New York. Nothing should have been more important than the prime minister's preparation.

'I remember thinking how indulgent, irresponsible, and arrogant it was to hold everyone hostage to her mood, even on Batam Island in Indonesia. This wasn't just *some* press statement; at the time, it was *the* press statement.'

Returning to the hotel for what was meant to be a brief pit stop before heading back to the plane, Abbott and Credlin went to an anteroom to have it out. Everyone else, including the Indonesian authorities, waited. And waited. And waited.

Finally, McMillan opened the door to the anteroom, and stuck her head in to remind them there was a whole entourage waiting to go and that the roads had been closed. Abbott called her in and insisted on a group hug. McMillan obliged. *Let's get this circus on the road*, she was thinking.

The volatility, the questionable judgement, the unnecessary meddling at every level, not only made for a dysfunctional office; it filtered through every nook and cranny of the government.

Consider this also. The prime minister of Papua New Guinea, Peter O'Neill, sent messages through intermediaries in 2013 to then opposition leader Abbott that he was anxious to meet with him in Port Moresby. For some reason (perhaps because he wasn't considered vital to Abbott's election prospects), Credlin refused to allow it. Abbott eventually spoke to his international affairs adviser, Mark Higgie, asking Higgie if he could talk to Peta to convince her to allow the meeting. Why the leader could not simply tell her to put it in his diary, and to make the travel arrangements, is a mystery. However, Higgie did as requested. When he put it to Credlin, he received a swift one-line response: 'It's not going to happen.' It didn't.

After he was restored to the prime ministership in June 2013, Kevin Rudd announced he had stitched up a deal with O'Neill to reopen the detention centre on Manus Island. Rudd had toughened Labor's stand on asylum-seekers, saying there would be no cap on the number to go to PNG; if they were found to be genuine, they would be resettled there or in a third country, but not in Australia. Abbott's other advisers surmised that this was what O'Neill had wished to discuss with Abbott.

Labor had already drawn even in Newspoll. Rudd fell back again, obviously, but those who knew the story about O'Neill were rightly nervous when Rudd made the announcement, worried that he might have struck on a strategy that would undercut the Coalition's policy to stop the boats. Abbott did not get to meet

O'Neill until after the election.

In the context of micro-management, what about this? There was a pre-Christmas staff dinner in 2011 at Chez Maurice et Linda, a French restaurant at Balgowlah in Abbott's electorate. The staff split into groups to play trivial pursuit, where all the questions related to details of office personnel, their birthdays, and so on. Every question was vetted by Credlin. Only one was vetoed. It asked how many times Credlin had chaired the 7.30 am staff meeting scheduled for parliamentary sitting days. The answer was 'once'.

Now, Credlin's day probably ended later than most, or began earlier on the phone with daily conference calls, but few can recall her arriving at the office much before 8.30 or 9.00 am.

Any notes for her had to be written on pink paper; notes for the prime minister were blue. Staff were instructed to shred the pink papers if they were returned with handwritten notations on them from her. No records were allowed to be kept of her written instructions. If staff wanted to slip something past her into his in-tray, they would wait until administrative staff were about to carry it into his office.

If they had a complaint with him, they felt free to tell him. If they complained about her, she would find out. They would be sent into exile.

When she was accused of micro-management, or control freakery, what insiders really meant was that she buried herself in minutiae — the design of staff business cards, the lettering on office nameplates, the seating plan for VIP aircraft — to avoid the big issues. Staff felt unsettled by the constant rearranging of seating in the office. Not only were they moved, but they were not allowed to choose where their furniture, such as filing cabinets, would be positioned. Administrative staff said they would have to 'text

Peta' to see if she approved of the positioning. Staff were even told which way their computer screens had to face—so, they presume, she could see the screens to ensure they were working.

Credlin agonised over the Australian gifts to international dignitaries—often finding a personal memento, such as an archived photo of President Park from Korea and her parents during a much earlier visit of theirs to Australia. While these gifts were thoughtful and well received by the media and the recipients, it was not usually a job done by the chief of staff to the prime minister.

Here is how one former senior adviser described it to me: 'While briefs and minutes piled up on her desk, and advisers and ministers waited to get clearance on policy and legislation, she was often found with the prime minister's chef, picking a menu, whittling down a wine list for the prime minister's events, picking the flowers for the G20, micro-managing office decorators, personally overseeing the installation of new artworks for the office, or even down at The Lodge approving the renovations. It highlighted a chronic inability to manage her own time and to triage the many issues that would make their way to the prime minister's office. Her insistence on seeing every brief, every minute, monitoring every decision, created a paralysis of her own making—paper, briefs, decisions simply didn't move for days or weeks on end.

'Interior design was her escape from reality, and hours and days were lost on matters that should have been the domain of the office manager, the PM's personal assistant, or his wife. While she would often manage Margie's involvement in government events, she made it her business to manage Kirribilli House as well. On more than one occasion, she made it clear that any functions at Kirribilli were to be paid for by the Abbotts, not the taxpayer (not something that was ever a threat of occurring). But she also insisted that staff at Kirribilli could not order food for Margie or shop for meals (even family ones), despite the Abbotts residing at the official residence.'

There are two thoroughly charming, hardworking women, Anna and Lucia, who clean the prime minister's office, and have done so for years. However, after Rudd's defeat, and before Abbott moved into the office, Credlin instructed Abbott's personal staff to scrub it top to bottom with sugar soap. A particular bugbear of hers was black fingerprints on doors (particularly from the press office, where staff got dirty from newspapers) or dusty windowsills. She instructed staff to clean the doors and sills weekly.

Right up to a few weeks before Abbott and Credlin both lost their jobs, the chief of staff—not the prime minister's wife—was still immersed in choosing the décor for the refurbished Lodge, where the cost blew out from the initial estimate of $3 million (announced by then prime minister Gillard) to a staggering $11 million by the time the Turnbulls moved in, with advice soon after that it could climb as high as $14 million, prompting the new prime minister to order an audit of the spending. Once the audit is completed, details of the extent and manner of Credlin's involvement at critical times should make fascinating reading.

A week out, she was obsessing about artwork, burying herself in trivia such as who was off on sick leave, rather than dealing with what everybody else could see was about to consume them. Their lack of preparation on that fateful night would astound even their allies.

'In the four-and-a-half years I was there, I never knew her to read a single copy of a draft speech I had written, to make suggestions or pass comment,' one senior adviser said.

Another adviser confirmed what one frontbencher had observed, and that was that the office was 'constipated'. It was irritating in opposition; in government, it was disastrous. Policy briefs piled up in her in-tray, then she would complain bitterly that she had not been properly informed on matters that the prime minister needed to know about. Absolutely everything had to be cleared by her—from each single draft cabinet submission, to all diary entries, through to the placement of office furniture.

They dismissed Credlin's defence that if she were a man her critics would not say she was a micro-manager—they would say she was across everything. 'That was bullshit,' one former Abbott intimate said. 'The reason people were pissed off was not because of that. It was the domineering, controlling, preventing them from getting to Abbott—silly stuff like that. Politicians don't like it when staff members, no matter how senior they are, behave like that. Or like taking part in cabinet discussions. Peta was the type of person who couldn't help herself. She wants to say what is on her mind.'

At one of the last meetings of the national security committee of cabinet, over which Abbott presided to discuss the expanded Syrian refugee intake, Scott Morrison had barely begun speaking when he was interrupted by Credlin. Abbott's practice at the NSC meetings was to go around the table in hierarchical order, which was as good a way as any, so Morrison had patiently waited for his turn, only to face a challenge, mid-sentence, from the chief of staff. 'If I can finish without interruption,' Morrison shot back firmly. Abbott mumbled something about how everyone should have their say, Morrison picked up where he left off, and the discussion continued. Old hands who sat and watched that, and who had also watched sensitive intelligence material make its way into the media, were horrified.

If the prime minister had a bad question time, which happened a few times in the disastrous aftermath of the first budget, Credlin would call an emergency meeting of all staff as soon as she got back to the office. It was not unusual for chiefs of staff to do this when things went awry. But her way of handling it was certainly different.

'It was basically to tell us loudly how hopeless we all were,' a senior adviser said.

There was a standard script, which went along the lines of: *I am fucking well fed-up with being the only person in the office who can get things done, I am fucking up at 5.00 am every working day, working until midnight, I look around at 9.00 pm for people, and there is no one here, and no one is answering their mobiles.*

'I must have heard that speech thirty times,' another senior adviser recounted.

They recall she was particularly tough on finance adviser Kathryn Lees. Lees would be called into the office, where she would be screamed at over something going wrong that had not been her fault. It was so loud, with Credlin telling her she was hopeless, useless, or incompetent — the usual rant — that others in the office could hear. Or she would simply do it in front of other staff. They would roll their eyes, then comfort one another later, the stronger ones knowing they had not done anything wrong. It was just 'Peta being Peta.'

'It was a miserable, miserable place,' one experienced adviser said when it was all over. Another said it was like coming out of a bad relationship. You didn't realise how bad it was until it was over.

Most of the staff still talk fondly of Abbott. But one by one, senior or junior, those closest to him, those who had also been integral to his success, left. A few left because of Credlin's insistence that — despite the fact they had families interstate — they had to be Canberra-based.

In his charter letter to ministers after the election, Abbott wrote: 'Please note that most ministerial staff are expected to be based in Canberra.' This was applied rigorously, almost without exceptions. Over time, the strain and the expense of travel forced them out.

Murray Hansen, the chief of staff to deputy leader Julie Bishop, was harassed over this for two years. Julie Bishop is a West Australian, and Hansen's family was in Brisbane, so he was based there. Bishop was not at all troubled by this. Given that they were hardly ever home, where Hansen was based made little difference — except if it was Brisbane, he would occasionally get to see his family.

Credlin insisted he had to be based in Canberra. Eventually, because of Bishop's intervention to Abbott, he was allowed to remain based in Brisbane, but it was always only for six months, at which time he was ordered to relocate to Canberra. Every six months Hansen had to go through the procedure of getting approval. If approval came after the expiry date, if Hansen needed to travel anywhere, it would have to be at his own expense. Hansen did not claim special entitlement; in fact, he made it clear if the rule were imposed, he would leave. Bishop did not want him to go.

It became a test of wills between the elected deputy leader of the party and the appointed chief of staff to the prime minister.

The Canberra-based rule was also applied in the prime minister's office. Abbott personally convinced Benny Ng to come back as his social-policy adviser after the 2013 election. Ng had been with him in the health portfolio. Forced to live in Canberra, he lasted nine months, worn down by the travel and by separation from his loved ones.

In their lighter moments, staff would quote to each other something that Christopher Pyne purportedly said about the wisdom (or lack of it) of the directive: 'Now they're all getting drunk in Canberra and bonking one another.'

When I first reported this directive and the effect it was

having on the morale of a new government, which should have felt exhilarated, there came the obligatory call from deputy chief of staff Andrew Hirst to say it was wrong. Subsequently it became an established, undeniable fact, as good people left or were denied jobs. The other consequence of forcing people to be based in Canberra was that they had little contact with the real world or its problems. They were all trapped in the same bubble. Or cell. Credlin made the job of prime ministerial policy advisers harder still by imposing severe restrictions on their travel, which limited their ability to liaise with stakeholder groups outside Canberra. She travelled extensively; they were all expected to stay at their desks.

The prime minister's office staff would cop it from both ends—from Credlin, if she decided they were not up to it, and from ministers wondering what was happening to their submissions, which were usually stacked sky high in her notorious in-tray.

In the beginning, Credlin would insist on seeing everything, including all draft cabinet submissions. She would vet the submissions of all shadow ministers in opposition. However, in government, it is unsustainable—unhealthy even—for one person to act as a clearing house down to that level.

The instructions were unequivocal. In an email to all staff sent at 3.02 am on 1 May 2014, Credlin wrote:

Team
We have made some changes with the management of paper in and out from the Prime Minister to make his life easier.
Effective immediately, no paper (speech, news report, letter—anything) goes into the PM directly from staff.
All paper for the Prime Minister to be handed to Kate

Rutherford. She has a special in-tray in her office for purpose.

Briefs from advisers—which come via me with a 'blue' on them—will not change.

This rule applies to <u>absolutely</u> everyone please.

Thanks

Staff knew full well that, despite the fact it would be put in Rutherford's in-tray, every item for the prime minister would in fact be funnelled through Credlin.

A level of order was established when Matt Stafford, who had worked with Credlin in the Coonan office, was appointed cabinet secretary. Senior advisers say that without him the place would have fallen apart. He was trusted by both Abbott and Credlin. Gradually he persuaded Credlin not to try to handle every single draft cabinet submission. It created bottlenecks, and it inhibited proper discussion, because all drafts submitted to her would live or die depending on her notations, without even making it to cabinet. Stafford found ways to get through to her. He was firm, he was frank, and he did not challenge her authority in front of others.

Other cabinet ministers also trusted Stafford. He would often act as a go-between or honest broker. Malcolm Turnbull and Julie Bishop would enlist his support on issues. Credlin would also use him to deal with them, because she could not do it herself.

One of Credlin's management techniques was to first isolate people and then to eliminate them. Or she issued ridiculous requests that made working there increasingly untenable. When she was away, she would bombard staff with emails to remember to do things such as change the water in the flower vases. Tony O'Leary was frogmarched by a security guard from an area where even journalists were allowed to mingle on election night in 2013 at Sydney's Four Seasons hotel, because he was told he did not have

The Peta Principal 53

the right clearance to be there. Andrew Hirst later claimed that two junior staff had taken it upon themselves to get security to eject him. It was preposterous to think that two woodchucks would spontaneously decide to throw out someone of O'Leary's standing, who began working for John Howard as his press secretary soon after he regained the opposition leadership in 1995.

That same night, two of Credlin's former colleagues from the Coonan office — Jane McMillan and Sarah McNamara — were allowed into the private room where Credlin and members of her family, as well as the Abbotts, could mingle.

They were not yet on the payroll, but soon would be. McNamara became a senior adviser in the prime minister's office on the environment and agriculture. McMillan, who had only worked briefly with Credlin, was brought into the press office without reference to senior press secretary James Boyce (although she did not know this at the time), who had enjoyed an excellent relationship with Abbott. Pretty soon, Boyce found his access to the leader had dried up, there was one fight too many with Credlin, and (this was another technique), it was announced he was going on extended holidays. He never came back.

It ended very badly for McMillan, too.

Former staff painted a picture of optimism and enthusiasm on their arrival, only to be greeted by what they later described as exhausted, battle-weary staff who had been worn down by the hard slog of opposition, or what they say was Credlin's volatile behaviour.

Because people stayed silent, for whatever reason, new staff were oblivious to what had gone before, and were enticed to join Team Abbott with tales of the unity in the office and assurances that Tony was a nice bloke and great to work for. One of them said later there was no warning of 'the Credlin factor'. Even some of those who had worked with Credlin previously had not experienced her in full flight, which was now happening more frequently as well as more publicly.

Jane McMillan fell into that camp.

'Incoming staff gave up well-paying jobs and their lives to work for the prime minister and, combined with the many dedicated staff who had slogged away during opposition, for a time it was a very good office,' a disappointed McMillan recalled for this book.

'The dysfunction was hidden in the early days, spoken about in whispers, intimated. But it didn't take long for the initial courtesies to be done away with and for the dysfunction to surface.

'It took me a while to realise that veteran staff were giving me a wide berth because I was seen as a "Credlin acolyte". Anyone who had been brought in by Peta was treated with caution in the early stages, until they realised we too were being victimised, blamed, and punished.

'Peta had a narrative for everyone in the office, themed around their "general incompetence" and her superior intellect, work ethic, and political nous. But you only had to talk to those staff members to realise they had once taken her to task, and were now suffering the consequences and were being frozen out.

'The office was regularly held hostage to Peta's moods. She would disappear, be uncontactable — or, worse — be present to single people out in group settings, and bully them. It was often followed by attempts to make it up to them with over-the-top gestures of generosity.

'She made a mockery of the sacrifice of everyone in that office who worked long hours, didn't get to see their families, and had to do her bidding with ministers by arguing for unsustainable or irrational policy positions.

'Everyone's reputation suffered, but we were all dedicated to Tony and the hope that things would get better. They never did.'

During the two years of the Abbott government, good staff who could stand up to Credlin steadily disappeared. Others, like Lees, took refuge in the cabinet office, which became something of a safe haven.

McMillan went on holidays in December 2014 and, like Boyce, never came back, after a row in the office with Abbott, Credlin, and Hirst over a leaked story that had profound consequences for Abbott's leadership. More on that later. McNamara went to work for Ian Macfarlane after his chief of staff, Kirsty Boazman, resigned in despair.

Abbott's colleagues also witnessed her temper tantrums in front of him. Others also sat there uncomfortably during meetings when she did the same with Loughnane.

When his ministers weren't feeling embarrassed for Abbott, they were wondering why he didn't do anything about it. Credlin's triggers varied. Sometimes it was because of unfavourable mentions about her in the media. Bishop would be blamed for reports that were not her fault, including things I had reported.

Abbott would tell Bishop she had to make it up with Credlin. 'She's a staffer, mate,' Bishop would say.

Bishop was seldom allowed to use a VIP aircraft, even if they were available. It made visits to Pacific Island nations extremely difficult, given there were only weekly commercial flights to some of the islands.

Bishop grabbed hold of Pyne one day in question time. He had just come back from an extended official visit to Samoa, Fiji, and New Caledonia, and had been given a VIP plane to make the tour. Bishop asked him how he managed it. Pyne simply told Credlin that unless he had a VIP aircraft, it would be impossible to do the trip. He would have had to fly in and out of New Zealand twice.

Bishop was seldom mentioned in despatches, and if she had the temerity to pass on complaints to the prime minister from his colleagues about his office, particularly about Credlin's behaviour, she would be admonished. 'Without her, you wouldn't be here,' Abbott would tell the woman who, to that point, had been elected as deputy leader in her own right three times by his party room.

They kept treating Bishop like a minion. In December 2014, Credlin told Bishop she was not allowed to go to a global climate-negotiation conference in Lima, Peru, which was being attended by representatives from 190 countries.

Bishop raised the issue in cabinet. Her colleagues readily agreed she should go. Abbott said nothing. Nor did Credlin, who was sitting in on that cabinet meeting. Next thing Bishop knew was that she was being 'chaperoned' by the trade minister, Andrew Robb. Credlin had told Robb to pack his bags — he was going with Bishop, because they couldn't trust her to stick to the government's position.

Bishop's calls or text messages were not always returned. If she couldn't get Abbott, she would try Credlin. Many times, there was no response. 'Charming, isn't it?' she would say.

Finance had also been instructed by Credlin not to release funds for travel by ministers unless there was a written letter of authority from her. This made it especially difficult for the foreign minister, given the amount of travel she undertook. Bookings would be made, then the office would have to wait for approval. There were times when approval came only twenty-four hours before take-off. On one occasion, when discount fares had already been bought for a dozen officials to attend an overseas conference, the fares lapsed before approval came through, so taxpayers had to fork out the full going rate for the tickets. One cabinet minister complained that he had submitted the names of two staff to accompany him overseas, only to have Credlin reject his choices, then tell him which two he could take.

Eyebrows shot upwards at the full Coalition staff meeting before the 2014 budget when she told them they were not to be seen drinking or celebrating in the hallways. 'She said journos would be roaming, waiting to take a picture of one of us with a champagne glass,' one staffer recalled. 'This raised a few eyebrows, considering her record.'

This was a reference to Credlin having been charged with low-level drink-driving in May 2013, after ACT police caught her returning home from Abbott's budget-reply speech. She pleaded guilty to blowing 0.075 during a breath-test, but avoided having a conviction recorded.

Because she had control over all appointments, and also because she fed journalists, there were snitches everywhere. On 28 October 2014, Credlin turned up at the weekly press secretaries' meetings, normally run by Jane McMillan. Credlin told the press secretaries that there was altogether too much gossip going on, and what's more, she and the prime minister's office knew which of them and their bosses were talking to journalists. Although no names were mentioned, those attending believed her remarks were directed at two ministers—Julie Bishop and Scott Morrison.

She said they knew who was doing it, because the journalists wanted to be friends with the prime minister's office more than they wanted to be friends with the ministers or their press secretaries.

She warned them that, if ministers complained or gossiped too much, word would get back to the prime minister's office, and they would end up on the backbench. She told the press secretaries it was their job to control their bosses. The press secretaries duly reported this back to their bosses, who were incensed.

According to one minister, this is how his press secretary relayed Credlin's warning: 'Your boss: punted, backbench! You: no job.'

'I haven't heard of anything like this happening before, anywhere,' another frontbencher later told me. 'It's created a culture where people dob on each other. It's not a collegiate atmosphere, not healthy for a young government. I think it is profoundly wrong.'

In one screaming match with the Senate leader, Eric Abetz, Credlin told him, also with use of the F-bomb, that he was no good, had never been any good, and she always believed he was no good. After the election, she refused to allow him to appoint respected long-time Coalition staffer Chris Fryar as his chief of staff. Abetz kept Fryar on as a senior adviser. Abetz, who was also unhappy about Credlin's attendance at cabinet meetings, complained to Abbott about Credlin's behaviour, then subsequently advised him to move her and Hockey. But his shabby treatment did not stop him from defending Credlin in public, nor from desperately trying to muster the numbers for Abbott on that last night. For Abetz, loyalty to the conservative cause outweighed any personal humiliation.

The industry minister, Ian Macfarlane, had his moments with Credlin, but denies one anecdote that he complained to Abbott after she challenged him in a meeting of the expenditure review committee. Macfarlane walked out of a cabinet meeting, closely followed by Credlin after a blow-up with colleagues on ethanol. Abbott soon joined them, gave Macfarlane a bear hug, and told him they would sort it out.

Macfarlane and Credlin clashed over other issues. Credlin was infuriated by Macfarlane's appointment of former Labor cabinet minister Greg Combet to negotiate a rewrite of work practices at SPC Ardmona. They had another run-in where she threw a few expletives around when she lost an argument. He did not let it get to him.

However, Macfarlane's chief of staff, Kirsty Boazman, who had been recruited back to his office from Hong Kong after the election, left after barely a year into the term, deeply disillusioned. She had worked for Macfarlane in the Howard years, and believed she would be coming back to the same collegiate, constructive, professional environment. As one of six senior female staffers enticed from private-sector roles, wincingly tagged 'Abbott's Amazons' (they blame Credlin for coining the phrase), Boazman was among the first to resign in obvious dismay over the lack of management skills and policy processes in the prime minister's office. Within two years, the group was largely dispersed. It became a sad postscript to the treatment of women inside the government.

'I consider the nature of Australian conservative politics fundamentally changed for the worse because of the partisan manner in which that office operated,' one of them said later. 'It ruined "public service" for many of us.'

According to another cabinet minister: 'There was not a single member of the cabinet she [Credlin] did not undermine.'

This may or may not be true. The fact that they believed it was true showed how little trust there was inside the government.

If they weren't being undermined, they were certainly being reprimanded. Volubly. Credlin was sitting in cabinet one day when the bells rang for a division; at the time, there was confusion about whether the ministers had arranged pairs or not for the vote.

The heavy cabinet room door swung open. An irate Credlin stepped out first, turned on her heel, and, in a raised voice, said to the assembled ministers so that everybody outside the room could hear it, too: 'I will fix it. Make sure you get pairs next time.'

So many people were frozen out—Mark Textor and Tony Nutt, to name just two. Textor is renowned around the globe for his expertise in polling and providing advice to conservative political parties and their leaders. He had helped John Key in New Zealand, and Boris Johnson and David Cameron in the UK. Textor had run successful campaigns in the United States, Fiji, Malaysia, and elsewhere. His counsel was rarely sought by Abbott and Credlin.

As John Howard's principal private secretary, Nutt knew where the bodies, along with their secrets, were buried. MPs in trouble went to him for help. He would either solve their problems or inter them. He worked briefly for Abbott after the election, in an office the size of a telephone box across the corridor from the main suite in the cabinet policy unit, before he went to New South Wales as state director. After the spill in February, friendly journalists were briefed that he was coming back. Nervous MPs were told the same thing. They were reassured, or rather lulled into thinking, that he would be back soon to provide a steady hand, as well as invaluable political-management expertise. Nutt, meanwhile, was telling close friends that he had no intention of going back while Credlin was there—unless, of course, the prime minister requested it, in which case Nutt would have had no choice but to go back. But the prime minister didn't ask. Nutt could not publicly contradict what the prime minister's chief of staff was briefing to gullible commentators. He eventually spoke with his feet, arriving in the prime minister's office on the afternoon after Abbott was deposed to help Malcolm Turnbull with the transition.

But it was the treatment of Abbott's wife, Margie, that troubled staff the most. People in the inner circle reported that it was rare or exceptional for Credlin and Margie to be in the same room or at the same event together.

Margie was initially a reluctant conscript, but, once she got comfortable in the role, she was willing to do more. She said so to Boyce and to another press secretary, Jude Donnelly. It never happened. It was as if she was kept as a prop of last resort. She was prominent during the election campaign, then around the time of the February spill.

As soon as the 2013 campaign ended, a campaign in which Margie and the three Abbott daughters — Frances, Louise, and Bridget — had appeared indispensable, they seemed to become superfluous.

The evening after Abbott's election victory, businessman Alf Moufarrige hosted a celebration at his plush Hunters Hill, Sydney, home for Abbott, his family, all staff and their partners, plus a few other selected guests and their spouses. Arriving guests saw place settings for the entire Abbott family arranged on one table. When they next looked, the settings for Margie and the girls, which had included specially created laminated placemats, featuring photos of the Abbott women, were gone.

Disappointed Abbott staff, there with their own partners, who had been looking forward to congratulating Margie and the girls for their efforts during the campaign — as well as hoping that Margie would become a regular fixture in the PM's schedule — asked what had happened. The response from Moufarrrige was that the chief of staff had decided the event would be office-only, so the family was now not coming. Abbott spent most of the celebration in huddles with Credlin, Hirst, and Boyce.

The absence of Margie and the girls was baffling to the other staff, especially as John Howard was there with his wife, Janette, and Philip Ruddock was there with his wife, Heather.

Credlin continued to keep an iron grip on the prime minister's diary. Every single invitation, no matter in what combination, for the prime minister and his family—whether to Abbott, to Abbott and Margie, to Margie alone, or to their daughters—was vetted by her. Credlin would then decide which invitations were passed on, or not, and when. Support staff were not permitted to inform the prime minister's wife, or family, about any invitations until Credlin had sifted through them. Former staff confirmed that a request from Margie for diary details was denied. According to one former adviser: 'Margie was kept in the dark.'

According to another: 'Peta did not want Margie to have access to staff, despite staff wanting to go to events with her.'

One by-product of the diary restrictions was that staff would only know when Abbott was coming and going from his Canberra office by peering out into the courtyard to see if his car was there. The other was that when Margie was eventually told about invitations, it was usually at such short notice that she could not arrange to join the prime minister at official functions. It played on their consciences. Someone suggested that Margie should get a briefing from the Finance Department on her entitlements, so she would know what she legitimately could or couldn't do. One staffer told me this never happened while she was there.

Early on, Abbott asked an adviser to prepare some notes for Margie, who had been invited to attend a diplomatic function where she would be making a brief speech to the wives of heads of mission. The adviser did as requested, then sent the notes by email to Margie, copying in Credlin. When it lobbed in her in-box, Credlin exploded. She angrily berated the adviser, telling him this was not the White House: he did not work for the prime minister's wife; he worked for the prime minister.

'If you get any requests for briefings for Margie's ladies' lunches, it's not going to happen,' she told him.

Credlin exercised an unprecedented level of control over the activities of the prime minister's wife. This was spelled out in an email to the staff of the prime minister's office sent on Tuesday 18 February 2014. The subject matter was: 'Assistance for Mrs Abbott.' Credlin wrote:

Team

Any contact on issues regarding Mrs Abbott's involvement (media, invitations other requests) should all be sent to Sam Cusack so we have a central place of input. If Margie rings the office, all calls should be sent to Sam so she can deal with them. Please don't give ad hoc advice on anything. This is important so that we are very careful on entitlements usage as there is no specific entitlement to travel, comcars, expenditure or staff time for the spouse of the Prime Minister (unlike the US where the 'First Lady' is actually a constitutional position with a budget, office, chief of staff etc).

Thanks

The email should have been entitled 'No Assistance for Mrs Abbott.' Like the email about paperwork, this also signalled to staff that everything to do with Margie would eventually be funnelled through Credlin, or vetted by her. Staff familiar with the process told me that invitations or requests would be sent to whoever was in charge of the diary, who was then under instructions to pass them on to Credlin. Credlin would then decide which were to be forwarded to the prime minister's wife. Naturally, nothing could be forwarded by the support staff until it came back from Credlin.

The restricted access to the diary, as well as the deliberate exclusion of the prime minister's wife by the late passing-on of information or invitations, was confirmed to me by several staff with intimate knowledge of the operations of the office.

Prime ministerial staff have routinely helped the prime minister's spouse or partner. There has seldom been a problem with 'entitlements', because everyone recognises that families of politicians are, in effect, part of the package, if only because of the volume of requests for them to be patrons of charities or to speak at public functions. Apart from being their nearest and dearest, they remain key to the success of the politician. Requests to spouses to attend events or to travel overseas flow directly from the prime minister's role.

Janette Howard would ring senior advisers directly if she needed assistance. In other prime ministers' offices, part of the duties of one member of the administrative staff would be to help out with correspondence or requests directly relating to the spouse. In cabinet ministers' offices, staff would regularly respond to inquiries from families. No one ever calculated the 'cost' of doing this; it simply added to the working day. In any case, if the concern was about the proper use of public monies, the federal secretariat could have been asked to pitch in.

Certainly, no one would think to question Margie's food intake at Kirribilli, unless it happened to be a truckload of Beluga caviar, or a ferryload of Grange — yet, incredibly, according to staff, Credlin forbade household workers from ordering food for her at the official residence.

There were also rules about Margie's physical access to the office. According to one source, when Margie arrived to attend the Press Gallery's mid-winter ball with her husband, she was escorted to the sitting room, adjacent to the main office, and separated from it by the foyer. On VIP aircraft, if she happened to be there, and if the prime minister needed to be briefed, she would move from the front to the mid-section. This was not so unusual — spouses would make themselves scarce if sensitive matters were being discussed—but the edicts on Margie's isolation, such as making her sit well away from others in the office when she was there for a social engagement, made staff uncomfortable, especially those who had worked in other offices for either leaders or senior ministers.

Staff struggled for explanations for Margie's exclusion. This was one: 'Credlin thought Margie was a distraction for Tony, that Tony was too concerned about whether Margie was OK rather than focussing on the job,' a former senior adviser said.

'Yet when she [Peta] was behaving like a schoolgirl, she was just as distracting, because he never wanted her to be upset.'

One senior Liberal MP, lamenting the strict rules that the prime minister's office imposed on the travel of spouses, suggested another reason was that because Credlin could not travel with her husband, others should not be allowed to travel with their partners.

People would often ask why Margie appeared with him so infrequently. I refrained from writing much about this until after the coup, because I did not want to embarrass Margie. But it is important for people to know what happened, and how the peculiar dynamic between the prime minister and his chief of staff, and her level of control, affected every aspect of his life—usually, to his detriment.

Abbott and Credlin were rarely apart. For anyone who has worked in a politician's office, it is easy to see how an us-and-them mentality develops, and how tightly bonded the people in it become. However, there is no doubt that this prime minister and this chief of staff had a very different type of relationship.

A minister recalls the time he was in the prime minister's office after a meeting with Credlin. As he made to leave, he turned back to see her and Abbott walking down the corridor side-by-side. They could not see him. Suddenly, Abbott gave her a slap on the bum — open-handed, playful, with a loud thwack. She smiled at him, and they kept walking.

Others recall occasions that were much more awkward.

One Liberal MP was invited by Abbott to dine with him and Credlin in Melbourne at one of their favourite Italian restaurants in Little Collins St. Their regular table was towards the back of the dining room, where they sat with their backs towards most of the diners. The MP sat next to his staffer (a male), who had accompanied him to the dinner, facing the prime minister, who was seated beside his chief of staff.

What happened made the staffer sit bolt upright, then shift back in his seat. To their dismay, they watched Credlin feed Abbott — who had a voracious appetite, and had already polished off his main course — mouthfuls of food from her plate with her fork. They had all heard the stories about her finishing his sentences for him at meetings with business leaders, but this took their behaviour to a whole other level.

The MP noticed that a couple of other diners sitting nearby had witnessed the spectacle. Asked to describe the reaction of the other patrons, he told me: 'It was like *I am not seeing what I am seeing.*'

According to the MP, Credlin also fed Abbott some of her dessert — again, from her fork, off her plate. As the meal was ending, she put her head on his shoulder to complain about being tired, to which Abbott said they must go soon. By this time, the MP and his staffer were highly uncomfortable. When he told me the story for this book, I asked him what he was thinking as he watched what happened.

'I have only ever done that with my partner or a date,' he said. When the dinner ended, he and his staffer spent some time discussing it. He did not wish to be named because, even though they were no longer in office, he feared there were still people close to Abbott and Credlin who could launch reprisals.

One cabinet minister felt embarrassed at the dinner table one evening after what he regarded as an inappropriate tactile moment between the prime minister and his chief of staff. This senior member of the government thought it was 'creepy', but also thought that if he had behaved similarly with a member of his staff, his wife would not have been at all happy.

True, Abbott was a hugger — with male staff, too, to celebrate a victory or cut the tension. However, there were times when his hugs with Credlin after spats made onlookers squirm. These more personal, un-blokey type of encounters usually occurred as he tried to comfort her, after her reminders to him about the sacrifices she had made for him. 'I was always relieved there wasn't a camera around,' one staffer confided.

She would apply his make-up before an event, then touch it up in front of people if necessary. They had never seen another chief of staff do this. Mind you, if she wasn't there, she would insist that another staff member, including male advisers, had to do it. During the 2013 campaign, she arranged the purchase of expensive matching Tumi luggage for herself and Abbott, inscribed, in gold, with their initials.

There was one story that sent a quiet ripple through the Coalition when it became public. On 26 July 2015, the *Daily Telegraph* published online, then in print the next day, photographs of the prime minister on 'a rare weekend off' at Perisher, skiing with Credlin, his daughter Frances, and his foreign policy adviser, Andrew Shearer.

The weekend had been organised by Credlin, who is an avid skier. According to the *Telegraph* report, it was 'believed to be only the first or second weekend that Mr Abbott, who is known for his remarkable workload, has taken off this year'.

Even though Frances was there, Liberal MPs were aghast, quietly asking each other how come he had chosen to spend his one weekend off with Credlin and other staff. Margie had apparently been visiting her homeland, New Zealand.

Party officials who intervened got short shrift from Abbott.

Michael Yabsley, the party's former federal treasurer, was one of the first to raise with Abbott the conflict of interest involved in having Brian Loughnane as federal director while his wife served as the leader's chief of staff.

My husband, Vincent Woolcock, worked full time for every Liberal leader from Billy Snedden to Malcolm Turnbull the first time around — handling logistics, not policy — then retired, but helped out occasionally on a part-time basis, including during Abbott's election-winning 2013 campaign. Nevertheless, he has often paid a professional penalty because of my scribblings, including unhinged suggestions by angry white male conservative commentators, after Abbott was deposed, that I had helped make it happen so Vincent could get a job with Turnbull.

However, the problem that Yabsley identified, first reported in my column in *The Australian* as early as 2010, was obvious and much more serious. Liberal MPs, staff, or people from the party organisation who encountered a problem with the federal secretariat felt they could not report it to the leader's office. And people with a problem with the leader's office could not report it to Loughnane.

Yabsley says that when he raised this with Abbott, Abbott accused him of being gender-driven. After a bit of argy-bargy, with Yabsley accusing Abbott of engaging in subterfuge, Abbott told him to get stuffed. Yabsley quit as federal treasurer, not just because of this, but partly because of it.

Yabsley's replacement, Philip Higginson, also quit in a blaze of glory and for largely the same reasons. He had been friends with Abbott for twenty years. Abbott had recruited Higginson to the party, then pleaded with him to take on the job after Yabsley resigned.

Abbott did not want Loughnane to go, and told him so after the 2013 election, when it was widely expected that he would leave, and he especially did not want Credlin to go. He wanted to keep the winning team together.

It was Abbott's interview in December 2014 with Lyndal Curtis on ABC 24, echoing Credlin's constant refrain that he doubted she would have copped as much criticism if she were a man, which further infuriated his MPs.

'The point I want to make, first of all, is this is the same office which ran a very effective opposition, it's the same office which has got an enormous amount done this year, sometimes under very difficult circumstances,' he said.

'The other point I make, do you really think that my chief of staff would be under this kind of criticism if her name was P-E-T-E-R as opposed to P-E-T-A?'

When he was asked if this was a direct message to his colleagues, Abbott said, 'I think people need to take a long, hard look at themselves with some of these criticisms.'

They were looking, all right. At him. And at her. They were not happy with what they saw.

A month after he seconded the spill motion, I spoke to the West Australian MP Don Randall. Randall had just been to a morning tea with other MPs. Their conversation was still revolving around the spill and everything that had flowed from it. Randall told me he had been speaking to fellow backbencher Peter Hendy, who told him he feared he had blotted his copybook because he had told the prime minister what he thought about Credlin. He had the uneasy feeling that she was listening on the other line. It is possible.

Others reported that they thought she was eavesdropping on their supposedly private discussions with the prime minister, because the interconnecting doors between his office and hers were open.

It did not necessarily work both ways. She had a large sign printed up and attached to her door, facing into his office, with a firm instruction, obviously meant for him, in bold type and in capitals: 'I am in a meeting. Please do not interrupt.'

Christopher Pyne told Randall at that morning tea that he thought things were going really well, that it had been a really good week, and that most people believed what he had done was right, because it had brought everything to a head. According to Randall, Pyne told him the bloodletting had resulted in a whole lot of behavioural and procedural changes. Without his actions, Pyne told him, the government would still be moribund.

Randall said he told Pyne at morning tea: 'She is still a shocking woman. Chiefs of staff usually want to help, but she is only interested in punishing people.' Randall affirmed then that Abbott 'only had four to six months to sort it out'. Andrew Southcott observed to Randall that although Natasha Griggs was an Abbott supporter, she had a sense that his demise was inevitable. She had voted for Abbott because she thought he had to be given time to turn it around, but was not confident he had the capacity to do it. Randall reported there was some surprise at how well Abbott had done in the week before we spoke. It was possible he might even get in front, Randall mused. 'If that's the case, fine; if he doesn't, and grinds down to bad Newspolls ...' The sentence was left unfinished.

Randall was a straight-shooter who seldom missed his target. I asked Randall if it was true, as someone had told me, that he had described Credlin to Abbott as an effing bitch, that she had to go, and if she didn't go then the party room would get rid of both of them. He said that was a bit 'extrapolated'.

He said he had told Abbott she was a bitch, that everyone hated her guts, and that unless he removed her, nothing would change. He told him this in the party room before the vote was taken, when Abbott went over to shake hands with him and the mover of the spill motion, Luke Simpkin. Randall says Abbott told them: 'No matter how the spill goes, we will move on — there won't be any malice.'

'I told him nothing will change unless you get rid of that bitch,' Randall told me.

'People were interpreting that to mean that they would both have to go. That's obviously what the case would be.' Randall's mood about the functioning of the government had not been improved by an event the previous week in the party room that John Howard had addressed. While it brought back good memories, it did nothing to improve his frame of mind. 'It brought it all back,' Randall said. 'He [Howard] and his office were inclusive. He brought people with him.'

When it was all over, in her first public appearance at an *Australian Women's Weekly* awards ceremony in September 2015, Credlin conceded nothing, apologised for none of it, and began the rewriting of history. She claimed she had only done one interview in her time in the job, and that was with Samantha Maiden about her unsuccessful IVF program. This was not true. She had given a few, including an exclusive interview to *The Australian* on 3 November 2014, where she said she had set up a Coalition Women's Network after the silence of the sisterhood when Clive Palmer launched a disgraceful attack on her.

On 17 July 2014, at a staff meeting held the day the carbon tax repeal bill was passed, Credlin asked all male staff to leave so she could address the women. She wept, saying how much she had been hurt by Palmer's comments, how hard it was to get to the top, and said she was there to help and mentor them—amongst other things.

She cried twice when talking about the sacrifices that had to be made. Women who were there, whose promotions or pay increases had been vetoed, were seething. Others squirmed.

One of the logistics staff, Michelle Moffatt, began the applause. Others followed. Moffatt then stood and applauded. In true old-Soviet or modern North Korean style, fearful to be seen not to be clapping hard enough or not standing, they all slowly stood and clapped. Fairly or not, many believed the network was a vehicle designed to protect or promote Credlin, or deflect criticism of her behaviour, particularly towards women, whenever it surfaced.

A Liberal member of the ACT Legislative Assembly, Giulia Jones, falls into that camp. Jones made disparaging remarks to another former Abbott employee about Credlin's treatment of women when she heard that Credlin was establishing the network, supposedly to mentor women. She then received what she regarded as an intimidating phone call from Andrew Hirst. He told her that word had reached the boss that she had been talking about Peta, and he didn't want to have to go back and tell the boss it was true. Jones, distressed both by the tone and the content of the call, told him to tell the 'boss' that she was always loyal to Tony.

Jones was no stranger to the office dynamics, having worked for Abbott in opposition. She left the office to run as the federal candidate for Canberra in 2010. After she lost, as she was always bound to do, she contacted Credlin to say she was looking for a job and was prepared to help in any way she could. Jones was called by the office manager, and was told that there was no job for her. She had a new baby, a mortgage, she had put her hand up for an unwinnable seat in what is traditionally hostile territory for Liberals, and yet there was nothing for her. Jones says she had also had a couple of unpleasant encounters with Credlin in the office before her departure. Jones remains dismissive of Credlin's women's network. She was elected to the assembly in 2012, and stands by her comments about Credlin's poor treatment of women, but nevertheless feels for Abbott. 'I really admire Tony. I value the values that he stands for, and I feel this is a terribly sad outcome for the country and for him,' she told me.

In the interview with *The Australian*'s Sharri Markson on 3 November, when Credlin was asked about there being only one woman in the cabinet, she said she thought it was the first time in history that 50 per cent of ministerial chiefs of staff were women. By the time Credlin left, many of them were already gone—disillusioned or burnt out.

She also told Markson that the toughest articles written about her were written by other women. 'I agree with Julie Bishop that there's a special place in Hell reserved for women who don't support other women,' Credlin was quoted as saying.

As this article appeared days after a column by me on the network, relaying complaints by women MPs miffed that not one of them had been invited to attend its launch by the prime minister, friends rang me to discuss it. Maybe I will end up in Hell—although I doubt for that reason—but I suspect I will have company.

As the year drew to a close, concerns about Credlin and the government's standing were growing.

John Howard was deeply worried about how the government was travelling, and how Abbott's office was being managed. More personally, Howard was also unhappy about the way his former chief of staff, Arthur Sinodinos, had been treated. Backbenchers were complaining to Howard about the problems, blaming Credlin, appealing to him to intercede.

He had tried to counsel Abbott, before as well as after the February spill, making it clear that he believed Abbott had vested too much of his authority in Credlin. Abbott insisted Credlin was doing a good job. He was not going to move her.

As close as he was to his then chief of staff, Grahame Morris, Howard had had to let him go at the height of the travel-rorts scandal in 1997, when Morris had overlooked vital pieces of paper.

Morris knew he was damaging his boss, and knew that political staff with a controversial profile could not properly perform their duties. As he says, it took him less than two seconds to know he had to go. At the time, Abbott told Morris his actions showed he was 'the prince of minders'. Morris returned the compliment by texting Abbott after his farewell press conference as prime minister that he 'would always be a prince of the Liberal Party' for having led them back into government.

It is difficult to nominate a single influential figure who did not think Credlin should have done the princely thing and stepped aside — including Rupert Murdoch, who tweeted in early 2015 that Credlin should resign. Abbott ignored everybody, from global media mogul (what would he know about running an office?) down to not-so-humble backbenchers. And so did she. Even if she had offered to resign, he would not have allowed it. He would have been completely lost, so low was his opinion of his own abilities.

Credlin was almost certainly right when she told Connie Fierravanti-Wells that Abbott would not have been able continue without her. It was utterly bizarre.

Just before the spill in February, in a column published in *The Australian* on 29 January 2015, I wrote this: 'There is no guarantee the Prime Minister will perform better if he is forced to sack his chief of staff, Peta Credlin. Government insiders fear he has become psychologically dependent on her, a view supported by the private comments of friends who worry he would feel bereft without her.' Wallis Simpson.

It was the first time this had been articulated publicly in such a way. It was one explanation for a pattern of baffling behaviour, it encapsulated the fears of his colleagues, and it became part of political folklore.

There are those who feel Credlin has been viewed too harshly, and that more people should have stood up to her, citing examples of those who did and won. In any case, ultimately, it was Abbott's responsibility, and an insight into his own character.

'At the end of the day, you are the politician, and you are responsible for the conduct of your office,' one puzzled cabinet minister said, wondering why Abbott lacked the will or the emotional intelligence to fix it.

According to another cabinet minister who stayed loyal to Abbott: 'Most people didn't push back. She is a big, striking, opinionated woman, and many people were intimidated by her. The control meant there wasn't the flow of information and advice to the prime minister there should have been. He allowed that to happen, and the buck stops with him.'

Assessing the combination of Abbott and Credlin, one senior adviser to a cabinet minister said: 'He knew he wasn't up to it, she knew he wasn't up to it, so they both hunkered down.'

Finally, his MPs realised there was only one way to get rid of Credlin. They came to realise that if they wanted to be rid of her, they also had to get rid of him. Their view was, if that's what it took, so be it. He was collateral damage, one of them said later to a former Abbott staffer.

A senior member of the government who made the transition from Abbott to Turnbull summed it up thus: 'John Howard knew what you felt before you felt it. Tony couldn't see that. He didn't have a feel for the party. This is where the lack of counsellors around him became critical. He had one source of advice. A great number of ministers and backbenchers did not trust in the judgement of that person or the person herself. We could not speak honestly to her.

'We were not intimidated by her. We got sick of the attacks, the undermining, the leaking.'

In January, before the spill, Peter Hendy received firm instructions from one of his branch presidents in his bellwether seat of Eden-Monaro. He told Hendy that the next time he wanted to hear from him was after Abbott had been removed. Hendy was listening. Not long after receiving this instruction, Hendy told people: 'Don't forget, we have been putting up with this for five years.' They had had enough.

CHAPTER THREE

Pressing Problems

At the Press Gallery reunion to mark the 30th anniversary of the election of the Hawke government on 9 March 2013, a young woman approached me and introduced herself as Clare Arthurs. At that time, she was working for the ABC.

Clare confided that in her previous life, not long after she had agreed to join the staff of former Labor minister Greg Combet, she was told that if she wanted to know what her life would be like as a press secretary, she should read my book, *So Greek*. She reached the bit where, early one day, my old boss, the treasurer, Peter Costello, sent the receptionist, Philippa, to get me out of the toilet in his Melbourne office, and I ended the same day by dropping the F-bomb on him in his Sydney hotel suite. This experience appeared in the opening pages, providing the title for what I thought would be my one-and-only book. Clare wobbled when she read that passage. She lasted six months in the job.

After publication of the book, my career, which I thought had ended, was resuscitated. I began writing a weekly column in *The Australian*, as well as appearing regularly on *Insiders* on ABC TV, and *Afternoon Agenda* on Sky, where I would freely offer my advice to all and sundry. My first experience as an interviewee after the publication of *So Greek* was on *Lateline*, when I was interviewed by Leigh Sales, whom Malcolm Turnbull has described to colleagues as one of the most beautiful women on television.

When her producer, a dear woman called Cath, was trying to get a handle on how much time I would need for make-up before the pre-recorded interview, she asked: 'What are you, Penny Wong or Julie Bishop?'

'Somewhere in-between?' I ventured.

A while after that, I was in the make-up chair at *Insiders* when Penny Wong arrived. To my surprise, she was embarrassed about being seen without make-up. To reassure her, I told her she looked fine, then related my experience with Cath. We all had a good laugh, including the lovely Sarah Klein and Thelma Henson, who performed like magicians those early Sundays. Eventually, I encountered Julie Bishop in the make-up room. The fact is, she did not take very long at all. I spent more time in the chair than she did.

It only took one appearance on *Insiders*, my first, to remind me that unless I said something completely dumb, there were more important things to pay attention to. After the show ended, my brother, Steve, rang to tell me I was great (he loves me, after all) but the HR manager for Coles had called him to point out that my nail polish didn't match my jacket. I would spend days swotting on everything from the budget to climate change to tax reform to leadership speculation, only to have people compliment me on my sweater, or ring the executive producer, Kellie Mayo, to ask where I had bought a pair of red ankle boots.

When I worked with Costello, my own appearance was the least of my worries—I used to fuss over his. But when I look back on my time there, it really wasn't so bad. Certainly, when I compare it to what press secretaries before and since have endured, it was nothing. The hours were long, the demands never-ending, the stress phenomenal, and the fear of stuffing up overwhelming, but I wasn't sacked, my boss wasn't sacked, and the government managed to do many, many good things. It was a privilege to be a small part of a successful operation.

One reason it worked well was the clear delineation of responsibilities. For starters, there was never any doubt who was the boss. It was the treasurer. Or, in Howard's case, the prime minister. Also, Costello always had a clear view about which were the next two most important positions in his office: the chief of staff, followed by the press secretary—get the policy right, get the message right. Occasionally there was overlap, as there is in any collegial office, but they were separate and distinct roles. That's not how it worked in Abbott's prime ministerial office, where the chief of staff usurped all poistions, leaving experienced operators like Tony O'Leary, James Boyce, and Jane McMillan with no choice but to resign, severely degrading the media-management skills of the office.

To get a wider perspective of the experience and the role of press secretaries, as well as their importance in the scheme of things, I gathered the recollections of a few to see what it was like in their day. Most of them had a much harder time of it than I ever did; however, their experiences, whether through tragedy, or farce, or the brutality of politics, underlined the importance of leaving media management to the experts.

At the farewell in his honour before he left Australia in 1971 to take up an appointment at the Commonwealth Secretariat in London, Tony Eggleton described his job as a press secretary by saying he was 'a valet, a chauffeur, a decoy, a bag carrier, a sounding board and a whipping boy'.

Eggleton was all that and much more—probably the best press

secretary ever to work for conservative prime ministers, probably the best press secretary ever in Australia, full stop.

He had had experience in print, radio, and television before John Gorton offered him a job as director of public relations for the Department of Navy in Canberra. It was 1960. At the time, Eggleton was chief of staff for ABC TV news in Victoria. He had been part of the team responsible for putting together the first-ever TV news bulletins for the public broadcaster in Sydney and Melbourne. He remembers Melbourne staff being issued with Wellington boots to negotiate the construction site between the Nissan huts to the studios in Ripponlea. Heady days—nothing like the days he would encounter later. As the spokesman for the navy, it was his handling of the *Voyager* disaster on 10 February 1964, when 82 men on board the vessel were killed after it collided with the aircraft carrier HMAS *Melbourne*, which drew him to the attention of the then prime minister, Robert Menzies.

In September 1965, he went to work for Menzies, who called him 'laddie' and made him martinis, which Eggleton discreetly poured into the pot plants at Kirribilli (Menzies couldn't come to terms with a journalist who didn't drink), kept on through to Menzies' retirement, and then stayed on. I spoke at length to him about three particular episodes in his career: the first, the day that Harold Holt disappeared; the second, the night that John Gorton swept a young journalist by the name of Geraldine Willesee off her feet and into an adventure that got her the sack; and the third, 11 November 1975.

On 17 December 1967, Eggleton was mowing the lawn, getting ready for the arrival of his wife Mary's mother for Christmas, when he got a phone call from Herschel Hurst, then head of the Melbourne *Sun News-Pictorial* Canberra bureau, inviting him to drinks. A short time later, Hurst rang again to tell Eggleton there were rumours that the prime minister had disappeared while swimming at Cheviot Beach.

Eggleton dismissed this by saying plenty of prominent people holidayed in that part of the world, and it was probably one of them. Hurst rang again ten minutes later to say the rumours were stronger that it was Holt. Eggleton then rang D24 (as police headquarters were then known), to be told they were investigating Holt's suspected disappearance. Eggleton tracked down Holt's wife, Zara, who was catching up with a long-time friend visiting from Queensland, to tell her the media were reporting that the prime minister was in trouble. Zara was untroubled. She told Eggleton that Holt often swam out to the rocks and stayed there, sunning himself. Eggleton rang Holt's private secretary, Peter Bailey, told him what was going on, and arranged for a Mystere, one of the smaller planes in the VIP fleet, to be put on standby.

Bailey rang John Bunting, the head of the prime minister's department, who was at his holiday house at Dalmeny on the New South Wales south coast. Nothing back then was as simple as it sounds, and for those who complain about the effect of social media and 24-hour news cycles, think about this: Bunting did not have a phone at his house. Bailey had to ring the local post office, whereupon the postmistress got on her bike, rode to Bunting's house to tell him there was an important call for him, and he went back to the tiny weatherboard structure on a hill overlooking the beautiful Yabbra beach to take the call, which informed him his boss had disappeared into the ocean.

Zara became more anxious as time passed with no news. She rang Eggleton to tell him she would pick him up in fifteen minutes in the Bentley to drive to the airport and fly to Melbourne. With her was her friend Allison Busst, and Holt's GP, Marcus Faunce. The pilot asked her if she wanted a helicopter to pick them up to take them to Portsea. She refused, saying she would rather the helicopter be used to find Harold.

When they landed, Eggleton saw Zara, Mrs Busst, and Dr Faunce into one car. He deliberately chose to travel in the other, because he wanted to listen to the radio to get a handle on what was happening. Of course, the car did not have a radio. Not all cars did back then. Fortunately, the driver had a little transistor radio, which they dangled from the rear-vision mirror.

Eggleton took the time on the drive to think about how he would handle such an extraordinary situation. Above all, he wanted to be open with journalists, to provide as much information as he was able to. He was fully conscious of the magnitude of it all. What struck him on the drive to Portsea was the number of people in the small seaside towns along the way who lined the streets in their beachwear as Zara drove by, their heads bowed. He found it incredibly moving. A row of outside broadcast vans lined the clifftop, and the number of journalists kept growing. They had been cordoned off, but Eggleton arranged for a hall to be set up for regular press conferences.

Anyone old enough to remember that time remembers Eggleton's composure. He says the journalists were fantastic. Maybe, but he was brilliant: calm, articulate, sombre, informative, and altogether impressive. Mrs Marjorie Gillespie had been with Holt when he went swimming. He immediately asked her to dictate her recollections, and gave a section of the transcript to an ABC reporter, who asked Eggleton about it at one of his briefings so that Eggleton could respond. As well as the worldwide media interest, and the sheer human tragedy of it, there was politics to consider, too.

Billy McMahon had already called the Portsea house a couple of times before Eggleton arrived. The family asked Eggleton to deal with McMahon. McMahon wanted to come down to Portsea, but it was not clear why. Eggleton had to talk him out of it. Bunting told Eggleton that, as the man on the spot, he would have to deal with all of it, but gave him one piece of advice — not to declare on that first day that Holt was gone. Declaring a prime minister dead at sea was a big deal. So was the succession. It would buy more time before the governor-general had to swear in an acting prime minister. This would be Jack McEwen.

Eggleton's life changed in that day. He became what most political staff strive not to be: a national figure. But it had happened for all the right reasons, and he had managed it in the best way possible. He had handled the most difficult situation imaginable superbly. He had lost his prime minister and his job. Frank Packer rang to offer him a replacement job, but when Holt's successor, John Gorton, asked him to stay on, he agreed. Eggleton had interviewed him for the Bendigo *Advertiser* when Gorton was first elected to the Senate. They got along well. Eggleton also got along very well with Gorton's young personal secretary, Ainsley Gotto.

Eggleton's relationship with Gorton was sorely tested on the night of 1 November 1968. It was the annual Press Gallery dinner, with Gorton as the guest speaker. Eggleton accompanied Gorton to the dinner. They arrived late, so there was not much mingling beforehand. That came later. Eggleton saw Gorton talking to one young woman, but thought nothing of it; it was not unusual for Gorton to make a beeline for attractive females. Eggleton rustled up the car to leave, and went to tell the prime minister that it was time to go. Gorton began to walk out with the young woman, Geraldine Willesee — sister of Mike, and journalist with Australian United Press — in tow. Following them were the male journalists, with their jaws hanging somewhere around the floor.

Eggleton thought—hoped—that when they got to the car, Gorton would turn and bid her goodnight. No such luck. Eggleton saw a look in Gorton's eye that told him the prime minister was determined on a certain course of action. He was taking her with him. Eggleton told him that was not a good idea. He insisted. Eggleton opened the rear car door for Willesee. She slid across, and Eggleton jumped in beside her. Gorton was furious. He wanted to sit in the back with her. He grumbled that, as the prime minister, he should be sitting in the back. He glumly sat in the front, then slid his hand around between the front bucket seats towards the back so he could hold her hand.

When Eggleton talks about it now, he laughs loud and long. Not so much back then. Gorton was insisting on taking Geraldine to the Black and White Ball at the Canberra Rex Hotel. Eggleton told him that was not a good idea, and besides, the American ambassador, Bill Crook, wanted to see him. Ainsley had told Eggleton to take the prime minister to the embassy residence after the gallery dinner. Gorton insisted on taking Geraldine with him. Eggleton got out of the car, knocked on the ambassador's door, and forewarned him that the prime minister had brought a friend. They walked in, and who should be there but Ainsley? She was looking daggers at Gorton and Geraldine. Geraldine was starting to get nervous. Eggleton thinks Ainsley was both jealous and furious—jealous because he was with another younger woman, and furious because of the impropriety.

Eggleton does not believe Gorton had an affair with Ainsley, although Gorton did admit years later that he 'loved' her. I asked Eggleton, in preparation for this book, how Gorton's wife, Bettina, felt about all this. Eggleton remembers Bettina as a 'remarkable lady' who behaved with considerable dignity. She was not worried about Ainsley in a sexual sense. She did not believe they were having an affair, but she felt she was being excluded. Stop if this sounds familiar.

Bettina had convinced her husband to run for parliament, and had taken a keen interest in his political career. One day, Eggleton visited her at the Lodge. She was a bit upset. She said she did not mind the friendship between her husband and Ainsley, but she was disappointed she no longer had an opportunity to work with him as she used to. Eggleton reassured her by saying her constant support of John was invaluable, but prime ministers inevitably became surrounded by a bevy of personal staff and departmental advisers.

Eggleton says he spent a lot of time with both Gorton and Ainsley, and saw nothing to suggest an affair. On late nights, after parliament rose, they would stay and drink together. They would invite him to join them. Eggleton, who did not drink anyway, would rather go home to his gorgeous wife, Mary.

Eggleton recalls Lennox Hewitt, the head of the prime minister's department, having an office alongside the prime minister, and for most of Gorton's rule he was the key adviser. 'As we know, Ainsley had a very close rapport with the PM, and an unusual degree of influence, but for the early years Len had the real clout. Later, Ainsley managed to replace Len in many respects,' Eggleton remembers.

Gorton's wayward ways were his undoing. Not even Eggleton's consummate media skills could save him from the retribution of his colleagues.

Then there was 11 November 1975. Before he left to go to Government House that morning, Malcolm Fraser told Eggleton he wanted him to wait in his office in old Parliament House until he got back so they could decide, depending on the meeting, what to do next.

Eggleton, by then federal director of the Liberal Party, was sitting in Fraser's office, on his own, waiting, when the phone rang on Fraser's desk. He answered it. A man's voice at the other end asked if he was John Menadue (then head of the prime minister's department). Eggleton said no, he wasn't, and identified himself.

The male caller, who did not identify himself, except to say he was 'from Government House', said 'Oh, I am ringing the wrong number.' Then he told Eggleton to walk out the front of the building, wait for Fraser to get back, shake his hand as he got out of the car, and say, 'Welcome, Prime Minister.'

That is how Eggleton was first alerted — by an anonymous caller to the wrong number — of one of the most momentous events in Australian political history.

When Fraser drove up, Eggleton did as suggested. Fraser did not skip a beat. He told Eggleton to immediately call a meeting of the shadow cabinet. When they assembled, they sat there quietly, waiting for Fraser to speak. He appeared solemn, then kept silent for a few moments, before finally suddenly announcing, 'Doug, you are deputy prime minister.' (Doug Anthony was the leader of the Country Party, the Liberal's partner in Coalition.)

'Reg, get the supply bills through the Senate instantly.' (Reg Withers, the toe-cutter, was the leader of the opposition in the Senate.)

Whitlam had gone to the Lodge for lunch, having neglected to tell his Senate colleagues what had happened, so they voted along with the Coalition for passage of the bills.

Eggleton immediately set about planning the campaign, including getting campaign headquarters ready before unions shut down services such as phones and telex. Yes, it was a different era.

An important piece of advice Eggleton gave to Fraser was that he should go into the campaign not as prime minister, but as leader of the Liberal Party. Eggleton knew it would be a willing campaign, and he didn't want to inflame it more than necessary.

When it was over, once he was elected prime minister, Fraser never mentioned the circumstances surrounding Whitlam's dismissal to Eggleton again.

They worked together closely for forty years, including in the aid organisation Care for many years. Not once over a meal or in any meeting did Fraser raise it with Eggleton, nor did Eggleton raise it with him.

Eggleton does not hold with the view that Fraser spent the rest of his life trying to make amends for 11 November 1975. Fraser simply got on with the rest of his life, doing things that he had always been interested in.

Eggleton does not regard 'dismissal day' as his worst day in politics.

'The tragic drowning of Harold Holt on 17 December 1967 is much more often in my mind than the confronting events of 11 November 1975,' Eggleton told me. The "dismissal" day was traumatic and agonising, but the sad, incredible, and untimely death of a prime minister and friend was profound and personal.'

Another legendary Liberal press secretary was Tony O'Leary. O'Leary had worked in the Press Gallery on both newspapers and TV, and joined John Howard in 1995 when he regained the leadership. He remained with him until his defeat in 2007. So good was he at his job that Laurie Oakes reckoned he was just about the best press secretary he had ever dealt with.

O'Leary says his toughest day was 11 September 2001. The prime minister, the official party, and the media were all staying at the historic Willard Hotel in Washington, DC, preparing for a White House meeting with President George Bush.

O'Leary was walking down the corridor when he bumped into

Max Moore-Wilton, the head of the Department of Prime Minister and Cabinet under Howard. The most extraordinary pictures had just appeared on the TV, Moore-Wilton told O'Leary—a plane had flown into the World Trade Center towers. O'Leary took one look before sprinting to the prime minister's office. 'You better watch CNN,' he told the boss. Then he rang his family back in Canberra to tell them.

Soon after that, O'Leary's assistant Willie Herron rushed up to tell him that Glenn Milne, then Network Seven's correspondent, was setting up a camera in an anteroom next to the media centre so he could do a dirty doorstop with the prime minister before he began his formal press conference. Milne's camera was placed strategically in front of a television, which of course was broadcasting wall-to-wall coverage of the towering infernos.

O'Leary was incensed. This was a day of immense tragedy, and the last thing he wanted was to provoke any suggestion that the prime minister was seeking to exploit it by appearing in footage with the burning buildings behind him. Willie had asked Milne to move. Milne had refused.

O'Leary confronted him. 'Look, I know you applied for the job of press secretary to John Howard, and you missed out. Feel quite free to apply for it again. However, while I am doing the job, this is what will happen. We will not be doing a doorstop grab in front of that TV. It won't be happening.'

An angry O'Leary is an awesome sight, difficult if not impossible to refuse. The scene was witnessed by Howard's bodyguard, Garry Hanna, who was standing with a couple of Secret Service agents. 'Who *is* that guy,' they asked him. Clearly, that guy was not to be messed with.

Kevin Rudd succeeded John Howard, and Lachlan Harris succeeded Tony O'Leary. It was a bruising time.

'There were lots of tough days,' Harris recalls. 'Days when the major tragedies of life—bushfires, soldiers' deaths, or traumatic accidents—would dominate the day, and leave you wincing at the pain that life can dish out so harshly, and so indiscriminately, and days when the minor tragedies of politics, the betrayals, the stuff-ups, the bad luck, and the bastardry would leave you wincing at the pettiness and nastiness, of your opponents, your judges, your allies, and occasionally yourself.

'But by far my toughest day as press sec for the PM was the 23rd of June 2010, the day Julia Gillard announced she was challenging Kevin Rudd. It wasn't tough because it was unexpected, or because I was shocked by the brutality of it. I'd been around too long, and seen too many leaders lose their heads, to be shocked by that. It was tough because it was so dumb, so short-sighted, and so weak.

'Wandering the halls of parliament that night, watching conspiratorial groups of MPs and staffers slink between offices, it was easy to see that my beloved party had simply cracked under the pressure of government. Voters had given us a chance, and a tonne of responsibility, and we were about to go a bloody long way towards throwing that opportunity away. Everyone was talking that night, but no one was saying much. There was certainty in our proclamations, both for Rudd, and against him, but on both sides there was panic in our eyes.

'This wasn't the targetted execution of a PM who simply had to go; it was a panicked over-reaction to the harsh realisation that governing is very, very tough. Mistakes had been made, and a step-change in the way we were governing was well overdue, but as a party we lacked the structural integrity, and political maturity, to make those changes, fix our stuff-ups, and still get the job done.

'I'll never forget walking out of the PM's office that night, switching off the lights for the last time, knowing full well in the morning I would be coming in only to clear out my desk. Labor governments are meant to be the light on the hill, always striving our hardest to do our best, but as I left that night, you couldn't help but feel that light was flickering, and it was our own hand on the switch.'

In June 2010, Sean Kelly was also working for Kevin Rudd. He recalls a night in June when he was attending a meeting preparing for the next election campaign.

'Oddly, several members of Julia Gillard's staff were absent,' he said. 'Towards the end of the meeting, I got a text from a senior member of the Press Gallery, telling me it was on. He meant a leadership challenge. It was a terrifying text. The meeting wrapped up, and we rushed back into the prime minister's media office, where ABC news was reporting the challenge. Fiona Sugden went to collect Kevin from an event, and Lachlan Harris rushed round to Kevin's office.

'I told everyone to shut down the phones — no communication in or out. In a febrile situation like that, the tiniest word can have unforeseen consequences. There was an atmosphere of urgency, but it was a quiet urgency — the atmosphere thinned out, rather than thickened, the way it does when you're on the front foot. From that moment on, the office was under siege, a swarm of cameras waiting outside. Inside, there were tears and feverish bouts of discussion. I told the junior media staff they could go home. Nobody did.

'I spent the rest of the night talking to other worried staffers, sometimes watching the soundless, black-and-white CCTV footage of Rudd, Gillard, and John Faulkner talking in Rudd's office. Mostly, I spent the time feeling nervous and sick.'

Kelly stayed on to work for Gillard. As luck would have it or not, he had to go through it all again when Rudd challenged her the first time. 'My partner is a theatre director, and was making her debut with the Melbourne Theatre Company that night. I wouldn't have missed it, and I didn't, but it was a strange and awful night. I spent the interval whispering into my BlackBerry rather than holding my nervous partner's hand. Afterwards I went home and stayed up in our kitchen until 3.00 am, preparing for the days ahead. At 6.00 am the next day, I was on the red-eye flight to Adelaide to prep Gillard.'

Barrie Cassidy says his most difficult day as press secretary to Bob Hawke was his first, on 11 November 1986. 'Immediately after the Remembrance Day events at the War Memorial in Canberra, we flew to Perth,' Cassidy recalls. 'I figured it would be an ideal opportunity to speak at length with my new boss. Unfortunately, he spent the entire four-hour flight with his head buried in papers.'

'Afterwards, at the hotel bar, somebody wandered in and said: "I've just seen the prime minister for the first time in my life. He was standing at his hotel door, shouting *Where's my #@* form guide?*"

'It turns out it was his routine to mark every horse in every race in Sydney and Melbourne, rating them all according to times, weather, track, jockeys, and trainers. That's what he had just done. Four hours work, and I threw the whole lot in the bin, on my first day in the job. Fortunately, the federal police were able to track down the air crew and retrieve the documents.

'More seriously, though, the toughest time was the leadership challenge, though I was there only for the first. On the day of the first vote in June 1991, he asked me to check with senior journalists in the Press Gallery, to establish what sort of a vote it would take to permanently see off Paul Keating.

'The consensus seemed to be something akin to 60–40. He won the ballot 66 to 44. The next day I checked again, and I presume Graham Richardson got to them before I could. The new consensus was that the vote had achieved nothing. I reported back. Understandably, he didn't like it. Over the next few weeks I tried to have him at least consider voluntarily leaving, protecting his legacy and avoiding a party-room loss. He was determined to fight on.'

Cassidy left in August 1991 to work as a freelance journalist in Washington. 'One morning—late at night, Washington time—just before the second challenge, John Laws phoned, and I told him what I had told Hawke. Hawke was clearly upset by that, and phoned me to say that, coming from me, it was "a kick in the guts".

Cassidy explained he had become a commentator, and as such had to call it as he saw it. 'Eventually, he either came around to that view, or put it behind him. I'm not sure which. But it was tough.' Cassidy was also lucky he worked for a man who never held grudges.

The disastrous repercussions that can flow when press secretaries are by-passed was but one of the morals behind the story provided by Kerry-Anne Walsh, my regular Monday-afternoon date on the political panel with David Speers, who now reigns as one of the nation's sharpest interviewer/commentators on Sky's *Afternoon Agenda*.

Late one Sunday afternoon in mid-1984, Kerry-Anne, then press secretary to immigration minister Stewart West in the first Hawke government, returned to Canberra from a two-day road trip, to be greeted by the furious blinking lights of 30-plus phone messages on her home answering machine.

Kerry-Anne recalls: 'It was a tough time for both the government and the country: eminent historian Professor Geoffrey Blainey had lit the fuse under a fiery race debate by questioning the pace of Asian immigration to Australia.

'His forceful attacks on the non-discriminatory immigration

policy, which he claimed favoured Asian immigrants, curried favour behind the fly-screen doors of our 'burbs.

'While we were a country of more than 100 nationalities, cohesion was as thin as gossamer thread. It had only been a decade since the abolition of the White Australia policy, but a sizeable minority still clung to its sentiment.

'Blainey's attacks, fomented by an opportunistic opposition, turned immigration into the Hawke government's bloody conflict zone.

'We worked closely with the PM's office on careful messaging: the aim was to defend the principles of non-discrimination, but douse the escalating perception created by Blainey that Australia would one day soon become more Asian than Anglo-Australian.

'There was much to lose: the government's integrity; Australia's international standing; social cohesion at home. It was a torrid time, and was about to become more so.

'As I obliviously tripped about the countryside, in the splendid isolation of pre-mobile phone times, a senior staffer in our office decided to background a *Sydney Morning Herald* journalist on upcoming arrival statistics, dropping the explosive quote that 'the Asianisation of Australia is inevitable'.

'The story appeared on the Saturday morning of my bush trip. My post-holiday, abruptly ruined, Sunday evening presaged months of unrelenting, high-stakes political battle that led to the historic breakdown of a bipartisan immigration policy, forever altered the political and policy approach to immigration, and came dangerously close to permanently fracturing Australia's social fabric.

'It also gave me a fine insight into the power of language, the ugly politics of race, and how the media only ever knows a fraction of what really goes on behind the wall of a political crisis.'

Wind back a bit to 1977 when the then Sue McNish (later O'Leary) was working for Senator John Button primarily as his research assistant, although her duties included dealing with the media. They shared a tiny office in old Parliament House, where Button sat in a large chair under a print of a motley group of people, with the caption: 'Be good to us and we'll be good to you.' Visiting journalists were asked to take note. Nothing's changed.

Labor had lost in another landslide to Fraser, and Gough Whitlam began sounding out colleagues to ward off a challenge for the leadership from Bill Hayden. As they were working away, Button whispered: 'Suze—the door, look, look at the door.' Through the frosted glass loomed a giant figure. 'It's him. It's him,' Button whispered. 'Don't leave the room,' he told her. 'Stay where you are. Do *not* move.' Gough knocked loudly and walked in. 'Comrade!' Gough glared at her to leave. Button implored her with his eyes to stay. She left.

After twenty minutes, she went back, and opened the door slowly to hear a small voice saying: 'I need your help, Suze. Please move the desk so I can get out of here.' Gough had pinned Button to the wall. He was firmly stuck in his chair, and couldn't move. Gough had sat with his foot against the desk, and as the conversation had progressed and become more animated, the desk kept moving toward the wall until it could go no further. 'I guess that's where the conversation ended, and Gough had the senator where he wanted him,' Sue recalled.

As well as providing interesting insights into how tough political situations are managed, and the extreme pressures faced by press secretaries, these anecdotes illustrate the importance of having professionals in those jobs, then trusting them to do them. They also show when it's time for staff to butt out and leave it to the politicians—even if the politicians beg them to stay—or how the best always tell the boss what he or she doesn't want to hear.

This was another extreme failure in the Abbott office. There was no division of responsibilities; instead, there was a takeover. The chief of staff not only took over the jobs of the political advisers, the policy advisers, the administrative staff, the decorators, and the menu-planners, but she took over the jobs of the press secretaries, too. They were seldom allowed to dispense information, which meant that if journalists wanted to know anything, they had to deal with one person at the top (or two people, if you counted Abbott, who also had his favourites). Press secretaries were kept out of the loop while Credlin dealt directly with correspondents.

James Boyce helped her connect early on with the *Daily Telegraph*'s political correspondent, Simon Benson. Boyce told her that Benson was the man to know, because he was the window to western Sydney. The problem, according to the insiders, was that she took this to a whole new level. She would invite journalists for a drink, tell them a few stories—which, being journalists, they would want to write—and next thing you knew, the yarns were in the paper. The problem was that the press secretaries didn't know anything about the stories until they appeared in the paper or online.

Cabinet ministers and backbenchers complained that they had no access, that the chief of staff would not return their calls or emails. Not so, reporters.

Here is just one example. On Sunday 20 July 2014, at 12.44 pm, Benson emailed Credlin directly with a series of questions seeking to establish whether a suicide attack in Baghdad had been perpetrated by a 17-year-old teenager from Australia, possibly from Western Sydney, and if the PM was 'concerned that the use of teenage suicide bombers marks a new and disturbing phase in the radicalisation of young Australians'.

At 1.04 pm, Credlin flagged the email as 'Urgent' and forwarded it to the PM's security adviser, Andrew Shearer. Next day, the story appeared in the *Tele*, confirming it was indeed an Australian teenager, although from Melbourne, with quotes from 'senior intelligence sources'. No blame attaches to the journalist or the newspaper here. They are in the business of getting stories, getting them first and getting them right. There is also a role for advisers who are expert in particular areas to brief media, especially on technical details.

According to former colleagues, Credlin was 'obsessed' with national security, because it was a strong point for the government and for Abbott. She sat in all of the classified briefings of the national security committee and in meetings with Defence chiefs and officials.

She made it her mission, especially after terror scares dominated press coverage, to improve security at Parliament House, which was probably overdue.

A discussion took place in the prime minister's office, involving senior staff, regarding both the 'threat' and the changes that would need to be made to security. Andrew Hirst, Jane McMillan, and Kate Raggatt were involved. They discussed the need to brief staff in the building as well as the Press Gallery bureau chiefs. The view was that if there was a threat to the building, staff needed to know first and to be reassured that all appropriate steps were being taken to ensure their safety.

However, according to one former adviser, Credlin decided the *Daily Telegraph* should get the story first. According to this source, Credlin briefed Simon Benson, then told him to deal with Raggatt. It was a bit awkward when Benson contacted Raggatt while she was with McMillan, who was increasingly being cut out of the picture.

A front-page story with a picture of Parliament House, headlined 'Red Alert Over Plot to Attack Nation's Leaders', ran on Saturday 19 September, overtaking plans to hold briefings for appropriate stakeholders, including ministers, officials, the Press Gallery, and staff.

Benson's story reported 'a senior government official' as confirming that there had been a new intelligence briefing on threats to Parliament House, and on the vulnerability of the prime minister and other ministerial offices.

Benson quoted this official as saying: 'There are a lot of lives in this building. And it is a building that is currently very vulnerable to a random act of violence. The weakest point is the Ministerial Wing. You could take out two blokes sitting at a desk and walk straight into the courtyard with a line of sight into the PM's office.'

The next day, Sunday, had been set for the briefing for senior gallery journalists by the Australian Federal Police and ASIO. Credlin also participated in the briefing, using language similar to that quoted by Benson. Gallery journalists were not impressed: first, by the fact the *Telegraph* had once again been given an exclusive drop on a story; second, because, as gallery doyenne Michelle Grattan observed, it did not help preserve security to have such sensitive material splashed all over the front of tabloids.

Credlin denied the leak had come from the prime minister's office, but the professional press secretaries were not surprised that the gallery was put offside both by the favouritism shown to the *Telegraph* and the lack of professionalism. In fact, they had warned that this was what would happen.

Credlin's constant involvement, at the expense of other duties, left her press secretaries looking clueless. And angry — especially when they had to clean up the messes that followed, for which they were invariably blamed. Few working journalists would ever complain or write about having access to the woman who had access to the prime minister, who provided them with information. Those who received it lapped it up, but there were too many left off the drip.

Press secretaries with a journalistic background also knew it was pointless trying to blacklist or seek retribution against reporters deemed hostile to the government, so it was rarely used as a long-term tactic. Of course there are always skirmishes, such as making regular calls to the ABC's Chris Uhlmann to complain about his reporting, or indulging in a bit of payback here and there. It is all part and parcel of a high-stakes environment.

Credlin had no problem with media exposure, so long as it was favourable. But she had a problem with no media exposure, despite what she later claimed about not seeking personal publicity.

After Malaysia Airlines flight MH17 was shot down, *Daily Telegraph* columnist Miranda Devine rang Credlin for background information on the story. During the half-hour conversation, Credlin provided some interesting detail, including about Julie Bishop's role, but a fair chunk of it was also about the role played by Credlin herself. Credlin told Devine she was going to write a book, a manual, for future governments to use on what to do in such a crisis, because no one had known what to do, and she had had to pull it all together, and so on. Devine used some of the information in her column, but did not mention Credlin.

On the day it appeared, she got a text from Credlin, asking why she had not been named in the piece. Devine texted back, asking why would she be named. Credlin responded to the effect that if she wasn't named, no one would know she'd been involved.

Credlin had nothing to complain about when Simon Benson's column appeared on 24 July 2014. Benson reported that: 'Abbott's office has also come into its own over the past week. Few would remember that his chief of staff, Peta Credlin, was a former international defence policy adviser to Defence Minister Robert Hill.' Benson cited the contributions of Credlin and Shearer, and also quoted from an email that Credlin had sent to staff, urging those not directly involved to stay focussed on their own work.

However, Credlin's text message had given Devine pause to think about how Abbott's chief of staff viewed herself and the way she approached her job. She wrote a scorching column about Credlin around the time of the leadership spill.

As far as Credlin was concerned, it was far worse to be mentioned in an unflattering way than not at all. As the number of her detractors grew, particularly among women inside the Coalition, so did the number of critical stories that surfaced about her. Credlin would seek retribution.

On 30 October 2014, in my regular Thursday column in *The Australian*, I began by writing about internal sniping against Scott Morrison for being too good at his job, and against Joe Hockey for not being good enough. Then I wrote this:

> Pretty soon there will be sniping about Julie Bishop. Either that or she will be written out of the script. Oh wait, that could be happening already. The deputy leader, the only female member of the cabinet and the (now) obvious successor to Abbott, was left off the invitation list for the launch by the Prime Minister last night of a new group set up by his chief of staff, Peta Credlin, designed to mentor and promote female Coalition staff, including getting into parliament if they want.
>
> The snub to Bishop was not personal but it was calculated. No other female MP — backbencher or minister, including Michaelia Cash, the Minister Assisting the Prime Minister for Women — had been invited, and boy (or girl) were some of

them miffed, their miffedness not abated by Prime Ministerial invitations to another function today to celebrate 'women of the future'. Talk about short-sighted. If the plan is to get more women into parliament, separating them from the women already there sounds counterproductive. And a bit weird.

A firm believer in mentoring, Bishop paid a gracious tribute to Credlin yesterday for organising the network. Through her performance at the National Press Club Bishop showed why she is where she is. No complaints, no excuses, no crutches. Just hard work and no nonsense. Talk about a class act.

It was a fact that Julie Bishop had not been invited, nor had Michaelia Cash. It was a fact that no other female MPs were invited, and that they were pretty upset about it. As noted earlier, many female staff were cynical about Credlin's motives in setting up the group. They saw it as a vehicle to promote Credlin. Bishop had many gripes with Credlin and the prime minister's office, but she did not have a problem with not having been invited, nor did she have an issue with my column. She did not complain either to me or to the paper. She knew it was 100 per cent accurate.

Credlin was furious. She had a meltdown in front of Bishop and Abbott. At 3.43 pm that day, she fired off a text to the editor-in-chief of *The Australian,* Chris Mitchell.

'I have enormous respect for you Chris but I've drawn a line in the sand this time,' she wrote. 'She must go. She is trying to damage the relationship between the PM and the Deputy Leader based on false claims that have never been put to the office. She's had a dozen or so stories like this but today is unprofessional, defamatory and damaging to the masthead.'

Mitchell responded a minute later: 'She won't be going Peta I can assure you of that. As I told Tony two hours ago.

'And in 23 years as a daily metro newspaper editor no COS or PM has ever made such a suggestion to me about anyone. Even Keating. As I said I will let you know what I decide to do, cheers Chris.'

Abbott rang Mitchell a minute later, alleging that Gillard had demanded the removal of Glenn Milne (a former columnist for *The Australian*). 'I pointed out Ms Gillard had demanded no such thing, and Glenn's fate was nothing to do with Ms Gillard,' Mitchell said later of his conversation with Abbott. Mitchell later texted Credlin, suggesting that the op-ed editor, Rebecca Weisser, and myself should meet up with her for coffee.

I rang Credlin and left a message to say I understood she was upset by my column, and asked whether she would would care to meet to discuss it. She never called back. It was not the first time the office had complained, nor would it be the last.

From around mid-2014, until not long before he lost the prime ministership, Abbott complained to Mitchell, every time he spoke to him, about either myself or Peter van Onselen. It is my understanding that he took it up with higher beings, too, although that kind of thing is way above my pay scale. In any case, both Rupert and Lachlan Murdoch trusted Mitchell to run *The Australian* and to make all the staffing decisions. Abbott also complained to Mitchell about critical editorials. Mitchell would point out repeatedly to the then prime minister that those editorials, along with columns by myself and van Onselen, received strong support and positive feedback from Abbott's own frontbench. The columns and editorials might have angered Abbott and Credlin, but they were certainly welcomed by large swathes of the Liberal Party.

Probably my last civil communication with Abbott was in early 2014. In an appearance on *Insiders*, I predicted that Bill Shorten would have no choice but to support Abbott's plans to hold a royal commission into corruption in the trade union movement, because otherwise he would be open to charges that he was 'running a protection racket for a protection racket'.

For weeks thereafter, it was like an echo chamber. Everyone from Abbott down pinched it, using it to flay Shorten, accusing him of running a protection racket for a protection racket. Around the third time the prime minister used it, I sent him a text to say, 'Hey, that protection-racket line is pretty good.'

'Yes,' he replied. 'I've shamelessly plagiarised it! Now I know where Costello got his best lines.'

I told him it was worth at least a cup of tea, so he told me to organise it with his deputy chief of staff, Andrew Hirst, which I tried to do. It never happened. So many things can be resolved over a cuppa, but then media management was not a strong suit of Abbott's or Credlin, either.

CHAPTER FOUR

Off to a Bad Start

The best professional strategists will tell you the most dangerous two weeks in politics are the week before an election, because that is when leaders are tempted to over-reach, followed by the week after an election if they fail to implement the appropriate structures to deliver good government.

Tony Abbott succumbed to over-reach on the very last night of the 2013 campaign, then failed to ensure that the right structures, personnel, and processes were put in place immediately afterwards to ensure a smooth transition from campaigning to governing.

Every bad thing that happened to him and his government flowed from those few days. Whether it was the first ministry, the first budget, the handling of inevitable day-to-day political problems, or his relations with his colleagues, everything but everything had its origins in those critical few days.

'The first budget, the first ministry, were the result of the failure to install the right protocols for the management of the government. They were the two disasters which played out to the day his leadership was terminated,' was how one key insider summed it up after it was all over.

The 2013 election campaign, from the logistical to the

advertising to the result, ran as smoothly as could possibly be expected, thanks to the experience of Brian Loughnane, his able deputy, Julian Sheezel, and the cunning of Mark Textor.

As Loughnane told the National Press Club a month after the election: 'Under Tony Abbott's leadership, in the last two elections, the Coalition has won a net 31 seats from Labor and achieved a 6.15 per cent nationwide two-party-preferred swing. On 7 September, the Coalition had swings towards it in every state and territory, and received a majority of the two-party-preferred vote in all six states for the first time since 1977. At the electorate level, the Coalition won a majority on primary votes in 51 seats. In contrast, Labor only won seven seats with a majority of the primary vote.'

The Coalition garnered a two-party-preferred vote of 53.45 per cent to Labor's 46.55 per cent. The two-party swing of 3.65 per cent saw Labor's primary vote fall to 33.38 per cent, its lowest in more than one hundred years. It was a stunning achievement, a testament to Abbott's leadership, his stamina, the discipline of those around him, including his staff, and the united teamwork of his colleagues.

The Coalition had the biggest bloc of votes in the Senate, but lacked a majority in its own right. The upper house was an unpredictable mix of independents, Greens, and PUPs spawned by the volatile, egomaniacal Clive Palmer, who had also won a seat in the lower house. It was extremely difficult, although not impossible, to deal with.

So why did it go so horribly wrong, so quickly?

First, the over-reach. The night before the election, God knows why, Abbott agreed to a live interview on SBS TV's World News. No campaigner relaxes until the result is known, yet there could have been nothing surer that night than that, in little more than twenty-four hours, Abbott would become prime minister. But while the professionals knew it was as certain as anything could be, it was hard for politicians to believe it. Politicians also worry that if the result looks too much like a done deal, there will be voter resistance, or they will think it's safe to vote for someone else. So Abbott chose a football analogy to warn of a tight race. 'This is like a grand final. There's only one try in it; either side can still win,' he told newsreader Anton Enus.

Enus, as an employee of a publicly funded broadcaster, then posed a completely predictable question. It contained no hooks; there was no cute language. For whatever reason, Abbott's answer was incredibly, unbelievably dumb. Perhaps it was due to tiredness, although there are those within the government who thought that, when it came out, it sounded scripted or premeditated.

'Well, what about public broadcasters, Mr Abbott. Another soft target. Are the ABC and the SBS in the firing line?' Enus asked.

Abbott should have been able to kick that one through the middle of the goal posts on the Penrith oval where he was standing. He could have been upfront, and said that his most important job would be to get spending under control, so of course the ABC and SBS would have to shoulder a small part of the burden to restore the budget to good health—every large bureaucracy was being asked to make efficiencies, etc—and left it at that. The penalty for an outbreak of honesty at that late stage would have been minimal.

Instead he went the full Monty, answering a question he wasn't asked, saying: 'I trust everyone has listened to what Joe Hockey has said, last week and again this week: no cuts to education, no cuts to health, no change to pensions, no change to the GST, and no cuts to the ABC or SBS.'

The morning note with the message for the day prepared for Abbott's team, sent at 6.58 am by Russ Neal from campaign headquarters that final day of the campaign, 6 September, to Peta Credlin, Abbott's senior advisers, press secretaries, and Loughnane, had set it all out carefully. For whatever reason, Abbott expanded it. He made it tougher, more emphatic, less ambiguous, leaving absolutely no scope for misinterpretation.

The message for that last day of the campaign boasted that the Coalition's costings had been independently reviewed by three of Australia's most respected experts in public finance and administration — Geoff Carmody, Len Scanlan, and Professor Peter Shergold. The prepared note pledged that a Coalition government would live within its means, there would be greater job security, and a 'Government with less debt and an improved Budget bottom line'.

According to the note, 'The Coalition will help to achieve this by pursuing a very significant infrastructure agenda while making responsible savings in the Budget by cutting Labor's waste.'

The note provided a tight answer on spending. If Coalition campaigners were asked 'will the Coalition cut health, education?', they were told to offer the following, much safer, answer: 'Contrary to Labor's false and misleading scare campaign, the Coalition's policy documents and costings reveal: funding for health will increase; funding for education will increase; and there will be no change to the GST.'

That was the script — which also did not mention pensions, the ABC, or SBS. But Abbott did not stick to it.

Probably the only people watching SBS news that Friday night were the dozens of operatives housed in the campaign headquarters of the major parties.

At the Liberal Party's campaign headquarters, there was disbelief when they heard what Abbott said. Some of the old stagers thought his answer sounded too rehearsed, altogether too redolent of Abbott's penchant for slogans: *No cuts to this, no cuts to that, nope, nope, nope.*

Long-time Coalition staffer Frank Jackson, co-opted from the office of Nationals leader Warren Truss into the campaign tactics unit, watched the interview live. Jackson was taken aback by the sheer force of what Abbott said. It was so completely unnecessary. He and the other members of the tactics group, Darcy Tronson, John Griffin, and Ian Hanke, knew full well that Labor had not set aside any money for Gonski's education funding, or for the National Disability Insurance Scheme, for that matter. 'It was a chimera,' Jackson said, knowing that Abbott's response would cause major problems down the track.

At Labor's campaign headquarters, where the slogan was 'He wins, you lose,' the party's national secretary, George Wright also saw it. He definitely did not think it was a slip-up on Abbott's part.

He took it as a sign that Labor's campaign had at least gone some way to setting the agenda and putting a handbrake on the swing to the Liberals.

'We had got our message through,' Wright told me later.

'So when he welched on it all in May 2014, I knew exactly where to go. And to go hard. We spent $1.5 million on an advertising campaign, post-2014 budget, using that footage. What it did was make sure not only voters knew that he had hurt them, but also that he had lied to them. I don't think he ever recovered from that.'

Wright was right.

Those words of Abbott's were the equivalent of Julia Gillard's pledge during the 2010 election campaign that there would be no carbon tax under a government she led. They set in train the events that broke trust with the electorate as surely as she had done, which not only undermined the integrity of Joe Hockey's first budget, but crippled Hockey himself, dragged his government down in the polls, and helped keep it there until he was gone.

Abbott didn't have to say what he did, but, like Gillard, having said it, there were things he could have done or said later to explain why he had to take the action that he did. She left it too late to explain or apologise. So did he. He helped destroy her because of it. All Bill Shorten's Labor Party had to do was follow Abbott's template to do the same to him.

Just like everything that went bad had its roots in poor management or poor protocols, everything about the first budget was simply bad: there was was no consistent, coherent explanation of the problem before the budget; the case for massive cuts was not made; the scene-setting on budget night and immediately before ranged from poor to inadequate to highly damaging; the document itself was a compendium of broken promises; and the sales job afterwards was deficient or hopelessly awry.

In opposition, Abbott had declared a budget emergency. The night before the election, he ruled out cuts in almost every portfolio area. Once in office, he took too long to get around to responding to the emergency he had raised the alarm about. And when he finally acted, he broke just about every promise he made.

Before the election, Abbott and Hockey had announced that, in government, they would set up an audit commission to review all government spending. Every experienced commentator, every serious political observer, saw this as a get-out-of-jail card. It could also have provided a stock answer to every curly budget question: the audit commission would be doing an audit of spending!

Everyone knew the drill. Get the independent commission's report out early, go through the *Oh My God, it's much worse than I thought* routine, wait for it to sink in, lay the groundwork for the budget, then bring down a tough but tamer document.

They ignored all the tried-and-tested rules of politics.

The other problem the government faced was that Hockey was not a good fit for Treasury. When Abbott had a chance to move him after the 2010 election, he failed to take it. John Howard had encouraged Abbott at the time to offer Hockey something else. Howard always believed that Turnbull should have been treasurer.

Andrew Robb considered a tilt for the deputy leadership then, which was not really about knocking off Julie Bishop, but designed to give him the right to choose portfolios. He would have chosen Treasury. When he heard what Robb was trying to do, Hockey was said to have threatened to 'bring the house down'.

Hockey stayed, creating a soft spot in the government's most important policy area. The government looked strong on national security, but all over the shop on the economy. Hockey's colleagues privately deemed this untenable. Success in the economic sphere for a Coalition government was, they thought, 'non-negotiable'.

Hockey had strong support with Mathias Cormann as finance minister, but the combination of his own personality and that of Abbott's was another critical factor in Abbott's loss of party-room support. It is possible for governments to survive with a prime minister who is sub-par on the economy. It is possible for governments with a weak prime minister and a strong treasurer to survive. But it is nigh on impossible for a Coalition government to survive if both prime minister and treasurer fail to inspire or fire in that most critical area.

While Hockey got off to a good start, particularly in parliament, where he was a strong performer, his deficiencies soon became apparent. He made plenty of mistakes on his own, then Abbott compounded them, inflicting irreparable damage on the Coalition's reputation for sound economic management, as well as on its trustworthiness.

Abbott's election-eve comments acted like a chokehold on Hockey, which was bad enough, but the treasurer was undermined by the way the prime minister and his office responded to the report of the audit commission, as well as by Abbott's decision — made without even telling Hockey — to sack Martin Parkinson as head of Treasury. Abbott's first meeting with Parkinson came the day after the election, the Sunday, when he and the head of Prime Minister and Cabinet, Ian Watt, briefed Abbott and Credlin. Incredibly, it was the first time Parkinson had ever spoken to Abbott. This was another indication of Abbott's lack of interest in matters economic.

Despite the stilted pictures that came out of it, the Sunday briefing went well. Parkinson and Hockey spoke on the Monday, then again on the Friday. Parkinson told Hockey that Treasury and Finance, with some input from the Department of Prime Minister and Cabinet, had drawn up draft terms of reference for the audit commission. Hockey was very appreciative. He told Parkinson on Friday how much he valued the support he was getting.

Imagine how surprised Parkinson was when he was called to a meeting with Watt the next day, Saturday, to be formally told that the government had lost faith in his ability to run the Treasury. This was public-service speak for 'You're fired.' Parkinson was told he could finish up immediately or in six months, after the budget. Parkinson, shocked, elected to stay.

He did not hear from Hockey all weekend. There was an Asia-Pacific Economic Cooperation meeting in Bali coming up in early October, and he needed to know about travel arrangements (did they want him to go or not?), so he rang Hockey's mobile on Monday morning. Hockey did not pick up. Parkinson then rang Hockey's chief of staff, Grant Lovett. Lovett was chirpy. How was your weekend? he asked Parkinson.

'Fucking awful,' said Parkinson. 'How was yours?'

Lovett: 'What's wrong?'

Parkinson: 'You sacked me. I was called in and sacked. I just tried to ring Joe, but couldn't get him.'

Lovett didn't know anything about it. Five minutes later, Hockey, who had been at the gym, called Parkinson. He didn't know anything about it, either. 'What the hell happened?' he asked. Hockey was upset, but sought to reassure Parkinson, saying, 'Leave it to me, I will fix it.'

It turned out that he couldn't. It was both an insult and an injury to the treasurer, as well as to his department head. Parkinson stayed until December 2014; but, as if the treatment of him was not bad enough, Credlin tried to bounce Parkinson's wife, Heather Smith, from a prime seat at the G20 meeting in Brisbane in November that was reserved for 'sherpas' (aides to the summiteers). Hockey won that one, at least, insisting that Heather stay where she was. Credlin had to sit elsewhere.

Parkinson believes he was removed because of his work on climate change, both in Treasury with Turnbull when he was environment minister under Howard, and then subsequently as head of Rudd's department of climate change. That was part of it; the other part was that Abbott and Credlin were suspicious of his closeness to Turnbull. They probably felt vindicated in that view, at least, when Turnbull appointed Parkinson as head of his own department after he became prime minister in 2015.

The interventions of Abbott and his office, here and in other matters, when combined with Hockey's own shortcomings, snuffed out any chance Hockey might have had of succeeding as treasurer, and as a consequence severely diminished the government's wider prospects of building credibility on economic management.

One of the nation's most respected business figures, Tony Shepherd, had already been chosen before the election to conduct the audit of government finances.

After a bit of toing and froing on the terms of reference, which the bureaucrats had largely formulated, Hockey had the announcement ready to go soon after the election. It sat in the prime minister's office, and was not announced until 22 October, some six weeks later. As well as Shepherd, the other members of the commission were Peter Boxall, Tony Cole, Robert Fisher, and former Howard government minister Amanda Vanstone.

The budget emergency that Abbott had campaigned on inevitably butted up against political considerations and a clunky administration.

In his discussions with Shepherd in early November, Hockey asked that the commission provide an analysis of government spending, then make recommendations about how to get to a budget surplus of 1 per cent of GDP in ten years' time. However, in a meeting with Abbott and his staff, Shepherd was told to be wary of ten-year projections. Even Shepherd got mixed messages.

It meant that a superhuman effort was required to get the report done by the end of January 2014, as required. Hockey granted a two-week extension, so Shepherd handed over the report in mid-February.

Hockey and Cormann wanted the report out as soon as possible. They argued their case for this in both cabinet and the expenditure review committee. Their view was that if the full report was not released, then at least the parts 'quantifying the problem' should be made public.

Cormann, who had played a key role in opposition demolishing Labor's mining tax, reminded his colleagues that Kevin Rudd had made a major mistake in releasing Ken Henry's review of tax at the same time as he announced the resource super-profits tax. The bungled handling of that contributed to Rudd's demise.

Cormann's view was that the government should not fear a robust public conversation; it should embrace it, because it would form an important part of the education process. It would set the scene, as well as enable the government to calibrate its response.

When Shepherd handed over his report, he watched as Tony Nutt, who was still in the prime minister's office before taking up his appointment as New South Wales Liberal state director, locked it in a safe. More than once, Shepherd feared it would never make it out of there. When he discussed the report with the prime minister, Abbott's reaction was both predictable and disappointing to Shepherd. Abbott seemed shocked by it.

He was extremely nervous about its impact, describing it to Shepherd as 'politically dangerous'. Abbott told Shepherd his view of the future might be right or it might be wrong. Abbott also told Shepherd he felt the report 'lacked humanity', was too prescriptive, and was not analytical enough.

Shepherd stood by the report, and to this day stands by its analysis, arguing that nothing which has happened since has detracted from the magnitude of the spending problem facing governments, particularly on pensions.

He argues that the report did not seek to make immediate nominal cuts in payments, but suggested changes that, over time, were essential if the government's 1 per cent surplus figure was to be achieved in a decade.

Shepherd's view, which was also being articulated internally by the economic ministers, was that the government should release the report well clear of the budget, then allow the debate to rip. *Get the bloody thing out*, Shepherd thought. It would lay the groundwork for the budget, leaving the commission to take the heat for the early blast of unpopularity of the findings.

'Throw us under the bus, that's what we're there for,' Shepherd says he argued. Hockey agreed with him. Even though Hockey had told Shepherd that only half his recommendations were doable, others were fanciful, and others still would be extremely difficult, he was anxious for the first phase of the report to be released. (The second, relating to less sensitive issues such as infrastructure and the public service, was completed mid-March). The prime minister's office delayed.

There were elections in both South Australia and Tasmania on 15 March. The Western Australia senate election had to be re-run because of a cock-up in counting by the Electoral Commission. That took place on 5 April.

With the elections over, there was still no report. Shepherd contacted Hockey several times to find out what was going on. They discussed the commission's suggestion that — rather than release the full report first-up, with all its scary recommendations — the government simply release the first chapters, which outlined the magnitude of the spending problem. While the government might disagree with the recommendations, the analysis was 'spot on', Shepherd would repeatedly argue.

Plough the field, prepare the community for what is to come, we will take the heat, Shepherd kept saying to Hockey. Hockey did not need convincing. In fact, he was in furious agreement. According to one cabinet minister familiar with the events: 'Abbott had this view that the savings could be made through efficiencies in the public service.'

It reached a point where Shepherd worried that the prime minister's office would never release the report. He thought it had been buried. In one meeting, he recalled, the prime minister and his economics adviser, Andrew Stone, said that 'growth would take care of' the budget problems, implying that the commission's growth projections were too bleak.

Shepherd's view was that, one day, Australia's luck would run out. The commodities boom was over; so, while twenty years of unbroken growth was brilliant, it would not, could not, last. He sensed that the prime minister's office, from top to bottom, was unwilling to release the report.

Finally, on 1 May, a mere twelve days before Hockey's first budget, the report was released. The timing was appalling.

The coverage was as predicted. Life as we knew it was going to end, because the audit commission had proposed 'cradle to grave cuts'. According to an ABC report: 'Family payments, child care, health care, education, unemployment and pension payments, aged care, and the National Disability Insurance Scheme are all among those areas in the firing line.'

'The audit also recommends swingeing cuts to industry assistance and the public service, and a radical shake-up of the way all governments tax and do business.'

The commission had tried to give Abbott an out on his paid paternity-leave scheme, suggesting it be pared back and the money put into child care. Shepherd even tried personally to get the prime minister to amend it. Abbott refused, arguing it had been a cornerstone of his election strategy. It stayed, but it was on life support, eventually amended after the pressure from his own backbench became unbearable. It became clear it would not pass the Senate, because not even his own senators would vote for it.

Hockey was out there quick smart to emphasise that the audit commission's report was 'not the budget', but because it was so close to the budget, people thought it was the budget. Could it get any worse? Yep.

The budget on 13 May bent or broke almost every promise the Coalition had made. It sought to impose a $7 Medicare co-payment to fund a $20 billion medical research fund; it proposed deregulated university fees; it increased the age at which pensions could be paid to 70; it flagged tough welfare changes, including a six-month waiting period for the dole for under-30s (which had not been recommended by the audit commission); it cut $43.5 million over four years for the ABC and SBS; it reinstated the indexation of fuel excise; and on it went. An accompanying document showed that the states would lose $80 billion in funding over ten years for health and education.

As an equity measure, there was a deficit levy of 2 per cent on people earning $180,000 or more.

There was a predictably ferocious reaction to the budget, including from premiers and chief ministers over the projected health and education cuts.

Days before the budget, Hockey and Cormann were snapped smoking cigars together in a courtyard. On budget night, Hockey allowed his biographer, Madonna King, and News Corp photographer Gary Ramage into his office to capture his big moment. He danced there with his wife, Melissa Babbage, to the tune of 'Best Day of My Life'. Soon, photos of the two of them together, with stories highlighting the cost of her dress, appeared online and in print.

As scene-setters for a tough budget, these images were disastrous. Hockey's reputation for being out of touch were further enhanced when, in response to questions about the impact of the expected petrol price-rise on poor people, he said they 'don't have cars, or actually don't drive very far'. It took three days to clean up that mess, and even then it was only after the prime minister got back from overseas.

Abbott had also done his bit to contribute to the disaster. He and Credlin had attended every pre-budget meeting, putting up their own ideas, rejecting advice from the public servants, challenging facts that contradicted their ideological positions, such as their determination to deny the dole to under-30s for six months—one of the harshest measures in the budget, which was imposed on the employment minister, Eric Abetz. It was the government's first budget, and the prime minister wanted to put his mark on it, so Hockey went along.

'They set him up to fail,' said one source familiar with the process. However, the damage extended well beyond the treasurer.

Ian Macfarlane had advised Abbott not to chair the meetings of the expenditure review committee of cabinet, the so-called razor gang. He told him he should follow John Howard's example, and only chair those he considered absolutely essential. This meant Howard was not locked in to each and every decision of the ERC. It meant that when he heard about them, he could reverse them. Macfarlane told Abbott to follow the same practice. Abbott ignored him—at Credlin's instigation, Macfarlane believes. Credlin also attended the ERC meetings, often arguing the point with ministers. Abbott's name was therefore attached to every measure.

The day after the budget, Abbott declared that if the Senate did not pass it, he would take it to a double-dissolution election. Credlin, similarly confident, told a meeting of Coalition staff the same day that they should be proud of the government's first budget, saying she was 'proud' of it and would fight an election on it.

Abbott had not cultivated the crossbenchers. Clive Palmer, especially, was rampant, so his PUP senators were in no mood to be threatened. Under Christine Milne, the Greens would not even back the fuel-excise indexation. For a while, Bill Shorten was the luckiest politician alive.

At this point, Grahame Morris was reminded of the negotiations with independents that had had to be conducted after the 2010 election. He was part of a bipartisan committee, along with Tony Windsor, Rob Oakeshott, Andrew Wilkie, and Bob Katter, appointed by Abbott to deal with proposed changes to the operation of parliament. Those negotiations went well, but negotiations on other matters, such as who would get the top job, did not.

Oakeshott approached Morris two or three times to say how well the negotiations were going with Gillard, and how badly with Abbott. 'Your bloke is making this bloody hard. He doesn't seem interested', Morris recalls Oakeshott telling him. Morris remains convinced it would have been possible, with the right approach, for Abbott to close the deal with the independents and to form government, thereby sparing Australia the disasters of the Gillard years.

From the outset, the prime minister declared that all negotiations/discussions with the crossbenchers had to be conducted through the government leader in the Senate, Eric Abetz, whose relations with them, particularly with Jacqui Lambie, were terrible. As the manager of government business in the Senate, Mitch Fifield had won the respect of all sides for his straight dealings, so he tried to insert himself into the process, but it was an unworkable approach. Less than two weeks after the budget, on 25 May, when it was obvious it was tanking, the prime minister hosted thirty marginal seat-holders at a private dinner. It was a Sunday, with parliament set to resume on the Monday. MPs had been back in their electorates for a week, gauging the mood of constituents. Unsurprisingly, they did not have any good news to report. People were as irate about the broken promises as they were with the actual content.

MPs were already chafing under the level of control that had started to be exercised almost immediately after the election. The employment of family members was banned, something that hit the West Australians particularly hard. All overseas travel, including if it was private, had to be approved by the prime minister's office four weeks in advance—no sneaking off with the missus to New Zealand on a weekend special.

This was spelled out in an email from Credlin:

From: Credlin, Peta [mailto:Peta.Credlin@pm.gov.au]
Sent: Monday, 14 October 2013 11:44 AM
To: Credlin, Peta
Subject: Proposed Overseas Travel [SEC=UNCLASSIFIED]

Dear Ministers, Parliamentary Secretaries, Members and Senators

Senators and Members are reminded that approval must be sought from the Prime Minister on any proposed overseas travel well in advance of expected travel dates. This includes any travel to be undertaken using either an accrued study travel entitlement, sponsored travel or privately funded trips. It does not include travel as part of approved Parliamentary delegations.

Approval should be sought by writing to the Prime Minister at least four weeks before any proposed travel.

It is the Prime Minister's expectations that no absences from Parliament will be sought, but where leave is unavoidable, approval from the Whip is also required please.

Regards

In an effort to ensure smoother relations with his MPs, Abbott would host regular dinners with backbenchers in his private dining room. Sometimes, after the first hour of listening to backbenchers' complaints, he looked like he was nodding off. At other times, such as on that Sunday night, he didn't seem too keen on the messages they were relaying.

His usual practice was to go round the table asking each member to say their piece. On this occasion, the 25 May dinner happened to be held three days after Wyatt Roy's 24th birthday. Roy, thinking he was being helpful—in fact, trying to be helpful—told the prime minister that he thought broken promises were the fundamental cause of the government's problems. It might be a good idea, Roy suggested, rather than indulging in verbal gymnastics, to apologise to people, as Peter Beattie used to do when he was premier of Queensland, then move on.

Abbott certainly did not take this in the spirit in which it was intended. He was furious. He rounded on Roy, yelled at him, and then, directing his remarks at all of the MPs, declared that there were no fucking broken promises and that no one should concede there had been. This incident was to stick in the mind of MPs, first because of Roy's bravery in broaching it, and then because of the prime minister's use of the F-bomb.

Roy had a bit of history with Abbott. When he was elected in 2010, aged 20, Roy had become the youngest-ever member of federal parliament. Before then, when the Liberals first heard that a 19-year-old wanted to become an MP, some of them were taken aback. *Get a life*, they thought. But when they met him, they revised their opinion. He was self-assured, articulate, shrewd. You could add 'ruthless' to the list.

At the time, Abbott was not impressed. In a heated confrontation, he tried to talk Roy out of running; then, when that didn't work, he began lobbying senior Liberal National Party officials, including the LNP's then president, Bruce McIver, to dump him, saying over and over that a candidate his age was 'not credible'. McIver encouraged Abbott to at least meet Roy. Abbott flatly refused.

McIver, who had voted for Roy in the preselection, also came under pressure from the federal director, Brian Loughnane, and the federal president, Alan Stockdale. McIver refused to budge.

Roy formed close bonds with both Malcolm Turnbull and Julie Bishop in that election when they travelled north to campaign for him. Abbott visited the electorate two days out from the vote, after it had become obvious that Roy was going to win the seat.

Roy grew especially close to Bishop, because she could empathise with his predicament. Her leader, John Howard, had opposed her run for the seat of Curtin in 1998 against his friend-turned-independent, Allan Rocher. It was Howard's then deputy, Peter Costello, who campaigned for her, then subsequently publicly identified her as one Bishop who could go all the way to the top.

It was a big mistake on Abbott's part to alienate Roy even further, as would become obvious later.

The budget continued to drag the government down, but every well-meaning piece of advice as to how it might be fixed was ignored. In late July, Peter Costello suggested in his column in the *Telegraph* that the government should include an updated version of the Intergenerational Report (usually contained in the budget) in the mid-year economic and fiscal outlook (MYEFO), normally due for release at the end of the year, so the government could make the case for fiscal reform.

It was a good column by Costello — not that the government welcomed his interventions. A while later, I sent him a text to congratulate him on another column. It was my first communication with him in almost seven years. After a few hours, he responded. At the time of writing, we haven't actually spoken; we've merely exchanged texts. It took thirty years for conversations between me and Graham Richardson to resume, so hopefully it will not take that long with Costello because, for one thing, I am pretty sure I won't live that long.

In my column a few days later, I picked up where Costello left off, suggesting that MYEFO be brought forward to October, and that it include refined or reworked budget measures so they might have some chance of passing; that the paid parental-leave scheme be recast; and that the prime minister reshuffle his ministry to remove deadwood, including Kevin Andrews. My then op-ed editor, Rebecca Weisser, summed it up beautifully with the headline: 'A new slogan for the PM: rethink, reboot, reshuffle.'

Abbott had deservedly received a lot of credit for his handling of the MH17 disaster when Russian-backed rebels shot down an aircraft over Ukraine on 17 July, killing 298 people, including thirty-eight Australians. It was the first time in five years as leader of the Liberal Party that they were given an opportunity to see him stripped of politics.

He handled it superbly — as well as Australians could expect of any leader. It provided an opportunity for him to recast his prime ministership, to use the goodwill generated by his early, firm handling of this horrific incident to restart the conversation on budget repair.

There were any number of opportunities to marry the two issues. Without a strong economy, nothing was possible; with it, everything was. But he failed to do it. He concentrated on matters of national security, because it was more in his comfort zone. As important as that was — and even there, he later went too far — no Coalition government can survive unless it succeeds on economic management.

Towards the end of November, wherever the tether ended, that's where most of his MPs were. There was the continuing saga of broken promises, cuts to the ABC, the Medicare co-payment.

Liberal backbencher Rowan Ramsey from South Australia,

who usually flew well below the radar, said publicly he thought that Abbott probably regretted promising there would be 'no cuts' to the ABC or SBS if he were elected as prime minister.

'The words of the prime minister on the day before the election, I think are unfortunate … and it puts us in a difficult position,' Ramsey offered.

The much-higher-profile Craig Laundy, from Sydney's western suburbs, tried another tack in the party room to try to get Abbott to see sense. He said he had promised his wife before the election they would take a holiday in January, but when it was obvious they could not, he sat down and explained why. 'She wasn't happy, but she understood,' Laundy said. Laundy told Abbott they were right behind him, they wanted to fight, but warned: 'People don't like verbal gymnastics.'

Abbott commended Laundy for his contribution, then said there had been 'no verbal gymnastics'.

Further enhancing my own status within the prime minister's office, Labor had picked up and broadcast far and wide a line I had used on the *Insiders* a few days before that 'A lie was bad enough, but lying about a lie is even worse.'

Finally, it penetrated. After the tetchy party meeting, in response to a question in parliament about whether he agreed with Ramsey that he regretted saying what he did, Abbott replied: 'He and I are pretty much always on a unity ticket, and I can certainly agree with him.' Backbenchers waited for the promised barnacle-eradication program, and the reshuffle that would have to follow.

The next day, Wednesday, Phil Coorey of the *Australian Financial Review* and Andrew Probyn of the *West Australian* both reported that the government was 'poised' to drop the Medicare co-payment.

Based on briefings from Hirst and Jane McMillan in the prime minister's office, other media outlets, including ABC TV 24, then hardened up the story even more, declaring the co-payment dead. And on the basis of another briefing, this time from 'well-informed sources', Fairfax Media's Mark Kenny went hard, saying that the co-payment was 'dead, finished' — only to be accused by the prime minister's office the next day, when the proverbial hit the fan, of over-egging the story. Credlin had also told at least one journalist on Wednesday that the reports of the co-payment's death were not exaggerated, and that the co-payment was 'dead in the water'.

The problem was that the co-payment's death came as news to the responsible cabinet ministers. It also appeared to come as news to Abbott. The health minister, Peter Dutton, attended the Orica Green Edge Cycle team breakfast in the Senate alcove with Abbott the next morning, Thursday 27 November. As they walked across to the event, he asked Abbott about the stories. Abbott said there was no change; the co-payment still stood.

Abbott told other ministers that there had been an 'unauthorised briefing'. This was code for a complete cock-up by his office, beginning with the chief of staff.

So unauthorised was the briefing that he was apparently ignorant of it himself. Abbott was attending a function on the Wednesday night after the stories declaring the co-payment was dead were aired, and was asked about the reports. At this point, not only was he unaware that he had killed it, but he sounded unaware that the stories declaring its death were running. His other policy advisers were in the dark about it all, too. Dutton and Hockey went out to declare the co-payment was still alive. It was another management/communications triumph, leaving backbenchers and ministers ropeable, and directing their fire at Credlin and the office.

Dutton had every right to be angry. Before those briefings,

where staff had decided the time had come to kill the co-payment, Dutton had recommended at a meeting of the expenditure review committee that the Medicare co-payment should be put up to the Senate for a vote before Christmas. There was no doubt it would be voted down, Dutton argued. That would effectively kill it off, and they could start the New Year afresh.

In the words of one cabinet minister, Abbott 'got the shits' with Dutton when he put it to the committee, telling him he had two options. Press on or resign. Dutton pressed on; however, the debacle over the 'unauthorised' briefings confirmed in his mind that the office was dysfunctional.

At the following party meeting, when Ken Wyatt, one of the gentlest souls in the parliament, stood up to complain — without naming anyone — of rude, arrogant staff, demanding that MPs be treated with respect, he was spontaneously applauded.

The co-payment, which had been put on the agenda by Abbott's former staffer, Terry Barnes, was eventually killed — this time, following Dutton's advice, so that the new health minister, Sussan Ley, did not begin her tenure as a lame duck. It was replaced by plans to cut the Medicare rebate, which caused its own round of problems.

As the year drew to a close, Hockey and Credlin remained the focal point of much of the discontent.

The first Abbott cabinet was the other early disaster that proved the critical importance of the week immediately after an election if the right structures are not established.

Bronwyn Bishop had been moved to the Speaker's chair. (Coincidentally, I had suggested this in a column yonks before, as one way of opening up places in the ministry. Oops.) Sophie Mirabella had lost her seat, which meant that the lone woman left in cabinet was the deputy Liberal leader, the foreign minister, Julie

Bishop. It was a serious mistake on Abbott's part, which rankled with women all the way to his demise.

It wasn't as if he hadn't been warned that this would go down badly.

It became the subject of heated discussion at a dinner in a private dining room at The Ottoman immediately after the election, attended by the tight-knit group that had held it together for four years in opposition. Sitting down to the restaurant's famous Turkish banquet, ostensibly to celebrate the victory, were Abbott, Credlin, Loughnane, Bishop, Hockey, and Pyne. With Mirabella gone, the prospect of having only one woman in cabinet was not regarded as a good look by Bishop, Hockey, or Pyne. All three argued that there had to be more.

They thought that unless other women were promoted, the new government would be crippled from the outset. They were urging Abbott to appoint at least two others. Bishop suggested either Marise Payne or Sussan Ley, or both.

Credlin was dismissive. 'We are not appointing women for the sake of it,' she told them. Bishop particularly noted her use of the word 'we'. The group also noted the reaction to the two other women — that Payne was too far to the left, while Ley barely registered on their radar.

Abbott said that none of the other women was ready. In response to the suggestion that Payne should be promoted, he said: 'I wouldn't be appointing Marise. I would appoint Connie Fierravanti-Wells. How would you like that?' It was sort of light-hearted, but had a real edge as Abbott became more and more irritated. As it turned out, he didn't appoint Connie, either, which was another mistake.

The dinner had barely begun when Abbott pulled up stumps and left early, around 9.00 pm. Credlin and Loughnane left soon after. The others were stunned that their opinions, once sought, had suddenly become unwelcome. That's not how it had worked in opposition. It was a worrying sign. They had been looking forward to kicking back over a few drinks, late into the night, savouring a magnificent victory. They stayed on, talking about what had just happened, wondering what it all meant. Little alarm bells went off in their heads.

Everybody knew from opposition days that Abbott had a woman problem. The party was also concerned about how few women were in the federal parliament. In his report on the 2013 election, former Howard government minister Rod Kemp recommended a concerted effort to boost the number of women. In the aftermath of the election, as he was writing his report, Kemp was also picking up on the widespread dissatisfaction with Abbott's first cabinet.

Kemp made two recommendations. The first was that the party leadership should make 'a major announcement on initiatives' to increase female representation in parliament for the Liberal Party. The second was for a special committee of the federal executive to be set up to encourage women 'to stand for pre-selection and be elected to Parliament'.

This meant, in the words of one insider, that Abbott as prime minister not only had to be sensitive to the requirement to promote women, but he also had to be seen to be promoting women. It was not enough to say he had a female chief of staff, a wife, and three daughters. Women needed to see more women included in the decision-making processes of the government. 'Peta Credlin should have been all over the emerging political problem, but there was an air of petulance about it, in putting political interests [dislike of certain women MPs] ahead of the political necessity of the government,' he said.

It wasn't that there were no good women there—Turnbull demonstrated there were with his first cabinet—but, as in the case of Kelly O'Dwyer, they were kept to the outer ministry, or ignored altogether.

O'Dwyer, intelligent, well qualified, and a good media performer, had replaced Peter Costello in Higgins, and was obviously a talent who should have been fostered. However, she was not liked in the prime minister's office: she was seen as 'too lippy' or too outspoken. They called her Missy Higgins. Abbott asked O'Dwyer after the 2010 election to write a supportive op-ed on his captain's pick paid paternity-leave scheme. Inside the party it was well known that she opposed the policy in the form he had announced it, after he had consulted only a few people, including Credlin and his friend Christopher Pearson. It was designed to counter his problem with women, but it only made things worse. It was overcompensating in more ways than one.

O'Dwyer refused Abbott's request, saying that once he got Josh Frydenberg (a particular prime minister's office favourite) to write the op-ed, she would know he was serious about the policy. At a party meeting in December, O'Dwyer asked Abbott when there would be a discussion about the PPL scheme. Abbott snapped at her, saying that if she was complaining about lack of consultation, she should speak to her old boss. He saw her later to smooth it over, reassuring her that she had a bright future.

On another occasion, when she was undertaking an inquiry into foreign investment in real estate, Abbott rang her to check an issue with the inquiry, then sounded peeved he didn't know about it. O'Dwyer had run it past Mathias Cormann, Scott Morrison, Andrew Robb, and others. She had put in repeated calls to Credlin, and sent emails to discuss it. Credlin had failed to respond. She told Abbott this. His reaction? Silence.

Much later, around the time of media criticism of Scott Morrison, Abbott lectured ministers and MPs, saying in effect, 'When we speak to the press, we must never undermine our colleagues.' O'Dwyer offered up her own advice, sagely as it turned out: 'You should probably give that message to senior staff as well.' Again, he said nothing.

O'Dwyer wasn't lippy. She was certainly direct. She said what she thought. Clearly, this was not welcomed.

The fact that there was no room at the table for O'Dwyer after the election drew a lot of critical comment. Journalists rang her for a response. She was due to appear on Sky the next day. O'Dwyer could not get on to Credlin, so she asked Andrew Hirst what she should tell the media when the inevitable questions were put to her about why she hadn't made the cut.

Hirst went away, then came back to tell her she should say the selections had been made 'on merit'. Cue raucous laughter here. Then Hirst told her not to worry—it would all blow over in twenty-four hours. Cue more raucous laughter here.

The treatment of O'Dwyer—and Tony Smith—who was dropped for no good reason from the frontbench altogether, fostered the view that there was a special antipathy within the office to anyone connected to Costello. Partly it was because of irritation with Costello over his regular columns and commentary, in which he would often give the benefit of his advice. How dare he!

The other reason offered up by insiders related to Victorian power plays. When Kay Patterson, who had hired Credlin in 1999, announced she would be retiring from the Senate when her term expired in 2008, Credlin made an appointment to see Costello in his electorate office. She sussed out with him, as well as other senior Liberals, her chances of securing preselection for Patterson's vacancy. She was offered neither encouragement nor discouragement. Although she was from country Victoria, she had no history of involvement in the Victorian party. Wiser heads also knew that the way to get a seat was to put your hand up and go for it. That's what everybody else had to do. Helen Kroger got that vacancy. Later, when Rod Kemp announced his retirement, Michael Ronaldson asked a few party friends what they thought Credlin's chances would be of getting the vacancy. *Around zilch* was the answer, because she was not really known inside the Liberal Party. Scott Ryan got that vacancy. Neither Kroger nor Ryan was popular with the prime minister's office.

Arthur Sinodinos was also treated shabbily from the outset. He was appointed a junior minister, assistant treasurer, rather than brought into cabinet as finance minister, as he had been promised. When announcing Sinodinos's lowly status, Abbott explained that it had nothing to do with allegations about business practices involving Sinodinos being investigated by the New South Wales Independent Commission Against Corruption—otherwise he would not have been on the frontbench at all. So there was no real reason proffered, leaving the impression it was personal.

A few months later, after his appearance at ICAC when it was obvious the government was being damaged, Sinodinos stood aside, without formally resigning, from the assistant treasurer portfolio.

Despite the accusations (he was subsequently advised there were no findings of corruption against him), Sinodinos remained a revered figure inside the Liberal Party for his contribution to the success of the Howard government as the prime minister's long-time chief of staff. Howard regarded him as one of the country's best advocates on matters economic. His business sense might have gone awry when he left the office, but his political/policy brain was unmatched.

The year dragged on without a finding from ICAC, so Sinodinos agreed in December to formally resign so that a replacement could be appointed. After discussions between him and the prime minister, it was agreed there would be an exchange of letters, to be released on Sunday 21 December, to enable Abbott to announce a ministerial reshuffle.

On the night of Thursday 18 December, James Massola from Fairfax rang Jane McMillan, the director of Abbott's press office, to tell her he was putting a story online to the effect that Sinodinos was quitting, paving the way for a reshuffle of the ministry in which the defence minister, David Johnston, would be dumped. She told people later that Massola had told her he had spoken to Credlin.

When she took Massola's call, McMillan was out with friends. She had not been privy to the discussions between Abbott and Sinodinis, or the discussions inside the office generally about any proposed reshuffle, so had no idea about what was behind the story. She set about contacting Abbott, Credlin, and Hirst to find out what the hell was going on. Mobiles ran hot with text messages. Sinodinos was alerted to the online story by his adviser Fiona Brown around 10.00 pm. He was furious that such a sensitive story had leaked. Sinodinos and Brown decided to meet in his city office to work out what to do. By now, it was after 10.30 pm. Sinodinos immediately tried to contact the prime minister to find out how a story known to only a very small group of people had come to be published.

Eventually, about 11.00 or 11.30 pm that night, Abbott and Sinodinos spoke. Sinodinos told him he was unhappy the story had leaked, because he had not told anyone of their discussion. Abbott told him there had been a media inquiry made to the office, and they had tried to play it down. Sinodinos told him he felt he had been blindsided. He believed Abbott's office was trying to finish him off.

'Don't be so melodramatic,' Abbott responded. Sinodinos had worked through the odd reshuffle with his old boss, John Howard, so he knew the sensitivities involved; he knew how much discretion was required in handling such changes. He thought the leak was designed to lock him in so there would be no chance for him to change his mind, even though he wasn't going to.

The next day, in the prime minister's office, McMillan confronted Credlin, in front of Abbott and Hirst. Credlin admitted she had spoken to Massola, but claimed she was not the source — Massola was already on to it, and she was merely trying to straighten it out.

However, in his online piece, Massola seemed privy to the prime minister's thinking, down to the possible appointment of Josh Frydenberg, who replaced Sinodinos in the portfolio. Massola wrote: 'Discussions are said to be tightly held, with Mr Abbott, chief of staff Peta Credlin, Liberal Party director Brian Loughnane and deputy chief of staff Andrew Hirst part of the discussions.'

McMillan flat out did not believe Credlin when she said she was not the source, even though the prime minister and Hirst attempted to argue Credlin's case. It had happened once too often for McMillan's liking — a briefing from a loquacious chief of staff gone awry, without reference to the press office, which the press office was left to clean up. It was just like Credlin's interventions to ban the burka in Parliament House, or to brief in advance on national-security matters. The confrontation occurred on the day McMillan was due to go on holidays. She, too, went on leave and never came back.

There were attempts later to blame Julie Bishop for the leak. However, those close to her said the first she knew about it was when Abbott called to tell her — after the story appeared online. Bishop was seldom consulted on such matters, her opinion hardly ever sought. The well-sourced article also made no mention of Bishop being a part of the discussions.

It was a very bad end to the year for Abbott and his office. Sinodinos, already worried about the government's lack of direction, the loss of public trust over broken promises, and the lack of commitment to economic reform, now worried about its internal integrity. He released a statement on the day, expressing disappointment that his intended resignation via an exchange of letters on the Sunday with the prime minister had been 'pre-empted'. He also made it clear later that, as a humble backbencher, he was now free to speak out on issues, and he would exercise that right. Which, at very critical points, he did.

To be fair, there had been some successes for the government that year. The most spectacular was the stopping of the boats carrying asylum-seekers. The architect of the tough policy was Brigadier Jim Molan; its executor was the immigration minister, Scott Morrison. The success that Morrison achieved in that portfolio not only stopped the drownings at sea, but it saved the budget $3 billion. It fulfilled one major pre-election commitment. It also enhanced Morrison's leadership prospects no end.

After some posturing by Palmer, the carbon tax was abolished. The infamous mining tax, the only tax in history to raise next to nothing, was repealed.

The environment minister, Greg Hunt, succeeded in securing the passage of seven major pieces of environmental legislation, including the repeal of the carbon tax, the passage of legislation setting the renewable-energy target, the passing of legislation to establish the green army, and the establishment of the previously widely ridiculed direct-action plan, in spite of stiff opposition and in the face of doubts that it could be done. Hunt had a game plan, and he had good staff, including the very savvy Wendy Black as his chief of staff.

The Senate was divided into three blocs against the Coalition: Labor, the Greens, and the crossbenchers, who were always very cross about something or everything. Hunt had only met Clive Palmer briefly before he arrived in parliament like a dervish, with three PUP senators on his coattails—Glenn Lazarus, Jacqui Lambie, and Dio Wang. Hunt set about building relations with all of them, as well as with Nick Xenophon, David Leyjonhelm, Bob Day, and John Madigan. He worked hard at gaining their trust, as did his two key advisers, Alex Caroly and Temay Rigzin. Where it was necessary, or useful, third parties—business people or other environmentalists—were brought in to brief the crossbenchers.

However, Hunt was brought close to disaster in October 2014 by Credlin after he had negotiated a deal with Clive Palmer to set up the $2.5 billion direct-action emissions-reduction fund. Hunt had agreed to Palmer's condition that the Climate Change Authority would not be scrapped, and that it would review PUP's plan to legislate an emissions trading scheme at a zero rate.

Credlin was furious when Hunt saw her to chase up what was happening with the agreement. Parliament was about to adjourn for three weeks, and Palmer was heading off on leave. If they didn't get it done then, it probably wouldn't happen that year, and who knew what would happen after that? The agreement was sitting in her infamous in-tray. Hunt confronted Credlin in her office. She told him it wasn't on—it couldn't happen. Because of Abbott's campaign against the carbon tax, everyone inside the government knew that he and Credlin had a bit of a phobia about anything remotely connected to it, and here was Hunt proposing they hold an inquiry into an emissions trading scheme.

Other staff could hear the screaming match going on inside her office. Early in the government's reign, Credlin had tried to block some of Hunt's staff appointments. He wrote to her, pointing out that Australia had a Westminster system of government that ministers were sworn to uphold, and he expected it to be honoured.

He made the same point again about his agreement with Palmer. The Coalition had been elected to implement the direct-action plan, and the prime minister's office did not over-rule a minister.

He went to Abbott, to tell him this matter was 'fundamental' to the way he did his job. The prime minister backed him. He had to. His only proviso was that Hunt take it to the leadership group meeting the next morning to get a final tick-off. Hunt did, and announced the deal at a joint press conference with Palmer later that day, 29 October.

In Hunt's view, abolishing the carbon tax was not enough; there had to be a credible alternative to it. It wasn't about the science or the targets, but the mechanism.

Hunt had not voted for Abbott when he'd toppled Turnbull in 2009. Nevertheless, Abbott had wanted him to stay on in the environment portfolio. Hunt had agreed on three conditions: that the science of climate change was never challenged; that there would be no fight over targets; and that he could design an emissions-reduction fund the way he wanted to. If Abbott had denied Hunt during his stand-off with Credlin, he would have reneged on his agreement to those three conditions. It was a rare win over the prime minister's chief of staff, although some ministers reckoned that if they could get through to Abbott, they were usually accommodated. The trick was getting through.

Morrison had also forged good relations with the crossbenchers, both as immigration minister, then as social services minister, where he found barren ground after the departure of Kevin Andrews from the portfolio.

Other ministers, such as Mathias Cormann, could find ways of working through complicated or contentious matters with the crossbenchers.

Abbott had fallen out badly with Palmer before the election. A connection was never re-established, nor did he really work at building relations with the other crossbenchers. They complained that they hardly knew him, and his ministers complained that he was too detached from the process — unlike Howard, who always stepped in to clinch a deal with independents or minor parties.

When things worked, there was little thanks from the public. There seldom is. Any successes were seen as the government simply doing what it was supposed to do — therefore it was owed little or no credit. Much more often, voters were completely underwhelmed by the procession of disasters, usually caused by poor management or poor processes.

Late in November, a third major trade agreement was signed with China, after deals had been clinched with Japan and South Korea. This trifecta, which the trade minister, Andrew Robb, had successfully delivered, should have been woven into the government's economic narrative of growing the economy and growing jobs. One problem, though: there was no economic narrative. The deals were left to loll around, treated like afterthoughts, until mid-2015, when the Construction, Forestry, Mining and Energy Union, and then Labor, began a concerted xenophobic campaign against the China deal. When the professionals surveyed the wreckage after the crash, their view that the first two weeks predetermined everything was only reinforced.

Asked to explain how Abbott could allow it all to happen, how he could replicate the mistakes of his predecessors, given that he

Above: Election night, 7 September 2013. Tony Abbott; his wife, Margie; and their daughters, Frances, Louise, and Bridget, acknowledge the applause of the crowd at the party to celebrate a magnificent victory. [ALEX COPPEL/NEWSPIX]

Below: Just 24 hours later, another victory party, this time at the home of Alf Moufarrige in Hunters Hill. The back of Tony Abbott's head is bottom right; sitting next to him is John Howard and his wife, Janette, and next to her is Philip Ruddock, whose wife, Heather, was also there. Conspicuous by their absence are Margie, Frances, Louise, and Bridget. Moufarrige told guests that the chief of staff had decided the event would be staff-only. [SUPPLIED BY AUTHOR]

Above: The sword-wielding Peta Credlin, with Tony Abbott hiding behind her, as drawn by *The Australian*'s Eric Löbbecke, published 5 June 2013. Abbott texted the author, saying he 'got a good chuckle' from the cartoon. *The Australian*'s John Lyons saw it hanging in Credlin's office when he went to interview her. [ERIC LÖBBECKE/NEWSPIX]

Below: Peta Credlin cleans up Tony Abbott after a Clean Up Australia Day at Auburn in New South Wales on 3 March 2013. Looking anxiously at the camera is Senator Concetta Fierravanti-Wells, who was later to ask each of them if they were having an affair. They both told her they weren't. [NIC GIBSON/NEWSPIX]

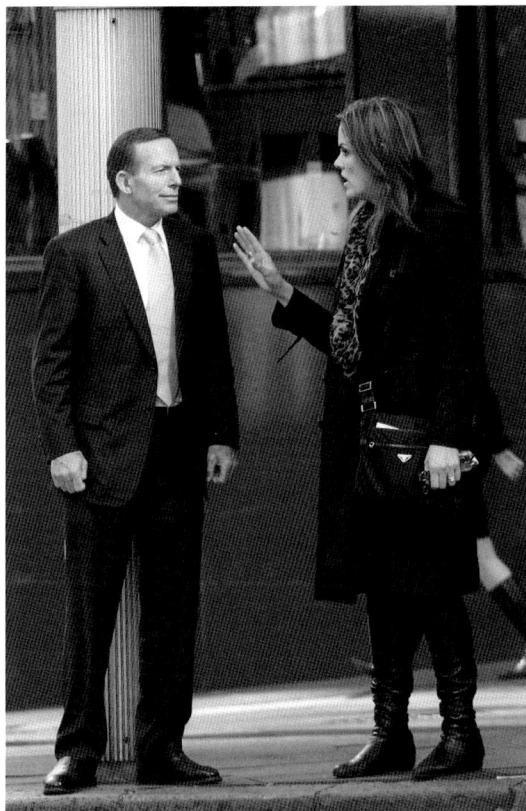

Left: Tony Abbott pays attention when Peta Credlin speaks. On the street in Sydney, Day 24 of the 2013 election, 28 August. [GARY RAMAGE/NEWSPIX]

Below: So who's the boss? The sign on Peta Credlin's door in the prime minister's suite that separated her office from Tony Abbott's. [SUPPLIED BY AUTHOR]

I AM IN A
MEETING

PLEASE

DO NOT
INTERRUPT

Below: Back in the frame. Tony and Margie Abbott together in Sydney, a few days after February's spill motion, at the official opening of the Chris O'Brien Lifehouse building in Sydney.
[BRAD HUNTER/NEWSPIX]

Above: The *Daily Telegraph*'s publication of the photos of and news article about the prime minister on a 'rare weekend off', skiing with his chief of staff, Peta Credlin, and other staff, on 26 July 2015, sent a quiet ripple through the government, even though his daughter Frances was also there.
[ANDREW MURRAY/NEWSPIX]

Below: Joe Hockey kisses his wife, Melissa Babbage, in his office before he delivers his first budget on 13 May 2013. They had been dancing to 'Best Day of My Life'. The harshness of some of the measures, as well as the broken promises, contributed to Hockey's and Abbott's steep decline.
[GARY RAMAGE/NEWSPIX]

Above: Another budget, another poor image. Joe Hockey's second budget went down much better than the first; however, a week out, it didn't help to have Tony Abbott look as if he was consoling his treasurer. [KYM SMITH/NEWSPIX]

Below: Tony Abbott with Barnaby Joyce. They used to be good friends, then fell out badly; nevertheless, Joyce still warned Abbott that Turnbull was coming to get him, a month before the challenge. [KYM SMITH/NEWSPIX]

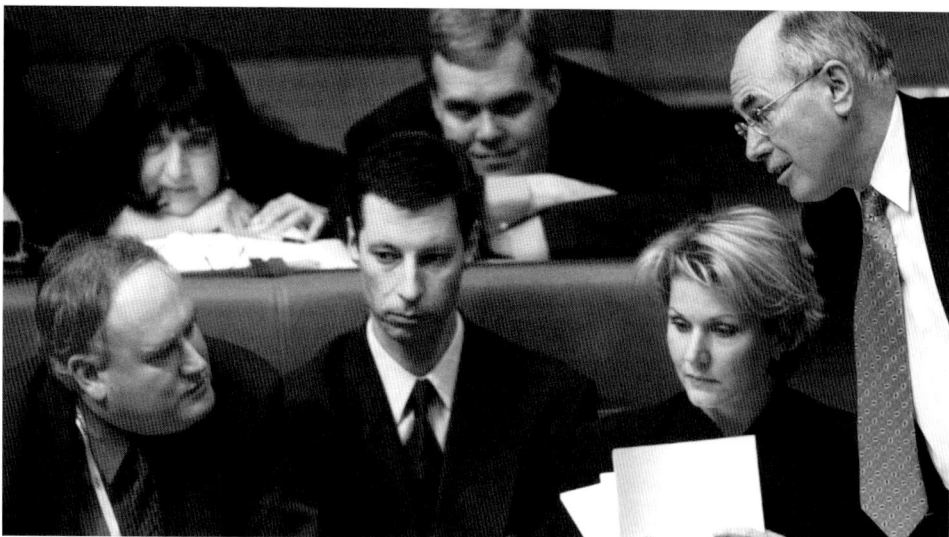

Above: Tony Smith and the author do their best to eavesdrop as John Howard seeks advice from Tony Nutt (left) during question time in the House of Representatives. In the middle is Howard's press secretary, Gary Dawson, and on the right is Ann Duffield, chief of staff to the then immigration minister, Philip Ruddock. Fast-forward 15 years or so, and Smith is elected Speaker by a thumping majority to rule over that very chamber. [PAUL HARRIS/FAIRFAX]

Below left: Tony Abbott kisses Bronwyn Bishop in front of the cameras after the party-room meeting that elected Tony Smith after he finally compelled her to resign. Bishop was not impressed. Nor were some of her colleagues, who told her it was like 'the kiss of Judas'. [KYM SMITH/NEWSPIX]

Below right: The moment that Malcolm Turnbull approached Tony Abbott in the chamber on 14 September 2015, after question time, to tell him he wanted to have a chat about a very important matter. They walked back to Abbott's office in silence. Once inside, Turnbull told Abbott he was resigning as communications minister to challenge him for the leadership.
[ALEX ELLINGHAUSEN/FAIRFAX]

Above: Malcolm Turnbull walks to the party meeting, surrounded by members of his G8, the group that helped him meticulously plan his successful coup. [STEFAN POSTLES/GETTY IMAGES NEWS]

Below: Nobody's patsy. Julie Bishop deliberately chose to walk to the meeting on her own. Tony Abbott had declared her position open as well. She had not called anyone, so she decided to send a message she was seeking re-election as deputy in her own right, and that she was — once again — not on anybody's ticket. [KYM SMITH/NEWSPIX]

Left: Tony Abbott waves goodbye to his staff as he prepares to leave from the prime ministerial courtyard for the last time, on Friday 18 September. [SUPPLIED BY AUTHOR]

Below: Malcolm Turnbull with the female members of his frontbench, five of whom made it into cabinet. [KYM SMITH/NEWSPIX]

Left: After he lost the leadership, Tony Abbott holidayed in France with his chief of staff, Peta Credlin, and press aides Nicole Chant and Adrian Barrett. This photo was taken in Paris. Margie had accompanied Abbott in London for the Margaret Thatcher lecture, then flew home alone. [SUPPLIED BY AUTHOR]

had witnessed them or forced his opponents into making them, how he could be so blind to history, especially as it had only been written yesterday, one professonal offered up the following simple explanation: 'The arrogance that some people gain from decimating their opponents in an election — it makes them unable (or unwilling) to transition properly from an opposition structure or mindset.'

CHAPTER FIVE

Knightmare

On 27 January 2015, just as Luke Simpkins landed in Singapore on his way to Thailand and Burma, he received a phone call from the prime minister, Tony Abbott. Talk about bad timing. Simpkins was already unhappy about the way things were going, but the day before, Abbott had announced he was awarding a knighthood to Prince Philip. As soon as he heard about that, Simpkins decided enough was enough.

Coalition MPs had finished 2014 as low in spirits as they were in the polls. While no one was talking openly about a leadership change, except for the occasional idle musing about what would happen if Abbott fell off his bike and under a bus, there was a feeling they were teetering on a cliff edge.

They had spent most of the summer break on a simmer, then they just boiled over.

They thought the reshuffle had been a fizzer. As parliament prepared to rise for Christmas, a cluster of backbenchers, including Don Randall, discussed the government's parlous state. They were concerned about the leadership, there were complaints about Peta Credlin, the polls were bad—and they were worried they would soon become irreversible. National business figures were already telling them Abbott had to go. Richard Alston, the party's federal president, was included in one conversation where MPs unloaded about the prime minister's chief of staff. He did not disagree.

In January, it only got worse. There was the continuing debacle over the decision to cut the Medicare rebate by $20 for short visits—the successor to the Medicare co-payment—which Abbott announced after parliament rose, without backbench consultation. Days later, as Christmas approached, he appointed a new health minister, Sussan Ley, as part of his ministerial reshuffle. Everyone went on holidays assuming the new policy would automatically proceed as they had announced it, because they had announced it. GPs were winding up patients, patients were winding up their local members, and their local members were transmitting the messages to the executive. Backbenchers were reluctant to go out and defend the latest iteration of the Medicare co-payment, in case it changed again.

Mal Brough had spoken to Abbott in December, saying he had a few ideas about how things could be improved. Abbott was receptive, so the two agreed to meet. The Lindt café siege in mid-December understandably swept everything else aside, so the year ended without the meeting taking place.

Brough swears he was prepared at that stage to do whatever he could to help Abbott make it through. But as he watched the so-called barnacle-removal program being rolled out, he thought Abbott was not improving matters; he was making them worse.

Brough had received a letter from a local GP setting out his concerns about the proposed Medicare rebate. When Brough returned to work early in the New Year, he contacted the GP, realised the rebate policy was a major problem, and set about contacting other GPs in Queensland marginal seats to ascertain the depth of their antagonism. He became deeply troubled, so he rang the prime minister's office to see what they thought about it. He was told it would be noisy for a bit, then it would calm down.

Brough responded along the lines that it would be noisy for a bit, then it would become a firestorm. He genuinely believed it was the sort of issue that could bring down a government. He told them about his calls to the GPs. He also told the prime minister's staff to tell the PM that if action was not taken within twenty-four hours by the government to stop it, he would go public with his concerns.

Abbott rang Brough to ask him to hold off. After a hook-up of the leadership group, the government decided to abandon the policy. The other concern was the impact the rebate cut was having on the Queensland state election that Campbell Newman had sprung early.

Ley, who was on a cruise ship around the islands of New Zealand, was called back to work to announce that the rebate cut would not go ahead. Ley might as well have been on the *Titanic*. In another triumph for internal communications, the prime minister's office forgot to tell the small business minister, Bruce Billson, of the change of direction. Billson was still strapped into his deck chair, declaring, despite the icebergs, that it was full steam ahead, only a couple of hours before Ley announced that this latest iteration of the Medicare co-payment was also dead in the water.

Backbenchers trying to explain to constituents what was happening were furious — not just about the decisions themselves, but the way they were handled. Abbott spent days in January ringing around, taking soundings. Craig Laundy, who held the New South Wales seat of Reid with a margin of less than 3 per cent, was one of several MPs who told him he had to get rid of Credlin and Hockey. Abbott went silent. For a long time. Laundy broke the silence by saying he knew it would be hard, but it had to be done. It then got very awkward. Abbott froze, and began talking like he would at a doorstop, saying they had a plan, and they had to stick with the plan, because the plan was working.

Stuart Robert also says he told Abbott he had to remove Credlin and Hockey. 'Mate, we are not throwing anybody under a bus,' Abbott told Robert. 'Well, unless you do, you might find yourself under it,' Robert warned.

In the third week of January, Abbott began his conversation with another marginal-seat holder by asking him what he thought needed to be done to make 2015 a good year. The MP decided to keep his answer to the policy barnacles, like the measly proposed pay increase for defence forces, which had been held below the CPI (a decision that Robert swears he was not privy to), and pension indexation. Abbott was agitated, dismissive, swearing. 'If we can't do that sort of thing, we can't do fucking anything,' he said. 'We might as well give the game away.'

Then he asked, to the bemusement of the MP, what he thought would happen 'if an election was held now'.

'We would lose,' he was told.

Abbott rang South Australian backbencher Andrew Southcott. Southcott told him the two major problems in his state were the Medicare co-payment and the submarines. He said people in South Australia had no sense the prime minister was engaged on the issues that mattered most to them. Southcott did not get any sense that Abbott took this on board; in fact, the opposite. Abbott rebutted both points Southcott had made. A few weeks later, Southcott, a friend of Don Randall's, voted for the spill.

Abbott rang Brough as well in that third week of January. That was extremely awkward timing, too. Brough was about to take constituents into a meeting with Turnbull. Brough went through the areas that he thought the government had to fix, including defence-force pay.

Others also tried to be constructive, urging him to give them something to grab on to. They needed a narrative, and they didn't have one. Dan Tehan had previously told him, *Give us something to fight for.* It was one message that penetrated. It might have had something to do with that other F-word.

The advice was similar, even if the words differed. Jane Prentice was one MP who told him the government needed a consistent narrative, then they discussed the issues running in her electorate of Reid in Queensland.

Whatever the plan was, it definitely was not working. Many backbenchers were reluctant to move against Abbott, but they wanted him to move his chief of staff and to shift Hockey out of Treasury. Credlin was on the nose with his colleagues; Hockey was on the nose with business. They were still prepared to cut the prime minister some slack.

Then, on 26 January, Australia Day, Abbott made a captain's call that might have gone down well in 1915. In 2015, it was an Improvised Explosive Device, constructed, planted, and triggered by Abbott himself. Each captain's call had been a disaster in its own way, beginning in the early days of his leadership with his Rolls Royce paid paternity-leave scheme, but the timing of his announcement that Prince Philip would be awarded an Australian knighthood could not have been worse.

The previous March, he had announced to the disbelief of his party room and the nation generally that he was reintroducing dames and knights. The first two to be so honoured were the serving governor-general, Sir Peter Cosgrove, and his predecessor, Quentin Bryce.

He had run the idea of the reintroduction past the attorney-general, George Brandis, who did not try to talk him out of it, but Abbott did not submit it to cabinet.

Abbott had also run the idea past John Howard, not once, but two or three times—the first time soon after the election. Each time, Howard had tried to talk him out of it, advising him to let it be. He did not listen. Howard had toyed with the idea himself in 1996, but dismissed it because he decided they were an anachronism. Howard understood that Australia had moved on from all that. Howard also knew he would have to hold a referendum soon on a republic, so he did not want to inflame republicans or do anything that might help their cause.

Abbott's announcement in March 2014 about the reintroduction of knights and dames was treated as a bit of a bad joke that was quickly subsumed by a whole lot of other stuff.

On Australia Day 2015, it was not funny at all. It was embarrassing. Humiliating. Unnerving. It seemed to sum up everything that was wrong with Abbott as prime minister: he did not consult; he was not in tune with his people; he failed to concentrate on issues important to mainstream Australians; he seemed incapable of living up to repeated promises to do better. By way of apology, he later accepted full responsibility and promised to consult more. His words fell on increasingly deaf and hostile ears. They had heard it all before. Often.

Even his conservative allies inside the government were bewildered. Mathias Cormann arrived back from overseas to attend a community event on Australia Day, missing his usual early-morning media briefing, only to find himself besieged by locals and journalists seeking his view. The finance minister could only say it was not a decision of the government. Privately, he was flummoxed. *What the fuck were you thinking?*, he asked his friend later.

One of the most troubling aspects of it all was that he showed absolutely no comprehension whatsoever of the impact his announcement would have on Australians—that they would be infuriated or mortified, or both. In fact, he genuinely believed the opposite.

A week out from the announcement, at a lunch with mates, including Hockey, he was asked if he had selected decent candidates on whom to bestow the honours. He told them: 'I think you will find that people will be very happy.'

This was said without even a trace of irony.

It was the sort of thing people remembered. And not fondly, either. Months after he did it, only weeks before he lost the leadership, Abbott attended a fundraiser in Melbourne at a trendy renovated warehouse. Abbott was going around tables, speaking to guests. After the exchange of pleasantries, one businessman said to him: 'Prime Minister, I have been meaning to ask you—what were you thinking with the Prince Philip knighthood?' Barely skipping a beat, Abbott said: 'Look, I can't say this publicly, and if anybody said I said this, I will deny it. The Queen asked me to.'

After Abbott was deposed, Greg Sheridan (a friend of Abbott's) wrote in *The Australian* that Abbott had bestowed the knighthood on Prince Philip at the request of the Queen. Senior cabinet ministers actually believed it was Australia's high commissioner in London, Alexander Downer, who initiated it. Naturally, the Queen will not be drawn publicly. A query to Buckingham Palace to clarify if she had indeed asked for the honour for her consort elicited this response from a spokeswoman: 'In regard to your enquiry below, we have not offered a comment. It is a matter for the Australian government.' Hint, hint. *It wasn't us.* The Queen was clearly less than amused at being dragged into the imbroglio. Somehow, she could not find the time to see Abbott when he visited London not long after he lost the leadership.

Well-informed sources later emphatically denied that the

Queen or Downer was involved in the Prince Philip knighthood, categorically stating that it was Abbott's initiative. Abbott simply keeps saying he accepts full responsibility for what he quaintly describes as 'an own goal'.

Whatever the sequence, whoever initiated it, the fact is that if he had not reintroduced knighthoods, there would not have been one for Prince Philip. He would not have left himself, as well as his colleagues, open to ridicule. The imbroglio also reignited mutterings about his office, especially as Credlin held such sway in it. MPs believed she could make him do or not do pretty much everything. The letters setting the Prince Philip knighthood in train would not have written themselves, his cabinet colleagues mused. Why didn't she stop it?

'It was such a reckless way to spend political capital he didn't have,' one supportive cabinet minister said later. 'I don't know why his office didn't stop him. All correspondence had to go through her.'

Credlin told co-workers at the time, with a roll of the eyes, that she had told Abbott it was stupid, but, hey, he was the prime minister, he ultimately made the decision, so she went along with it.

The best that could be said of it was that it was completely in character. Almost fourteen years before, on 11 June 2001, he wrote to his then prime minister:

Dear John,

As you can see, I have been reminded by my friend, Justice Michael Kirby, of the desirability of a Golden Jubilee Medal to mark the Queen's 50 Anniversary. I gather there is ample precedent for this. I would be grateful for any information you could give me about plans to mark this important anniversary.

With all best wishes,

Yours sincerely,

Tony Abbott

The following year, fellow monarchists were complaining bitterly about the failure of state and federal governments to do anything to mark the occasion.

The knighthood on its own did not trigger the spill motion against Abbott; however, the camel was already buckling under an enormous weight when the last straw was loaded.

Simpkins had spoken to a number of his colleagues on Australia Day, after the announcement, to tell them he would be away for six days. He said to them: 'I have had enough. If something is going to happen when we get back to parliament, count me in.'

He spoke to both Steve Irons from Western Australia and Alex Hawke from New South Wales. He seriously thought that by the time he got back from Burma, 'something would have happened'.

So when Simpkins took the call from Abbott after he landed in Singapore, he was not impressed. Abbott asked him what he thought. Simpkins said that bringing back knights and dames was bad enough, but giving one to Prince Philip was worse. He also told the prime minister about his concerns over paid parental leave, and about the way the whole Medicare co-payment/rebate had been handled.

A few other things happened while Simpkins was away.

After winning government in Queensland with one of the largest recorded majorities in Australian history, Campbell Newman was turfed out on 30 January. The former federal president of the Queensland LNP, Bruce McIver, told me that Abbott did not cost Campbell Newman the election, but he certainly cost them votes. A week out, until Newman blundered by alleging that bikies were funding Labor through the union movement, tracking polling showed that the Queensland LNP's primary vote was at a healthy 47 per cent. It began to crash when Newman could not substantiate his claim, except to advise the media to 'Google it', and it kept falling after Abbott announced the knighthood for Prince Philip.

Newman's loss galvanised other backbenchers, not just in Queensland. Victoria had already been lost. There was an election due in New South Wales in March. While no one seriously thought Mike Baird would lose, the political atmosphere made people anxious.

When Jane Prentice said on ABC News 24 on the night of the Queensland election that 'we can't continue as we are,' and that the prime minister's scheduled speech to the National Press Club on Monday was 'make or break' for his leadership, the leadership speculation took off.

Wyatt Roy texted her to say he thought she had just thrown the prime minister 'under a bus'. Craig Laundy sent her a thumbs-up, which was intended as a compliment for her performance overall, particularly in swatting Wayne Swan during the telecast.

Earlier that day, Brough was at a polling booth when he was called by a journalist, asking if it was true he was planning to challenge for the leadership. Brough was taken aback, but he neither confirmed nor denied it.

Brough had concluded the government was dysfunctional — that the processes needed to keep government ticking over did not exist, and probably never would. He had rung around party elders, people like Howard and Reith. He was trying to get a handle on who could get through to Abbott. The answer was no one, except probably Credlin.

In 2007, Brough was one of the few members of Howard's cabinet who told the then prime minister he should resign and hand over to Peter Costello. He had the conversation with Howard at the time, but then he did nothing to follow through. He decided he wasn't going to make that mistake again. He told Abbott as much in February.

Brough had never been especially close to Turnbull. In fact, he had written a letter supporting Peter King in his preselection battle with Turnbull in February 2004. Brough also made some disparaging remarks about Turnbull to the then US ambassador, Robert McCallum, in June 2008, which were later broadcast to the world via WikiLeaks.

According to McCallum's leaked cable:

Malcolm Turnbull had lost support in the Coalition parliamentary caucus, Brough stated. Turnbull was only interested in Turnbull and his constant undermining of Nelson had hurt him in the eyes of many of his colleagues. Some in the Liberal caucus supported Turnbull as Leader only because they wanted to put him in a position to fail, Brough declared. He thought that Turnbull would become Opposition Leader at some point in the future and would land some blows on the Government as Leader but he predicts Turnbull would ultimately fail.

Brough's remarks in 2008 were prescient; however, in 2015 he accepted that Turnbull was the best option to replace Abbott, and decided he would do what he could to make it happen. He was playing for keeps in February.

Abbott's speech to the National Press Club on 2 February was both defiant and conciliatory. He promised the most consultative and collegial government the country had ever seen, dumped his paid parental-leave scheme, and then dismissed suggestions he would be removed by his party.

In an effort to ward off revolting backbenchers, he declared: 'It's the people that hire, and frankly it's the people that should fire.'

His backbenchers thought otherwise.

Simon Birmingham did not have a personal beef with either Abbott or Credlin. Abbott had promoted him into the ministry, and his dealings with Credlin were 'functional'. Birmingham was the deputy convenor of the South Australian branch of the Australian Republican Movement when he first met Turnbull around the time of the referendum. In 2009, he told Turnbull he would vote against the spill motion against his leadership, but if it got up he would vote against him. When it did get up, he voted for Hockey; then, when Hockey was balloted out, he went back to Turnbull.

Birmingham, as well as being philosophically aligned with Turnbull, believed the Abbott government's greatest problem was its breach of trust with the electorate over broken promises. The very weapon that Abbott had used to crucify Gillard had, in turn, been used by Labor to devastating effect against Abbott himself. Birmingham could not see how Abbott could recover from that.

Birmingham had met separately that week in Sydney with Sinodinos and Turnbull. It was the usual palaver, obviously with an added edge, about the chatter around the traps, and what it meant.

Birmingham's firm view was that Turnbull should be prepared for all eventualities, but should not take any action that would precipitate or provoke anything, or engage on the issue of a leadership challenge in any way. That apparently was Lucy's view, too.

Birmingham thought that what was happening in Canberra had parallels with Queensland. He thought Campbell Newman lost because he had done things after the election that he had not canvassed before it. He thought that if the Labor machine could make Daniel Andrews the premier in Victoria, and Annastacia Palaszczuk the premier in Queensland, it was more than capable of making Bill Shorten the prime minister.

Things had also turned very sour in Birmingham's home state of South Australia, where Labor had run heavily on Abbott's unpopularity to secure large swings in two by-elections in what were once safe Liberal seats. The Liberals retained one, but missed out on the other.

Colleagues were calling Turnbull: some, to see if he was doing anything; others, like Brough, urging him to do something.

Brough was also in contact with Sinodinos. They talked about going to see Abbott to tell him he should seek a vote of confidence from the party room. Then they heard mid-week that there was movement in the west.

While he was preparing to leave Singapore to return home, Simpkins received a phone call from Mathias Cormann. Simpkins told him straight that he no longer supported the prime minister and wanted him gone. Cormann tried to get Simpkins to see the consequences of what he was planning—Turnbull could end up prime minister. Simpkins said he didn't want that, he wanted Scott Morrison, or he was 'even prepared to wear' Bishop, so long as she was prepared to make concessions to the party's conservatives. Cormann reported back to Abbott and Credlin, and he also spoke to former Howard government minister Chris Ellison, who was close to Simpkins, asking him to speak to Simpkins to see if he could talk him out of taking what Cormann feared was the inevitable next step. Cormann also suggested to Abbott that he should call Simpkins. Abbott did not call him before the spill. Even if he had, he would not have been able to stop him.

Simpkins returned home on Tuesday 3 February. He spoke again to both Irons and Hawke. There had been lots of talk, but nothing was happening. Simpkins couldn't believe it. He thought surely something would have happened in his absence.

On Wednesday 4 February, Simpkins again spoke to Hawke, who is closely aligned to Morrison, as was Simpkins. He floated the idea of a backbenchers' meeting on the Sunday before the resumption of parliament to apply pressure on the prime minister to change. Hawke told him it wouldn't work, because MPs would not want to be seen going into the meeting.

Simpkins told him if no one else was going to do anything, he would. He also told Brough and Sinodinos the same thing. Simpkins said he was sick of being stopped on the street by people telling him that Abbott had to go. He was fed up with the lack of direction. Brough thanked him for what he was about to do, then asked if he had given any thought as to who might second his motion.

Simpkins tried colleagues in South Australia, Victoria, and New South Wales. While they were sympathetic, they were unwilling to put their names to it.

Christopher Pyne was picking up on the chatter. He warned Abbott that a spill was imminent, and that it could get anywhere between 30 and 40 votes. Abbott didn't believe him.

Pyne, who had never had a problem with Credlin, had nevertheless advised Abbott that in government he needed a 'crusty old bloke, or a crusty old woman' as his chief of staff. He believed Credlin should have been his principal private secretary. He even suggested that Malcolm Hazell, a long-time Liberal staffer and a former official secretary to the governor-general, should be chief of staff. Nothing came of that. A combination of Pyne's personality and his post as leader of the house meant that Pyne was well aware of the deep unhappiness inside the government about the running of the prime minister's office, as well as the discontent associated with the treatment of the deputy leader, Julie Bishop, by the chief of staff.

While Abbott and his office were dismissive, Pyne was alert to the backbenchers' planning. It was full steam ahead for Simpkins.

Don Randall had already told Simpkins that if he couldn't find anyone else from the east coast, he would second the spill motion. 'I was already aware that Malcolm and Don had spoken,' Simpkins said when recounting the events.

Simpkins was not a Turnbull man. He was a Morrison man, and at a pinch a Julie Bishop man. Above all, he had become an anyone-but-Abbott man. He spoke to Randall again on the afternoon of the fourth, and asked him to second the motion. He thought maybe Turnbull would step up, or perhaps Bishop would. He knew Morrison wouldn't.

The next day, the fifth, he says Brough and Sinodinos wanted him to spill the leader's position only, but he believed both positions should be spilled, and perhaps that would force Bishop's hand. He emailed the motion to Randall's office on the fifth at 4.47 pm, asking Randall's staff to get him to sign it, then scan it and email it back to him. He said in the email that if Randall wanted to make changes, he would get the revised version back to him, but wanted it done by nine the next morning. It came back, signed, at 8.53 am. He reckons Randall didn't want to spill both positions, but Simpkins was determined to do what he wanted — seeing as he was the one who was initiating it — not what others like Brough or Sinodinos wanted. 'I was doing what I thought was the right thing,' Simpkins told me later.

On Friday morning, 6 February, Simpkins called a meeting of his staff, which his wife, Lara also attended, to discuss the strategy for the day. He called the whip, Philip Ruddock, to tell him what he was doing and to ask for advice about procedures.

At 9.13 am (WA summertime), he emailed Ruddock, saying simply: 'Dear Philip, Please find attached my motion for the Party Room on Tuesday. Yours sincerely, Luke Simpkins MP.'

This is the motion that spelled the beginning of the end for Abbott:

MOTION

Federal Parliamentary Liberal Party

Mr Luke Simpkins MP moves:

That the Liberal Party Room resolve, via secret ballot, that the senior positions of the Federal Parliamentary Liberal Party be declared vacant.

Moved: Luke Simpkins MP

6/2/2015

Seconded: Don Randall MP

6/2/2015

Ruddock suggested to Simpkins that he should also email the motion to Credlin, which he did four minutes later, advising her that he was going to 'call the PM now'. Credlin advised him the prime minister was on a flight and would call him shortly.

When Abbott called him, Simpkins says that Abbott sounded 'reasonable', but told him that what he was doing was 'damaging the country'.

At 10.20 am (WA summertime), before he left the office to attend a meeting, Simpkins emailed his colleagues. He did not put out a press release. He did not need to. Six minutes after the email lobbed in their in-boxes, Simpkins was called first by Fairfax Media's Latika Bourke.

He did only one television interview that day, with Sky, which he now believes was a mistake. He thinks he should have done more, to explain to people why he had embarked on such a drastic course of action.

Abbott's supporters were furious, blaming Wyatt Roy and Mal Brough for putting the West Australians up to it, or speculating that Simpkins and Randall were acting as stalking horses for Bishop.

Friends of Simpkins support his version of events, confirming that what he said was what he felt. He and Randall were exasperated. 'No one was listening, nothing was changing, it was getting worse,' one cabinet minister later explained.

Simpkins set out his reasons in his email to his colleagues that Friday:

Dear Colleagues,

In the last two weeks I have been inundated with emails and walk ins to my Electorate Office all questioning the direction the government is being led in. The Knighthood issue was for many the final proof of a disconnection with the people.

These contacts have come from many people that I personally know and are firm supporters — in some cases they are booth workers as well. The last time this outpouring of concern happened was when we were being led to support the Rudd Government's ETS and faced with this erosion of our base support we acted.

I think that we must bring this to a head, and test the support of the leadership in the party room.

I have therefore submitted to the Chief Government Whip a motion to spill the leadership positions of the Federal Parliamentary Liberal Party. The spill motion should be considered via a secret ballot as the first item of business in our Party Room meeting. The motion was seconded by Don Randall who shares the same views as myself.

I look forward to your support in this matter. It gives you all an opportunity to either endorse the Prime Minister or to seek a new direction.

As I have said in the past, I have no front bench ambitions. I just want to make sure that the economic vandals do not get back into power and our children and grandchildren are not left to pay Labor's bill. I do this because I believe it is in the best interests of the people of our country.

Yours sincerely,
Luke

Simon Birmingham spoke to Turnbull, as well as to Turnbull's closest adviser, Sally Cray, after it lobbed. They were all asking one another *What the fuck just happened?*

It had all happened too quickly. None of the principals was ready. No one was really in control of it, there was no clear challenger, no one had been overtly positioning themselves. There was not the kind of pre-meditated, meticulous planning, or organising months or weeks in advance, which usually accompanied such actions. Backbenchers fed up to the back teeth had decided to force the issue, ready or not. At least, that's how it looked to some of those watching without actively participating.

Either way, both sides agreed it was extraordinary that, less than eighteen months into his prime ministership, Abbott was facing a mutiny. The Liberal Party was preparing to do to its prime minister what Labor had done to their two most recent prime ministers.

Despite everything, there are still those who believe that,

because they were all from the west, Randall and Simpkins were acting as Bishop's surrogates. Bishop insists she knew nothing of their plan in advance. She let it be known that there was no way she wanted to be cast as Lady Macbeth.

However, she was also, sensibly, trying to leave her options open. On the Sunday after the Queensland election, Abbott sought an assurance from Bishop that she would not challenge him. She refused to give it.

Sky's Kieran Gilbert was told the next day about the discussion between the leader and his deputy at Kirribilli. Gilbert asked Abbott at the Press Club if he had asked Bishop for a commitment, and if so, what she had said. Abbott dodged the question by praising Bishop, then saying he believed he had her full support.

Gilbert ran hard with his exclusive story on Sky the next morning, Tuesday, giving the leadership speculation another set of legs. Gilbert was incredibly well informed. On the night of the Queensland election, he texted a minister to ask what he thought the federal implications were. The minister texted back to say that, unfortunately, Abbott was finished, and that it could happen sooner rather than later.

Bishop had begun calling colleagues, not directly canvassing votes, more sussing out where they were heading. Her approach, such as asking 'Do you think Malcolm has changed?' was subtle. She hadn't signed up to anyone.

There was not much time for the anti-Abbott forces to organise. It was like herding cats. In a bushfire. Sinodinos and Brough began sounding out MPs in earnest.

There were conversations between the principal players. Scott Morrison was prepared to serve as treasurer if Turnbull became leader. Turnbull wanted Bishop to remain deputy. Of course. Bishop, on the other hand, who was riding a wave of popularity with the backbench, would have been prepared to stand if the spill were successful and Abbott vacated the leadership. Ultimately, she decided the numbers were not there for the spill to get up. She stayed out of it.

Morrison was not then a contender, but he was all for change. He knew it wasn't working, and had decided well before that Hockey was not up to the job. Turnbull and Morrison had been friends, going back to Morrison's time as New South Wales state director. They had a spectacular falling-out before Turnbull's leadership imploded in 2009, then made up some time later.

Morrison had also never been close to Abbott, although they worked well together. Morrison had helped Abbott deliver in the key area of stopping the asylum-seeker boats, but there was no mentor–pupil element to their relationship. Nor did they have regular dinners or get-togethers. Morrison was there on merit, not patronage.

Morrison's housemate, Stuart Robert, was another prime mover. He wanted to get the spill up.

The problem was that there was no challenger, and there was understandable reluctance in some quarters to move against the prime minister so abruptly and so early in his tenure.

'To vote against a first-term prime minister who had literally only been in office a bit over twelve months, without there being a challenger, was showing disrespect,' one Abbott supporter said.

Backbenchers who might have been inclined to vote for the spill motion wanted to know who, if anyone, was going to put their hand up. They had a right to know, before they voted, who they might be voting for if they decided to remove a prime minister in his first term.

Andrew Robb, highly respected inside the government for his work in securing three massive trade deals with Japan, Korea, and

China, one of the good-news stories from 2014, came out publicly and strongly against the spill. He also made it clear to anyone even thinking of challenging that they might find him in the ring as well. Robb was worried about the comparisons with Labor, he had his own history with Turnbull, and he believed Abbott should be given a chance. Later, in September 2015, Robb stayed quiet, playing no role. He refrained from working either against Abbott or for Turnbull.

Peter Hendy also did not think the time was right for the spill. He thought it was too early.

Abbott had called Hendy on the Saturday before the party meeting. Curiously, the prime minister did not ask him for his vote or his support, saying only, 'So what do you want to tell me?'

It was late at night, and Abbott was obviously tired. Hendy told him what others had already told him — that Hockey needed to go, and he needed a new chief of staff. Hendy, who had done that job twice previously, told the prime minister: 'You can't have a chief of staff with a higher media profile than a cabinet minister.'

On the Sunday night before the spill, word spread quickly through government ranks about the queue of backbenchers outside the prime minister's door as Abbott tried to nail down support. South Australian senator Sean Edwards later told colleagues: 'I sold my vote for the submarines.'

Brough also saw Abbott that evening. They had a very brief, pointed conversation. Brough made clear his desire for change.

James McGrath's campaigning genius had helped deliver Newman's historic victory in 2011, which saw the LNP win 78 out of the 89 seats. It also helped garner a net nine seats for the federal Coalition in 2010, and contributed to turning Labor into a minority government. He stayed aloof from the planning for the spill. But in a seven-minute conversation, he told Abbott exactly what he thought when the prime minister rang him that Sunday night.

McGrath told Abbott he did not know whose side the federal government had been on during the Queensland election campaign, but it wasn't on the side of the LNP. He told Abbott that he believed he would lead them all to catastrophic defeat federally. As politely as he could, he informed Abbott that he would indeed be voting for the spill.

Simpkins reckons Brough told him on Sunday night that he thought they had the numbers to get the spill up. Although Simpkins was pleased to hear it, he was not that confident. He had spoken to about ten colleagues, not so much to persuade them, but to explain why, and a couple of them, including rock-solid Abbot supporter Andrew Nikolic, from Tasmania, had got stuck into him.

'I always tried to do what was best for the country,' Simpkins said. 'Who is who in the zoo, who is going to vote where — others can do that stuff. I was certain this was the right thing to do. I wasn't certain about the numbers. Whenever anybody asked me, I said I was confident we had them — I wasn't going to say we were cactus.'

Hendy did a mental calculation of the numbers the next day, figuring there would be 40 votes against the prime minister. In the event, there were 39. On the morning before the ballot, news outlets were quoting Abbott supporters as saying the spill would garner only 15 or 16 votes. Journalists who ran the stories were convinced that the low number had been fed to surrogates by the prime minister's office.

Abbott looked confident as he walked into the party meeting. He went over to Simpkins and Randall to shake hands. Randall told him that nothing would change unless he got rid of Credlin — MPs hated her, and she had to go. Abbott said something like, 'Ah, mate, I don't think I can go there.'

Liberals cannot forget the look on Abbott's face when he read the result of the ballot that was handed to him on a piece of paper by the whip, Philip Ruddock. He was shattered. After it was over, having coffee with friends, he confessed he was shocked that so many of his colleagues had voted against him. He should not have been; once again, he showed that he didn't always take in what people were saying to him.

Josh Frydenberg, who had been helping Cormann with the numbers, went to the gym with Abbott on the morning of the spill. Frydenberg told him that while he would win, the vote for the motion would be in the high thirties or low forties.

Abbott simply said 'OK', seemingly taking time to let it sink in, but in reality not doing the maths. Reality only hit when he saw the number 39 written down. Without a challenger, barely eighteen months into his prime ministership, his colleagues had delivered him a mortal blow.

In his subsequent speech to the party room, Abbott called for unity, committed himself to consult more, and promised that the prime minister's office would no longer vet mid-level staff appointments, nor control travel. He said he would review Medicare reform, and confessed that as a former health minister he should have known you could not take on the medical profession and win.

He said he had just had a near-death experience. He promised he would change.

In view of what happened six months later, Bishop's speech was interesting. She thanked MPs for re-endorsing her as deputy leader. She reaffirmed that she had not been on anybody's ticket, and said that in her view she had been elected separately as deputy leader as a conduit between the backbench and the leader. Partly, her remarks were designed to correct an impression left by Abbott that there was a ticket when he'd insisted she appear with him in Queensland on the Saturday before the vote.

Bishop was furious that she had been compelled to attend the event at Townsville airport to announce the start of international flights there. She had had nothing to do with it. It was not something even remotely related to her portfolio, except for that one word, 'international'. But it was made clear to her by Credlin that if she did not attend, it would be seen as a vote of no confidence in the prime minister. It was also made clear to her that if she did not participate, it would be used against her to question her loyalty to the leader. Bishop resented being treated like a pawn, but the pictures of her beside him served Abbott's purpose at the time.

Bishop went out of her way to make it clear to the party room that day that she believed Liberal MPs had provided her with a separate mandate. She was the only one not appointed by the leader, who did not depend on him (whoever he might be) for her position. She had not at any time run on a ticket with the leader to get elected, although in each ballot she maintained her position of voting for the leader.

She would be reminded of her arguments about separate mandates later that year, in September. Eric Abetz told colleagues in the party room that the vote was a signal to Abbott to shake up his economic team. Abetz said he had already advised him to do this. Abetz also made it clear to people later he had told Abbott that if he did not sack both Hockey and Credlin, the party would sack him.

Days later, Abbott rang the whip, Philip Ruddock, to offer him a couple of ill-defined other jobs, one of which involved Indigenous recognition. However, his primary purpose was to sack Ruddock as whip. There was no explanation offered, and none was sought. Appointing the whip was the prime minister's call, but it looked like Ruddock was being blamed for not having told him things were so crook. In fact, it was not Ruddock's job to do the numbers, nor had he been asked to, although he had been doing his best to pass on to the prime minister the discontent felt by backbenchers, as had MPs themselves when they spoke to him directly.

On Monday afternoons during every sitting week, Ruddock would meet with his deputies, Scott Buccholz and Nola Merino, to exchange intelligence on the issues occupying the backbench. Ruddock would pass on the information personally to Abbott the next day; if he could not get to him, he would usually speak to Andrew Hirst. Around the end of 2014, the mood was especially bleak. Ruddock passed it all on.

Obviously, Abbott himself suspected all was not well. Otherwise, why was he ringing backbenchers in their summer holidays to ask them what he could do to make things better?

Friends of Ruddock's also suggested that Ruddock had not been enthusiastic enough when he announced to the media the prime minister's magnificent victory over an empty chair. Ruddock's sacking was 'like shooting your mother', Liberals said later.

Ruddock, elected in September 1973 at a by-election, was the father of the house. For many Liberals, he was an icon, particularly after his stint as immigration minister under John Howard. Ruddock had been through countless challenges — the first, between Billy Snedden and Malcolm Fraser in March 1975. Back then, he managed the rare feat of convincing both sides he would not be voting for either of them. Ruddock did not approve of Tony Staley's undermining of Snedden on behalf of Fraser, and told him so. When Snedden rang to ask him if he would vote for him, he said no. Both sides had him down as a no. He did, in fact, vote for Fraser. Ruddock was the exception which proves the rule that when counting numbers for a challenge, you can only believe those who say they will not vote for you.

Hendy made a mental note to himself in February. He thought that if things were still as bad come September, that would be the right time for a move against the prime minister. He stuck firmly to the timetable he had set.

Abbott's backbenchers had tried to tell him directly, but he simply wasn't listening, so they sent him a message in a way they thought he would understand.

Abbott had asked MPs, including Queenslander Luke Howarth, to give him a chance to restore the government's fortunes. He rang Howarth before the spill to tell him he was confident he could turn it around in six months. Howarth thought *Fair enough, yes, that seems reasonable.* A supporter of Abbott's, Howarth's chief complaint before the spill was that backbenchers were not being listened to. He wanted that fixed. Abbott told him to ring or text him directly if he needed to. He did, and says he never had any trouble getting through. Those who put up constructive suggestions in policy areas found Abbott receptive.

Scott Ryan voted for Abbott, and publicly declared his support before the spill. He did not want the Liberal Party to do what Labor had done. He also offered the prime minister constructive advice about what he could do to rebuild. Others had simply made up their minds. They had told him what they thought he should do, and he wouldn't do it.

They expected Abbott and his office would go out of their way to bind the wounds. They told him the system of patronage and punishment had to end. Instead, stories about 'turncoats' were briefed to the tabloids.

Within a matter of days, in spite of everything that had happened, Brian Loughnane was telling a regular meeting of thirty marginal-seat holders what the PM had recited to them in January. The fundamentals were sound. There was a plan, the plan was working, and it was important to stick to the plan.

Their frustration boiled over. They were unhappy about the continuous focus on national security. They were unhappy about a hangover of decisions from Kevin Andrews' time as minister for social services, they were unhappy about the level of consultation. In short, they were still really, really unhappy.

Their unhappiness only grew when they learned of a text that Peta Credlin sent to the Senate president, Stephen Parry, a month after the spill. Credlin was meant to be assuming a lower profile after all the controversy.

The content showed that while she was down, she was definitely not out. The carefully worded text, couched in supposedly friendly terms, was interpreted by Parry, as well as by the friends to whom he showed it, as threatening. Credlin wrote that she had been told Parry had criticised her at a state executive meeting. She said she was sure this wasn't true, but, by the way, journalists were asking her why there were so many Tasmanians in senior positions. The version at the time from sources close to her was that she was informing Parry that journalists had asked about rumours he was being challenged for the Senate presidency.

No one had heard of such rumours. There was no suggestion of any threat to his position. Few believed that journalists had initiated any such inquiries. Their take on it was that Credlin was delivering a warning that criticism of her came with consequences. Parry was a highly respected figure in the Coalition. He had won the presidency with a resounding 63 votes. As a former homicide detective, Parry was pretty good at stringing clues together, so he understood exactly what the message was that she was seeking to convey with the text.

Relations with the presiding officers—Parry and the House Speaker, Bronwyn Bishop—and the prime minister's office were already strained over the proposal to ban burkas in Parliament House, which the presiding officers had announced on Tuesday 30 September 2014. The next day, 1 October, the proposal got a big boost when Fairfax Media ran a front-page story saying that Credlin had told LNP backbencher George Christensen she was sympathetic to the ban on security grounds. The report was based on her alleged conversation with Christensen, who had earlier been advocating the ban.

Christensen told me back then that his conversation with Credlin had lasted less than a minute, and that she had simply asked him to cool it, which he reckons he had already decided to do after a knife attack by a young Muslim man on two police officers. He insisted she did not ask him to raise the matter with the presiding officers, and it was a mystery to him where Fairfax got the information it had on the front page that she had told him to make his case for the ban on security grounds. Credlin did not complain to the authors about the article prominently reporting her views, supposedly conveyed privately to a backbencher, although plenty of others voiced their objections. What was the chief of staff doing on the front page of newspapers, intervening on such a sensitive issue?

The idea for the ban was first put to Bronwyn Bishop by the Australian Federal Police, based on a review of security at Parliament House.

Credlin, accompanied by Andrew Shearer, ASIO, and the AFP, had already met with Bishop previously (a meeting that Parry did not attend) to outline concerns about security in the building.

Among other things, Credlin at that meeting had canvassed removing the Parliamentary Library from its central position atop the executive wing, so that parliamentary secretaries could be moved in.

Soon after, at another meeting with the Speaker, the AFP suggested the burka ban. Bishop's chief of staff, Damien Jones, passed on the proposal to Kate Raggatt, a senior adviser in the prime minister's office who worked hand-in-glove with Credlin. Raggatt said to leave it with her, as she would have to check with Credlin. Raggatt came back to Jones saying, 'Go with it, it has to be done.'

According to sources, security officials had privately confirmed that there had been some 'chatter' about an attack on Parliament House, but did not believe there was a specific threat to a particular person. At one point, Credlin, who took as keen an interest in national-security matters as the prime minister, also took great delight in informing senior advisers in the prime minister's office that the AFP was considering issuing her with Close Personal Protection officers. She told them that she hoped she wouldn't be 'beheaded — as that would cap off a really shitty year'.

The proposal to ban the burka triggered a huge public outcry. Bishop was scheduled to fly overseas on Friday 3 October, so Jones tried to get hold of Credlin on Thursday evening to see what they should do. She did not return his call. The person who called him back was Tony Abbott, who had earlier also described the burka as 'confronting', although he did say that Muslim women were entitled to wear it. The issue was building up a head of steam, the prime minister told Jones, and it had to be reversed. Jones said he would tell the Speaker. Abbott emphasised that it was in everyone's interests that it be sorted. Bishop rang Abbott later that evening and agreed to back down. Parry and Bishop ended up carrying the can for the prime minister's office, even though those involved said later that the office had been 'up to its armpits' on the issue. The presiding officers joined the queue of people who were unhappy with the office.

Although some of his supporters were convinced he could recover, it was folly to think that Abbott could come back from the February spill. The fact that there'd been no challenger made the reality that thirty-nine of his colleagues had voted against him not only humiliating, but ominous. If an empty chair could get that many votes, what would a credible challenger muster?

Only a truly exceptional leader could survive that. Abbott was not truly exceptional, as evidenced by the fact he was in so much strife so soon. He was right to call it a near-death experience. People who have had such experiences tend to re-evaluate their lives. They reform, they recast, they do what they can to make sure it never happens again. This particular political animal was never going to change, nor was the faux-leopard wearer whose paw prints MPs saw at the scene of every debacle.

It was also folly on his part to ask Liberal MPs to give him six months to turn it around. By doing so, he made himself hostage to the polls and to a deadline. In reality, his backbenchers, as a result of his own actions, had chopped him off at the knees. It was only a matter of time before the job would be completed, despite the fact that things went quiet for a bit after that.

Brough later remarked on the goodwill felt towards Abbott after the spill, saying he had also hoped that the prime minister would be able to turn things around. That hope evaporated as the year progressed. By July, Brough was back where he was in February.

It took considerable courage for Simpkins to do what he did back in February 2015. After it was over, he hoped it would work, that Abbott would make the changes necessary to recover.

'I was glad I did it. I don't regret doing it at all,' he told me later. He is conscious of his place in history, and the consequences of what he did. He does not resile from it. He has fairly and squarely taken full ownership of it.

'I was surprised it came down to me. I never thought I would be the one to do stuff like that. In the end, someone needed to act. No one else was going to step up. Bloody hell. You are here to do the best thing for the country. I wasn't going to let reticence hold me back from doing the best thing for the nation. You just can't be grey on these sort of matters—you have to step out.'

Simpkins resents suggestions he was ever doing anybody's bidding. He stressed that he had always done what he believed to be right. He rejected my view that Abbott was finished from the moment that vote was read out.

For a while, Simpkins thought it had worked. He had always liked Abbott. He believed his achievements in stopping the boats and scrapping the carbon tax were great. He thought Abbott was a terrific role model because of his fitness and community work. It drove him nuts when people poked fun at his red budgie-smugglers, even though they were a symbol of his volunteer surf life-saving. Unfortunately, Simpkins says, Abbott kept saying or doing silly things.

A few months later, it was back to the future for Simpkins, too. Once again, he concluded time was up. It hadn't worked. Nothing had changed.

CHAPTER SIX

Speaking of Disasters

Joe Hockey's second budget on 12 May 2015 went down a whole lot better than his first one, thanks to some inspiration from a new addition to Tony Abbott's team, but the lead-up was not without its dramas.

In late April, the party whip, the amiable Queenslander Scott Buccholz, was told by nervous backbenchers to deliver another message to the prime minister: if this budget went the way of the first, Hockey would have to go.

The subtext was even then, as emboldened backbenchers privately admitted, that if the budget tanked and Hockey was not removed, the prime minister would be.

Buccholz did what whips are supposed to do. He relayed the message for the prime minister to his office — not to Credlin — but to lower-ranking staff nominated to deal with backbenchers.

Having been told this had happened, I rang Buccholz to ask him about it. It put him in an invidious position. He could not deny it, because we both knew it had occurred, so he gave a one-line comment for publication, saying: 'I think Joe's done a good job in difficult circumstances, and I think he is well aware of the importance of this budget landing well.' This was as good as confirmation in the circumstances.

The morning the column appeared, on 7 May 2015, was the morning that Abbott was interviewed by Neil Mitchell on 3AW. Abbott described my account as a 'complete invention', then went on to say he had not spoken to Buccholz about Hockey. I never said he had. It was curious, though, that after such a message was relayed, the prime minister didn't bother to call his whip to discuss it — unless, of course, the whip wasn't going to tell him anything he didn't already know.

Abbott was obviously anxious, a week out from the budget, not to say or do anything that would imply any loss of confidence in Hockey, but here was another fib. Later that day, at the insistence of Abbott and his office, with one arm twisted halfway up his back, Buccholz wrote a letter to the editor of *The Australian*, saying he had not spoken to the prime minister on the matter.

The editor, Clive Mathieson, ran the letter with a note at the bottom to say the column had not stated that Buccholz had spoken to the prime minister. It had stated that Buccholz had passed on a message to the prime minister's office. Abbott succeeded in deflecting the story, but he also succeeded in confirming how fast and loose he was with his language. He did the same thing to Scott Morrison after he lost the leadership. Or, to give him the benefit of the doubt, perhaps both times his office neglected to pass on the message, or had put a different 'construction' on it.

In the wake of the budget, Newspoll showed the government had drawn neck and neck with Labor at 50–50. A package of measures to help small business gave MPs something to sell. They were grateful. The package was the brainchild of Michael Thawley, the new head of the prime minister's department. Relations between Abbott and his previous department head, Dr Ian Watt (who, readers will remember, had been the messenger obliged to give Martin Parkinson the flick from Treasury), broke down irretrievably after the MH17 disaster. The prime minister's office blamed Watt for not having notified them of the crash, and he was squeezed out. Abbott asked Thawley to take on the job.

John Howard, who had appointed Thawley ambassador to the United States, encouraged his former international/national security adviser to accept it, believing—hoping—he might be able to help Abbott stabilise his position by governing better, while also providing a separate trusted source of advice.

Thawley began work as departmental secretary on 1 December. He was under no illusions about the difficulties of the task he faced in rebuilding trust. He was concerned about the poor relations between the prime minister's office and the department. He was also concerned about how the previous budget had been handled. Thawley believed concessions were essential to encourage start-ups to drive jobs growth. Like many others, he was also aware of just how much the government needed to be able to tell an economic story. Thawley wrote an outline of a package for small business, the department attached figures, and he sent half-a-dozen pages to the prime minister so he could read it over Christmas. Before that, it looked as if childcare would be the budget's centrepiece.

Abbott took up Thawley's suggestions with relish. Four weeks before the budget, the small business minister, Bruce Billson, was brought in to complete it. When it was unveiled, the $5.5 billion package, which allowed small business to immediately deduct any asset costing less than $20,000, as well as a 1.5 per cent tax cut for companies with less than $2 million in turnover, went down very well. Hopefully, a new category of voter, Tony's Tradies, had been created to rival Howard's Battlers.

At this stage, Malcolm Turnbull was telling friends that even if there happened to be a vote on the leadership—which was not in prospect—it would probably go to Morrison. Having done their bit, backbenchers rightly thought that if any new moves to unseat Abbott were to be made, they would have to be initiated by those higher up the food chain. Turnbull tried to be zen-like, telling people that if Abbott took them to the election and they lost, he would happily go off and play with his grandchildren. He certainly would not go into opposition—he would leave parliament and do something else.

Turnbull's enemies inside the government were blaming him for leaks from cabinet, in the hope it would make him look disloyal or weak on terrorism. This infuriated him, because he had been locked out of security discussions directly relevant to his portfolio. When the national security committee of cabinet decided to toughen up laws on metadata retention in August 2014, it went straight to the front page of the *Daily Telegraph* before it even made it to cabinet—which was not always required, but it was always politic to do so. Turnbull had not been co-opted to the NSC for the discussion, and he exploded in cabinet over the leak. There was no prize for guessing the name of the chief suspect.

Then a whole lot of things happened that provided depressing confirmation for many backbenchers and frontbenchers that, since February, very little had in fact changed.

Bronwyn Bishop fell to earth in a helicopter. It took eighteen days to clear the wreckage. It might as well have been eighteen weeks, for all the damage that was caused to politicians generally, as well as to Abbott personally. Whatever goodwill had been generated by Hockey's second budget evaporated. Who wanted to talk about small business or Tony's Tradies, after Melbourne's *Herald Sun* broke the story on 15 July that the Speaker had arrived at a function, a fundraiser for the Victorian state election, no less, in a helicopter, at a cost of more than $5,000? What made it worse, or better, depending on your point of view, was that they had a photo.

Thank you, taxpayers. Goodnight, career.

It was not a huge amount—other MPs had spent more on charter planes to get to functions—but the visuals, the cartoons, were irresistible, and the way it was handled, risible. Yet this, too, was emblematic of Abbott's approach. If it had been the only issue that had gone awry during the winter recess, maybe they might have got away with it, although that is unlikely.

Before the helicopter crash there was Abbott's overblown, over-the-top rhetoric about Islamic State, a jihad against the ABC, and a cabinet leak that either made the prime minister look opportunistic or his senior ministers look like wreckers. There was a near-complete absence of trust, of respect, of order, of good judgement.

Stock markets in China were in meltdown, but Abbott's answer to that at a press conference called specifically to announce a new grocery code was … the new grocery code. When it came to the economy, sometimes it seemed the prime minister had little to say. When it came to national security, there was always a lot to say, although some of it was probably better left unsaid, or said differently.

The Liberal Party's federal council in late June 2015 was a non-event, which is usually the way the insiders like it, until Islamic State terrorists launched murderous raids in Kuwait, Tunisia, and France.

At a doorstop, Abbott delivered an apocalyptic warning that, 'as far as the Daesh death cult is concerned, it's coming after us'. Nobody was under-estimating the threat; nobody was minimising it, or was cavalier about it. We had all watched as terrorists flew planes into skyscrapers or blew up trains, or set off bombs in Bali that killed more than 200 people, including eighty-eight

Australians, or slaughtered innocent people on the streets of Paris or Sydney. So we all knew full well their capabilities, driven by their murderous intent. But his language and tone were all wrong for a national leader.

It seemed that his mission was to keep people in a constant state of anxiety, rather than to reassure them.

Where should we hide? Under the bed with the Reds, or in the cellar with the other reds? There was no escape. There were regular national-security announcements designed to keep the issue at the forefront of voters' minds. They were also designed to wedge Labor. Abbott would have liked nothing better than for Shorten to refuse to back him on a national-security measure. Shorten always failed to oblige him.

Peter Jennings and Anthony Bergin from the Australian Strategic Policy Institute offered sensible advice, saying the government needed to watch its language, and to work on ways to counter radicalisation. This was not taken up by Abbott.

Experts in the field worried about both the tone and the content of the prime minister's messages. Urging Muslims to be part of 'team Australia', advising Muslim leaders talking about Islam as a religion of peace to sound as if they really meant it, did not inspire confidence or encourage co-operation.

There was a marked change in both within weeks once Turnbull took over, to the relief of security agencies that had advised the new prime minister to try a less confrontational, or provocative, approach.

Reflecting subsequently on Abbott's performance, Jennings told me: 'I think there were a couple of factors at play which did not help the way the government was handling the issue.'

Highly respected, with a long history in his field, Jennings could not in any way be cast as dovish. He was fully behind military action against IS. However, he was troubled by Abbott's approach, by what he said, by the tactics that appeared to drive it.

'There was Abbott's own psychology. He got IS in a way that others didn't, because he is a person who has an Old Testament view of the world, he understood the millenarian [a belief that we are in an apocalyptic millennium] nature of their ideology. That's where the death cult came from,' Jennings observed.

'In some ways, that was a correct reading of what is motivating IS.

'[But] as a way of conducting public policy, that was miscast. It elevated IS standing in a way that should not have been allowed to happen. They were presented as more powerful than they are, and in a way that suited their propaganda. Something less emotional would have been better. The high point was that "coming to get us", which was way over the top.

'Also, there was a sense of how the political advantage was maximised. I don't blame the government for doing it, for seeing if it could push Labor to break, so it could then be seen as weak on national security. This became a parlour game the office was way too interested in.

'Every week there was a new announceable, with more money being spent with the thought that this might be the thing which will force Labor to break. So there was the combination of Abbott's end-of-days psychology and political games, which meant there was a failure to get the right narrative.

'Abbott and his office were conscious of how it played to the base, which always wanted more and more punitive ways to deal with the issue, rather than co-operate with the Muslim community.'

Experts also believed that Abbott had not done enough to work with the Muslim community, which felt more and more alienated by a 'punitive' approach that stressed arrests and disruption operations, but was less focussed on steps needed to counter the radicalisation of 15-year-olds well in advance of terrorist action.

Once again, it appeared there was too much reliance placed on the inner circle. His foreign affairs adviser, Andrew Shearer, and Credlin had the greatest influence here.

Connie Fierravanti-Wells also realised there was too much concentration on national security, and not enough on community engagement. Along with others, Connie was troubled by Abbott's language. Her extensive consultations with the Muslim communities, undertaken at Abbott's request as part of her duties as parliamentary secretary to the attorney-general, confirmed in her mind what she already believed: it was counterproductive. She urged him to change tack, and believed he was doing that before he was deposed.

After he lost the leadership, he reverted to type and then some in his calls for a reformation of Islam, accompanied by the assertion of the cultural superiority of the West. In a considered contribution to *The Australian*, without mentioning Abbott by name, and drawing on her more intimate knowledge of the feelings of the community that supported reform, Fierravanti-Wells stressed the need to support moderate Muslims, warning that 'megaphone politics not only distracts from this, but has implications for our relationships with our neighbours'.

The other conflict early that winter was the continuing war against the ABC. This time, *Q&A* was beyond the pale. Producers invited onto the program on 22 June a convicted criminal whose despicable, misogynist tweets about columnists Miranda Devine and Rita Panahi should have been enough to disqualify him from participation in a forum on one of the national broadcaster's flagship programs. In the same way that convicted paedophiles or convicted rapists do not deserve a platform, Zaky Mallah did not deserve one, either. The ABC's excuse was that it did not know about the tweets.

In 2003, Mallah had been charged, but subsequently acquitted, with planning a suicide attack in Sydney. He had admitted to doing 'some stupid things, including threatening to kidnap and kill' when he was younger. Only six months before he appeared on *Q&A*, he had tweeted:

Australia has two decent whores, @RitaPanahi and Miranda Devine. Both need to be gang banged on the Sunrise desk. #freedomofspeech love it!

When he was condemned for inciting gang rape against the two women, Mallah responded by tweeting: 'Gang raped? Please show me where I said "gang raped"? I remember saying gang banged! Rita and Miranda, if you'll consent, I'll be the first!'

So here was this offensive punk in the audience of a flagship program, asking the parliamentary secretary for foreign affairs, Steve Ciobo, what would have happened to him if the immigration minister, rather than the courts, had decided his case—a reference to the debate then raging over stripping home-grown terrorists of their Australian citizenship.

Ciobo told Mallah he'd be happy to see him kicked out of the country, despite the court's ruling.

'I am not familiar with the circumstances of your case … but from memory I thought you were acquitted on a technicality, rather than it being on the basis of substantial finding of fact,' Ciobo said.

'I got to tell you … my understanding of your case was that you were acquitted because at that point in time the laws weren't retrospective, but I am happy to look you straight in the eye and say I'd be pleased to be part of a government that would see you out of the country, as far as I am concerned.

'I would sleep very soundly at night. I don't apologise for this point of view.'

Ciobo had handled it very well; however, there was an issue here that had to be dealt with, which went to the propriety of *Q&A* allowing Mallah onto the program in the first place. Abbott was right to be angry over the way Ciobo had been set up. He was also right to express his anger. However, once again, his language was over the top. Playing to his conservative base, who despised the ABC, he branded the program 'a lefty lynch mob', asked whose side the ABC was on, demanded that heads roll, and accused the ABC of betrayal. All of this was consistent with his worldview that whoever was not with him was agin him. Ministers were banned from appearing on *Q&A* until it was sorted.

This controversy also dragged on for days, occupying space and time better spent on other issues such as, er, the economy or the budget.

Malcolm Turnbull did no harm to his standing inside the Coalition by taking on Barrie Cassidy on the ABC's *Insiders* on this matter, only in a more judicious manner.

The other issue that thrust Turnbull back into contention was when he, along with several other cabinet ministers, rolled Abbott in cabinet on the citizenship issue. The first whiff of the revolt was reported by Sky's Kieran Gilbert, but the issue itself had been put on the agenda by the chairman of the joint standing committee on intelligence, Dan Tehan, in an op-ed piece that appeared in Melbourne's *Herald Sun* on 16 May, four days after the budget.

Tehan's piece argued for the removal of Australian citizenship from dual citizens convicted of terrorism, and also from sole citizens if they could avail themselves of the citizenship of another country. He was prompted by the complaints of constituents who could not understand why the government was ready to take people back who had joined terrorist groups overseas. Tehan was not privy to discussions that had already taken place in the national security committee of cabinet, but his piece had been cleared in advance by the prime minister's office.

So when cabinet met on 25 May, the issue was already out in the public arena. Gilbert had put out feelers before the meeting began, then received a couple of late-night calls outlining what had happened. He says his informants were 'flabbergasted' by what had occurred. As to who alerted him, Gilbert says only that it was not the 'usual suspects'. He also did not get a sense that his sources were seeking to undermine Abbott; rather, they were offended by the process. Gilbert put questions to the attorney-general, George Brandis, around 6.30 the next morning on his program, but Brandis avoided answering by saying he had not seen Gilbert in the cabinet room.

In fact, Brandis was one of those who had strongly opposed a proposal to give the immigration minister, Peter Dutton, the power to strip Australians of their sole citizenship. The matter had already been before the national security committee of cabinet three times, and three times it had been rejected.

Abbott wanted Brandis and Dutton to sort it so they could bring a joint proposal to cabinet. They could not reach agreement. A paper was prepared by the prime minister's office, which was not circulated to other cabinet ministers in advance of the meeting, nor had there been any consultation with them about its contents, nor was the item listed on the cabinet agenda.

Under traditional protocols, cabinet 'submissions' are circulated to all relevant ministers for their comment and consideration before discussions take place in cabinet. Once again, due process appeared to have been subverted.

That cabinet meeting was drawing to a close, and officials were closing their folders preparing to leave, when Abbott almost casually raised the issue of the citizenship discussion paper.

One cabinet minister said later that Peter Hartcher's account in Fairfax Media of what then happened read like *Hansard*. There was a lot of finger-pointing about who leaked it. Turnbull was blamed by some; Bishop, by others; and Credlin, by still others, supposedly in a Machiavellian double-play to set Turnbull up for the rap.

There was no fight over stripping dual citizens of their Australian citizenship if they were involved in terrorism. The core of the dispute was whether the immigration minister should be empowered to strip sole citizens of their citizenship. According to the Hartcher account, later verified by others, Turnbull described it as an extraordinary proposition. Dutton had the full backing of the prime minister.

Barnaby Joyce, who was to have a spectacular falling-out with the prime minister later over coal-mining in his electorate, argued that the matter should be left to the courts. 'If you don't have enough evidence to charge them in a court, how can you have enough evidence to take away their citizenship?', he said.

Precisely the point, countered Dutton — evidence was not essential, because it was an administrative decision.

Brandis was offended by the concept. 'I am the attorney-general. It's my job to stand up for the rule of law,' he said. Christopher Pyne backed him. Bishop was annoyed that the discussion paper had not been circulated, so the cabinet secretary, Matt Stafford, had to rush around and get copies for her and the others. Bishop argued that no other country would accept discarded Australian citizens, in any case.

Even Kevin Andrews, perhaps Abbott's closest supporter, another who stuck till the bitter end, chimed in against it.

Turnbull later went public with his concerns. Stripping citizenship from terrorists had headline appeal in the community, but inside cabinet there were deeper concerns about due process, not only when it came to their own deliberations, but for all citizens.

The worries over how the government went about things spread from the cabinet to the backbench as the government showed its characteristic lumbering, heaving, flat-footed approach when the Bishop helicopter crashed.

The opposition, with Tony Burke leading the charge, ran hard on the issue. Burke was warned by his colleagues there would be blow-back. He ignored them. He was splattered later when the government belatedly began providing the media with details of Burke's own unwise entitlement claims. However, the payback came too late to have any hope of altering the result.

During Howard's tenure, after the loss of a platoon of staff and ministers, Tony Nutt was brought into his office as principal private secretary. It was part of his brief to handle delicate political problems like this one. Nutt had the expertise to sift through the documents, then to tell the politicians what they had to do to fix it. If it involved self-immolation, so be it. It was his job to look after the greater good, and the greater good meant protecting the prime minister.

He would have had a full handle on the Bishop saga within a couple of days: she would have been convinced to make an unreserved apology; then, if it was shown in quick time that that had not worked, she would have been asked to hand in her resignation before further damage was done. While he was conducting his forensic investigation, the media would have been inundated with information about Labor MPs and their 'misuse' of entitlements.

For all the reasons previously stated, Nutt was not there.

There was no grovelling apology from Bishop until it was way too late. According to sources, Bishop was apparently keen to go out quickly, publicly, to try to kill off the story. Her chief of staff, Damien Jones, discussed tactics with Kate Raggatt in the prime minister's office. Bishop wanted to go out on the Friday, and say sorry. Raggatt said *No, hold your fire.*

On Saturday, Bishop was at the football when Jones got a call from Raggatt to say that Bishop had to get out there and do a press conference immediately to fix it. However, Raggatt also advised that, in the process, Bishop should not say 'sorry', because that could be construed as an admission of wrongdoing. The press conference was a disaster. Bishop did not say sorry, she did not grovel, and she gave Hockey a flick for giving her a flick.

It spiralled out of control across all media, traditional as well as social. Over succeeding days, stories appeared about other spending by Bishop, who was a prodigious fundraiser for the Liberals, and who travelled extensively. Although it is possible that the details were leaked by the Finance Department to Labor, Bishop remains convinced the leaks sprang from the prime minister's office, because they held all the information — all of it supplied by Bishop's office.

She slowly bled to death. Unfortunately, they all bled with her. Abbott's tardiness in dealing with it incensed MPs who, while they sat on the backbench, were in the frontline copping all the flak.

Abbott could not, would not, confront Bishop. Some commentators excused this on the grounds that he was staying loyal to her. However, that loyalty to her was taken inside the government as disloyalty to them, and disloyalty to his party, or as cover for poor judgement. Julie Bishop, Malcolm Turnbull, and Scott Morrison refused to defend the Speaker in public when they were asked to do so.

On Wednesday 29 July, Bishop met with Abbott and Credlin at the prime minister's office in Sydney to discuss a strategy to try to resolve the crisis. Bishop suggested she do an interview with the *Daily Telegraph,* where she would make an abject apology, then follow up with an interview with Alan Jones. Credlin vetoed the *Telegraph* interview, because she did not think the paper—which had been running heavily against Bishop—would treat her sympathetically. Credlin impressed on Bishop the need for contrition.

Bishop did the interview with Jones the next morning, in which she expressed her remorse, then flew to country Victoria. Credlin texted Bishop after the interview to commend her on her performance. Abbott gave Bishop a lift on the VIP plane to Perth for Don Randall's funeral, on Friday 31 July; in conversations with him on the plane, Bishop thought she still retained Abbott's support. She believed this up until less than an hour before his press conference when he announced her resignation.

By the time she delivered an abject apology, her position was irretrievable. Labor was preparing to move a no-confidence motion against the Speaker when parliament resumed, and a number of government backbenchers—maybe up to half a dozen—were saying privately they would abstain; they would not vote with the government to support Bishop.

Until then, Luke Howarth believed that Abbott had been fulfilling his pledge to turn his performance and standing around in six months. He believed the budget had put the government back on track. But he was dismayed by how long it was taking to fix choppergate. He texted Abbott to give him the feedback from his electorate. It was all bad. The mover of February's spill motion, Luke Simpkins, who had also believed that Abbott was turning it around, again lost faith. He was back where he was, mentally, at the beginning of the year. MPs everywhere were being monstered in the media or by their constituents.

The other cost of the failure to clear the wreckage of choppergate in a timely manner was that it allowed Shorten time to reposition himself. He secured a victory at the party's national conference, thanks to the backing of lefties such as Kim Carr, to allow a Labor government to adopt the Coalition's previously much-maligned policy to turn back asylum-seeker boats. It was critical for Shorten to try to defuse this as an issue.

It also smothered concerns over Shorten's appearance in early July at the royal commission into trade union corruption. Shorten's performance was woeful, and there were serious questions about payments by companies to the Australian Workers Union during his stewardship. Although the royal commission subsequently found no evidence of criminal or unlawful behaviour by Shorten, it was tricky for the opposition leader at the time. Subsequent revelations by Fairfax reporter Latika Burke that the royal commissioner, Dyson Heydon, had accepted an invitation to speak at a New South Wales Liberal lawyers' event that turned out to be a fundraiser also bought Shorten important breathing space.

However, it was choppergate that helped Labor survive what might otherwise have been a very cold winter recess.

In between all this was the disgraceful booing of Adam Goodes by AFL football fans. It was a national story, it was about race, and the prime minister was silent on the subject. Conservatives were getting stuck into Goodes, while Liberals were appalled by the absence of the prime minister from the debate.

Abbott couldn't appear in public anywhere because of the Bishop saga. He called in to radio 2SM to appeal for Goodes to be treated with respect.

Where other ministers had held back in support of Bishop,

Christopher Pyne was out there, defending her to the hilt. Apart from his long-standing friendship with Bishop, Pyne told colleagues he had also been convinced by the prime minister's office that if Bishop went down, many others would soon be in the frame over their misuse of entitlements. He was told they couldn't let her go, so he was out there backing her to the bitter end. Raggatt was giving the same message to Bishop's office about the need to protect other colleagues.

Bishop spoke to Abbott on Saturday 1 August to give him an update on where things were at. There was no hint from him that he wanted her to quit, or that he was about to sack her. However, Cory Bernardi rang her that same day to tell her the whole affair was a major distraction for the government, and that, for the sake of the conservative cause, she should go. She thanked him for his call.

On Sunday morning, she was scheduled to attend a surf life-saving event at Palm Beach. As she was walking into it, she saw there was a message to call the government leader in the Senate, Eric Abetz. She decided to wait until the event finished before calling him back.

Not long after, Abbott called Damien Jones to ask if Bishop had checked her messages. It was close to lunchtime, and Jones explained she was at a function. Abbott told him he had to pull her out of it. Bishop then rang Abetz, who told her they needed to 'stop the bloodletting'. Abetz told her she needed to 'take one for the team', and should resign. She also thanked him for his call.

Abbott had tried to use emissaries—two conservative men who he knew were philosophically aligned to Bishop, but they were not her friends. He would have done better to have used Christopher Pyne, or George Brandis or Julie Bishop, although it's doubtful they would have been able to convince her.

Finally, after friendly columnists had been briefed hours earlier that she was gone, the prime minister had to cut the umbilical cord himself. Abbott had once described himself as the political love-child of John Howard and Bronwyn Bishop. Now, after having ignored his 'father', he was forced to kill his 'mother'.

Abbott called Bishop around 2.00 pm. He asked her to resign. Bishop said she was not prepared to make that decision.

'If you don't resign, I will have to announce you have lost the confidence of the government,' Abbott told her. He gave her ten minutes to decide, and said he would call her back. Exactly ten minutes later, when he did call her back, she told him she would resign. 'You have left me no alternative,' she said.

Abbott spoke to Bishops' chief of staff, Damien Jones, again, shortly before his press conference, to discuss the wording of the retirement announcement. Abbott began the conference by saying, 'Ms Bishop called me to let me know that she will be resigning' (which, strictly speaking, was not true), and said it had been a 'very difficult day' for Mrs Bishop, but that she had done the right thing by the people of Australia.

'Today is not the day to offer an appreciation of Bronwyn Bishop's long parliamentary career, her long career in public life,' he said.

'I have a great deal of personal respect for Bronwyn Bishop, and without wanting to underplay the significance of some of the errors of judgement, which she herself has conceded and apologised for, I think she has certainly done the right thing today.

'No one who saw Bronwyn on television the other day could be under any doubt as to her remorse.'

He also announced a 'root and branch' review of MPs entitlements — the second such review in two years.

Despite the deep involvement of his office in the debacle, the media were later briefed that, once again, Abbott had ignored Credlin's advice, and that she had told him to remove Bishop. Funny, how at the scene of every disaster it was made known that the chief of staff had had nothing to do with it. Funny, how the prime minister never demurred from this version of events. If true, it meant he was not listening to her—in which case she should have gone. If it wasn't true, her judgement was as flawed as his—in which case she still should have gone. That's what happens in normal professional relationships. Political staff also tend not to brief the media about internal matters, either to claim credit or avoid blame.

MPs were dismayed by this apparent briefing against the boss. That was definitely not normal. Everyone knows that when things are going great, the boss takes the credit. As soon as they go belly-up, it's the fault of the staff.

After Bishop finally resigned—a week from the resumption of parliament—what happened next should have been enough warning to Abbott of the restlessness of his MPs. Once again, he refused to take heed.

Backbenchers were determined to choose their own person to replace Bishop as Speaker. They were certainly in no mood to countenance another captain's pick by Abbott. They wanted to see some integrity restored to the party, as well as to the parliament. In the circumstances, it was widely agreed that the person best equipped to deliver this result, as well as to offer a cleanskin image, heralding a shift to the next generation, was Tony Smith. He was by far the best candidate, and Abbott would be the ultimate beneficiary if order were restored to the house.

Once again, though, Abbott failed to pick up on the mood of his own people. They were cranky and defiant. They were not prepared to tolerate any interference by him or his office in the process, but he could not leave it alone. He let it be known, to Christopher Pyne among others, that he did not want Tony Smith to get the job. Abbott wanted someone, anyone, else. 'Anyone but Smithy,' was the message. Abbott's loyalty was often trumpeted by his supporters, but he was also renowned for holding grudges. In the 2010 campaign, in an interview with Kerry O'Brien, Abbott kicked a big hole in his party's communications policy when he confessed he was no 'tech-head', and yet Tony Smith ended up carrying the can for the failure to sell the policy, and was demoted after that election. For some reason, Abbott also thought Smith would panic in the chair. Smith's demeanour, and his performance, showed otherwise; however, Abbott, in his typically stubborn way, refused to see it.

The whip, Scott Buccholz, rang half-a-dozen backbenchers to lobby them — they think for Russell Broadbent, but it was hard to tell, because Buccholz was trying to say it in code. Interventions by the whip could only happen at the prime minister's instigation. MPs liked Buccholz, but they resented his attempts to turn them away from Smith. In any case, Libs thought of him as a Nat, so they were extremely reluctant to be guided by him on this issue.

The opposition to Smith was irrational. It seemed personal. Smith was well liked by his colleagues, and it was clearly time to move on to the next generation.

Smith, who had been in parliament fourteen years, had also earned the respect of his colleagues, because he had got on with parliamentary work after Abbott dropped him from the frontbench altogether after the 2013 election. Although he felt the loss of position keenly, he refused to moan about it. Abbott had appointed him head of the Joint Select Committee on Electoral Matters. His work there, on Senate voting and on the debacle of the Western Australia Senate election, won him the respect of his colleagues, as well as of Labor and the Greens.

He reached out to mentor new MPs such as Lucy Wicks and Michael Sukkar, who now nominated and seconded his nomination in the house, where he was to be elected unopposed.

From his student days on, Smith had never lost any ballot he had ever contested. In this campaign, he received some critical support from his close friends Mitch Fifield and Kelly O'Dwyer, despite the fact they knew that Abbott preferred someone else. And as soon as Scott Morrison heard Smith was running, he swung his full support behind him, too. It wasn't personal against Abbott on Morrison's part, but he got along very well with Smith. He knew Smith would do a good job, so he was keen to help. Smith also spoke to almost every Liberal MP. Even staunch Abbott supporters such as Andrew Nikolic liked the fact that Smith had put his head down and bum up after having been dumped, with no moaning over his disappointments.

There were three other candidates: another Victorian, Russell Broadbent; South Australian Andrew Southcott; and Queenslander Ross Vasta. Smith won the final ballot by 51 votes to 22 against Broadbent. This was a thumping victory for Smith, and a thumbing of the nose at Abbott. As MPs left the party room after the vote, and while the television cameras were rolling, Abbott went up to Bronwyn Bishop and kissed her on the cheek. If looks could kill, Abbott would have been turned to stone in that moment. Colleagues told Bishop later that it was the kiss of Judas.

After Smith's election in the house, Abbott made a perfunctory speech, congratulating Smith and paying tribute to Bishop. Smith, whose performance over the following weeks and months justified the faith put in him by his colleagues, made a point of saying he was a man with friends on both sides of the parliament.

Importantly, what the whole process had revealed to Smith, apart from the inexplicable, continuing antagonism from the prime minister, was that there was considerable unrest on the backbench. When he rang them or they rang him to discuss the ballot, what they really wanted to talk about was how badly the government was travelling. The backbenchers weren't doing anything except talking at that stage. They had made it clear after February that if there was to be another tilt, it had to come from the ministry. The message coming through from them now was that they could be receptive to a move. Nevertheless, when parliament rose for the winter recess at the end of June, MPs had been hopeful the government would stabilise. The budget was working. Adjustments had been made to the prime minister's office, loosening the iron grip on backbenchers. As one senior Liberal said: 'At least they got better at pretending to listen.'

But the winter recess was like the summer recess that preceded the February spill, except worse. 'Everyone came back thinking, *Holy crap, what happened?* one frontbencher recalled.

CHAPTER SEVEN

Same Sex, Same Problem

As the second anniversary of his election approached, Tony Abbott's prime ministership was once again at a tipping point. Many MPs saw little to celebrate. Abbott's survival relied on the support of his conservative base; but in his anxiety to secure it, or perhaps motivated by his desire to wedge Malcolm Turnbull, he lost outright the support of moderates such as Christopher Pyne and George Brandis, and MPs on the right such as Scott Ryan. The issue that did it for Abbott was same-sex marriage. He was being pushed by deeply conservative MPs to hold the line against it, and pulled by the moderates, as well as capital-L liberals, to allow a free vote.

In a strange sort of way, this worked against Abbott like climate change had worked against Turnbull in 2009. Both leaders, at different times but on issues that went to their core beliefs, made the mistake of believing that outcomes mattered more than processes, while forgetting that while majorities might rule, the interests of minorities have to be accommodated, too. Outside politics, outcomes might be more important; however, inside, they carry equal weight—how you get there can be as important as what you eventually do when you arrive.

Although he might have ultimately landed in the right place, Abbott's handling of the same-sex marriage issue was a critical step on his road to ruin. The prime minister's trickiness, at best, or outright deception, at worst, in order to secure a victory that day, 11 August, cost him most dearly.

Talking amongst themselves later, as they went back over what had happened, and in conversations with me, Liberal MPs regarded this as a pivotal day (one of many pivotal days, it must be said) in Abbott's leadership. If it wasn't the reason they shifted, it provided them with the excuse to decamp and to let it be known that they had.

One cabinet minister summed it up by saying: 'He was not acting as a leader of the whole party, he was the leader of the right. He was not acting like a Liberal — I mean capital-L Liberal — acting in the traditions of the party to deal with the issue.'

Backbenchers thought it was bizarre that Abbott had not once discussed the handling of the same-sex marriage issue with either the full cabinet or the leadership group. Even supporters of marriage equality believe that if there had been a free vote, in all likelihood it would have been defeated in the parliament. This would have dealt with the issue for the time being; and, equally importantly, he would have been seen to have discharged his obligations as leader in an honourable way.

'I have rarely been as angry and as outraged as I was that night,' one Liberal MP said. 'It felt like our first caucus meeting. It was a meeting called and arranged with the intention of delivering a particular result under the veil of consultation.

'Tony is just an ends-justifies-the-means kind of guy.'

That meeting was critical in shifting Scott Ryan to Turnbull. Ryan later provided a thoughtful explanation to me of the impact of that day on him.

'I hadn't publicly argued the case either way on same-sex marriage—it simply wasn't a strong priority for me,' Ryan said.

'While years earlier I had opposed change, my view was evolving as I gave the issue deeper consideration, influenced by friends and colleagues, and particularly senator Dean Smith. But I hadn't indicated this publicly at all.

'I had previously been a little annoyed that advocates for change who were on the frontbench were seemingly free to disagree with party policy, while those of us who felt strongly about other issues did not have the same freedom (such as on taxes and the local government referendum). But I realised that this reaction was the wrong response.

'In the party-room debate, a number of colleagues referenced late 2009, when frontbenchers resigned and senators crossed the floor to oppose Rudd's CPRS. I thought this was the right thing to do in 2009. But I explained that this period wasn't something we should seek to replicate; it was a situation we should seek to avoid.

'When a large number of colleagues feel so strongly about a significant issue that a genuine compromise or consensus is impossible, we should seek to accommodate this rather than contrive a process designed to bind a large minority to a position they conscientiously disagree with.

'In this case, the [significant] minority wanted nothing more than to be able to vote according to their own beliefs, at no cost to anyone else. They were not asking the majority to vote against their principles in any way—only for everyone to be free to vote with their own consciences. There was strong precedent for this issue being treated as such.

'In this case, by inviting the National Party into the room [they were not present during the CPRS debate in 2009], the handling of the issue caused additional and entirely unnecessary angst amongst a significant number of colleagues, including those who opposed changing the definition of marriage.'

Abbott already had a rocky relationship with Queensland MP Warren Entsch, who was a staunch advocate for allowing same-sex marriage. A straight shooter, Entsch had always been forthright in his advice to him. Entsch had raised with Abbott the Credlin-Loughnane conflict before the 2013 election. He believes this cost him the whip's job in government.

Entsch is upfront in his dealings with the media as well as with his colleagues. By the time this issue was done and dusted in the party room, Entsch felt betrayed and duped. Others felt that traditions they held dear had been trampled.

Entsch had been an advocate for same-sex marriage for years. In the 2010 election, the parliamentary party stuck with the Howard position that marriage was between a man and a woman. In the approach to the 2013 election, Entsch wanted options kept open for a free vote in the Liberal Party room. He believed he had Abbott's agreement to this. It was further agreed with Abbott that nothing would happen on the issue in the first year, then agreed again that it would wait until after the second budget to give the government some clear air to sell what was a much more benign document.

Entsch was fine with this. He was patient, and he did not want to rock the boat. Bill Shorten, in the wake of the successful plebiscite on the subject in Ireland in May, moved a motion in the parliament to grant marriage equality. Entsch voted against it, because he believed Shorten was being opportunistic. At the time, to the dismay of his conservative wing, Abbott told parliament that this was an issue which should belong to the whole parliament, strongly implying that a vote would happen soon in the parliament, and it would be a free one. Entsch had cross-chamber support, with the backing of independents, the Greens, and Labor, for his own measure.

Abbott had also met separately with other Liberal MPs, including Simon Birmingham and Kelly O'Dwyer, before and after the second budget to discuss the issue. They also canvassed a timetable, and were likewise happy to wait until the budget was settled. They agreed it was best to do it in August after the winter recess. While Abbott did not give an explicit assurance to them that there would be a free vote, that was the clear impression he left with them. Certainly, there was no indication from him that there would not be one, or that he would seek to block it.

On 7 July, Abbott met in his office with Malcolm Turnbull to discuss ways of dealing with the issue, including allowing a free vote, which appeared to be the way Abbott was leaning at the time. They also discussed a plebiscite, and if one were held, what the best timing for it would be. Turnbull's view was that it would chew up a lot of oxygen; the government would spend four weeks talking about it when it could ill afford to look preoccupied with an issue that, important as it was, was not really core business. Turnbull left, assuming the issue would go to cabinet, where ministers could discuss it, and where they would also get essential input from Brian Loughnane and Mark Textor on when — either before the election, simultaneously with the election, or after — as well as how to do it.

Parliament resumed on 10 August. Entsch met again that day with the prime minister. He wanted to introduce his private member's bill, and wanted a discussion beforehand in the Liberal Party room on the question of allowing a free vote in the parliament. When he left the meeting, he was certain he had an agreement from the prime minister on a free vote. He says he told Abbott that if he wanted to wait another week for the discussion in the party room, that would be fine by him.

Entsch later related that he told the prime minister that day: 'Tony, I am not asking you to change your point of view, but you have to get away from these negative stereotypes. Everybody is expecting you to be tricky.' He advised him, in effect, to surprise everyone and allow the free vote. People would reassess him. If he blocked it, he would be reinforcing all the negative opinions of him.

'He said: "I know where you are coming from, Entschy. I have to take it to the leadership group. I will get back to you later today,"' Entsch later told me.

The Liberal Party meeting was set for 9.00 am the next day, Tuesday. At 8.07 am, Entsch received a text from the prime minister. Abbott wrote: 'Warren, I said I'd get back to you re SSM. As you know, I'd prefer it never came up, but, if it must, I suppose today's party room would be as good as any! Cheers Tony.'

Entsch responded immediately: 'Thanks mate, I really appreciate your co-operation. Best.'

Christopher Pyne—a member of the leadership group that Abbott had told Entsch he needed to consult—later told people that as he walked into the party-room meeting with Abbott that morning, he asked Abbott if he thought same-sex marriage was going to come up. Abbott's reply—'Who would know?'—was disingenuous, to say the least. It provided even more context to Pyne's subsequent remarks.

An hour after receiving Abbott's text, Entsch stood up in the party room and raised the issue of same-sex marriage. What Entsch didn't know was that even if he had not raised it then, conservative MPs who had been caucusing separately were going to bring it on that day. Abbott was fully aware of this because of his regular discussions with those on the right.

Victorian MP Michael Sukkar and ACT senator Zed Seselja had

been working on the issue for months. They had assembled a group of about twelve, which became highly active after the successful plebiscite in Ireland. They kept in regular contact with Abbott, particularly after the Irish vote. They were troubled when he said the issue had to be owned by the whole parliament. They wanted to be clear where he stood, to make sure he had not weakened on the policy. In their conversations with him subsequently, he confirmed to them that his position had not changed.

Sukkar and Seselja had set about drawing up lists of MPs, showing who stood where. It was divided into those who opposed same-sex marriage and opposed a free vote; those who favoured a free vote and opposed same-sex marriage; those who supported same-sex marriage as well as a free vote; and those undecided. That list would come in handy a month later, in another context.

The conservatives were split on what they thought would happen. Some thought that if a free vote were allowed, the bill would pass the parliament with a handful of votes; others, that it would be denied, but only by a tight margin of two or three votes, which would do nothing to resolve the issue in the medium term. They believed that, with the right tactics, they could kill it off in the party room. Sukkar, in fact, thought a plebiscite would be the best way to go, and had told Abbott this. Seselja had also previously canvassed a referendum or plebiscite.

When Entsch raised the issue in the Liberal Party meeting, Abbott said he believed the Nationals should be included in the discussion. This went against what Entsch had wanted, and what he believed to have been agreed with Abbott.

Pyne, who had been in the frontline of every debate with the prime minister, including defending Bronwyn Bishop, exploded. He said the prime minister was traducing the great traditions of the Liberal Party, and accused his leader of branch-stacking by calling in the Nationals. The Nationals had already discussed the issue separately, he argued, but the Liberal Party had been denied a similar right. They had not been given any chance at all to discuss it separately.

Pyne's objections were ignored. After the Nationals came into the party room, Pyne continued his outspokenness, saying they should not be there. He let colleagues know he was disappointed that the issue had not been discussed in advance by the leadership group or even by cabinet, as it should have been.

Seselja was fully prepared. He had taken a folder into the meeting with him, and after Pyne's tirade he flicked through it to find the quote from Abbott before the election, in which he said the matter would be resolved by a meeting of the joint party room. He texted it around his group, and before the meeting ended, Tasmanian MP Brett Whitely stood up to read out Abbott's quote, which vindicated his calling-in of the Nationals.

The prime minister then deferred debate for another time, citing pressure of other business. This sent the conservatives wild. Seselja rang Abbott's office, asking *What the fuck is going on?* Others got in touch with Abbott directly. They wanted it dealt with then and there. They pressed him to bring it on. The day before, they had elected a new Speaker, and that day the government had actually announced a good policy position, achieved through proper cabinet processes, on emissions-reductions targets of cuts between 26 and 28 per cent by 2030 on 2005 levels. It disappeared into the ether. If only the same principles had been applied to the same-sex debate.

The marathon Coalition party-room debate over same-sex marriage not only overwhelmed discussion on the renewable-energy target, but it also swamped news of the passage of legislation to set up the $20 billion medical-research future fund, a brilliant initiative unfairly derided because it had been tied to the Medicare co-payment in the 2014 budget. Joe Hockey announced it, but the finance minister, Mathias Cormann — not for nothing known as the Belgian Bulldozer — made it happen, with the help of the Greens Leader, Dr Richard di Natale. It passed without comment or fanfare.

Even though the issue of same-sex marriage had been on the radar for months, and even though he had agreed that it be brought on in August, there did not seem to be a clear strategy from Abbott on how to deal with it. The pressure from the conservatives once again spurred him on.

The next thing that Entsch and almost everybody else knew was that a special joint party meeting had been called to deal with the matter later that afternoon. The prime minister had held urgent conversations with the government leader in the Senate, Eric Abetz, who was one of the most strident opponents of same-sex marriage, as well as with other senior conservatives. Abetz later boasted to colleagues that he had convinced the prime minister to bring it on that day.

The special party meeting forced the cancellation — or, rather, circumvented — a scheduled Liberal leadership group meeting that afternoon, which would have included the prime minister, Eric Abetz, Christopher Pyne, Julie Bishop, and George Brandis, where the issue would have been raised.

During the subsequent marathon joint party meeting, Bishop and others complained about having been ambushed. Entsch was gobsmacked. He went over and showed her the text from the prime minister telling him that today was as good as any to bring on the discussion. Pyne was also shown it. He felt as if he had been deceived. Entsch was staggered that the PM had not discussed the subject with the leadership group, although clearly he had discussed it with some and not others.

Months later, Entsch was still fuming. 'He (Abbott) was deceitful,' Entsch told me. 'Once they saw the text, they knew it wasn't me that was doing the ambush. All he needed to do was just be honest with me.

'I was working very hard to support him. If he had asked me to put it off for a week, I would have been happy to do that,' Entsch said. 'Clearly, by his actions he had no respect for what I was doing, or for me. I was not going to be taken for a fool. I had been treated with no respect, treated like a bloody fool.

'I was prepared to give him 100 per cent respect. Respect begets respect.'

Despite their earlier differences, Entsch says he voted against the spill motion in February. At the end of 2014, he had gone so far as to lodge a formal complaint against Abbott when he accused his colleagues of sexist bias against his chief of staff.

Nevertheless, he reckons he stuck by Abbott in February because there was no challenger, plus he believed that Abbott at least deserved a chance to set things straight. 'I spoke to him the day before the vote. He said to me if he survived, he realised that he would have to dramatically change the way he was doing things. I said to him that if he changed, I would support him 100 per cent, and I gave him the opportunity to change. My mantra was this is not about changing the leader, it's about changing the leadership.'

If there was any possibility at all that Entsch would ever back Abbott again, it was lost the day of the same-sex marriage debate. 'It just convinced me he did not have the capacity to make the changes,' he said.

Although MPs gave credit to Abbott later for allowing the debate to run in the party room, the way he ran it rankled. Ministers and parliamentary secretaries were not given the call to speak until last. Most of them supported a free vote. It was not until they spoke that some of the newbies realised that a tradition going back to Menzies had been violated. While, traditionally, frontbenchers do not speak in party meetings, Sukkar and Seselja were intent on ensuring that backbenchers spoke first, thereby setting the mood. Bishop had been acting as spotter, telling Abbott who wanted to speak. He noted them, and then he decided the order of speakers. By the time Teresa Gambaro spoke, she was only the third one in favour of a free vote. There had already been sixteen speakers against. That also was no accident. Abbott knew who to call. By the time the frontbenchers spoke, it was too late to change or persuade any waverers.

The way the debate was framed in the party room—by asking whether MPs wanted to stick by the existing position that marriage was between a man and a woman, rather than whether there should be a free vote—influenced thinking as well.

The marathon joint meeting ended with forty-six Liberals voting against a free vote, and thirty-three in favour. The proportions probably would have been similar without the Nationals, or even if Abbott had gone through the proper processes. The prime minister might have spared himself a lot of heartache, and avoided the charges that he was not a true Liberal leader.

Maybe he also would have been spared the loss of Brandis and Pyne as supporters, although there was an air of inevitability about their departure. Pyne was already assumed by colleagues to have shifted; however, his comments in the party meetings that day sent an unmistakeable signal that he had made a complete break with the prime minister. MPs such as Seselja and Sukkar, who suspected that Pyne had crossed months before, got the message loud and clear. They thought, however, that Abbott was taken aback by Pyne's vehemence.

204 THE ROAD TO RUIN

Pyne's electoral survival was under threat. The wily independent senator Nick Xenophon had announced he was forming his own party to run in lower-house seats in South Australia. Xenophon's high standing, and Abbott's low standing, especially after he had reneged on a promise to build new submarines in the state, meant that South Australian Liberals faced annihilation at the federal election.

Pyne was unrepentant about what he did that day, but was still smarting later when he told friends that the prime minister and his office were in La La Land, thinking that everything was going really well. They thought they had Shorten's measure and that they would destroy him in an election. Pyne thought otherwise. He was convinced by then that he would lose his seat and that the government would get smashed.

Pyne had also told colleagues he felt he was in a 'constant state of warfare' with the prime minister over the mismanagement of issues. Pyne always believed that Abbott and his office had made two major foundational errors. They had treated Julie Bishop very badly, and they were completely paranoid about Turnbull. It infected their thinking as well as their actions, to the detriment of the government and to Abbott's eventual cost. Pyne was subsequently completely dismissive of suggestions that either of them had undermined Abbott, or that Bishop had in any way behaved inappropriately.

After the meeting ended, the prime minister left it unclear at a late-night press conference whether the same-sex issue would be left for voters to resolve at either a plebiscite or a referendum. Scott Morrison went in hard, publicly, for a referendum. Other conservatives sensed that Morrison was positioning as the alternative to Abbott, which they didn't mind at this stage.

'It was a little too cute,' one of them said later of Morrison's push for a referendum. Morrison, who had also had many discussions with Abbott on the subject, including about the possibility of a plebiscite, was anxious to lay down markers. His real intent was a compulsory-vote plebiscite with a binding outcome. Morrison was also taken aback by the prime minister's tactics, echoing the view of proponents of same-sex marriage that the outcome would have been the same with a more structured, respectful process that did not seek to 'smite' opponents.

Brandis, who had stuck by Abbott in February, because he wanted him to recover, and because he thought the reaction to Prince Philip's knighthood was overblown, was having none of that. He had spoken strongly in favour of a conscience vote at the joint party meeting.

When it was over, he was not unhappy with the idea of a plebiscite, because it would give people a say. However, he wanted the issue dealt with fairly.

He quite deliberately went on Sky to contradict Morrison, saying that a plebiscite was the right way to test public opinion on vexed or important social issues, rather than a referendum — which, he argued, was completely unnecessary.

He said the issue had been resolved by the High Court in December 2013 in a case against the ACT government. 'That is an unambiguous, a unanimous and a recent statement by the High Court that the marriage power as currently written is ample to provide the parliament with the power to legislate for same-sex marriage, should it choose to do so. No constitutional referendum is necessary in this case,' Brandis said.

It was not only the failure to consult that some MPs resented. It was the sneakiness of the tactics that infuriated them.

'At the end of that process, there certainly was a sense of betrayal,' one minister said. 'Not because I thought he was going to allow a free vote; I never thought it would be easy. I did not expect him to manipulate the party-room outcome in the manner in which he did.'

Liberals around the country were infuriated by Abbott's tactics. Victorian opposition leader Matthew Guy accused Abbott and his supporters of 'poisoning the well of goodwill for all other elected officials in the country'.

Guy told reporters the next day: 'I've got to say, I think Australians are utterly sick of federal politics, and I'm not surprised why.

'People who feel they should be bound on matters of conscience by a party vote … need to go back and look at the rationale in which our party was founded by Robert Menzies. It wasn't one of binding votes; it was one of conscience. We should be proud of that, and members should be able to exercise that—full stop.'

Months later, it still made Guy angry. 'You can't rig a vote,' he told me, contrasting Abbott's tactics with Howard's conduct of the republic referendum.

There had been a bit of grumbling about Turnbull's performance during the party meeting. Some MPs, even those who liked him, thought he was too strident, but that angst soon dissipated.

It was the opposite with Abbott. He ended up winning the battle, but it cost him the war.

When Turnbull later sounded out Entsch, the Queenslander was as direct with him as he had been with Abbott. He told him that he did not want a job, but he told Turnbull that he, too, needed to change 'dramatically'.

'I told him as an opposition leader, he was a bloody disaster,' Entsch said. 'Malcolm said, "That's a bit harsh."

'But you know, back then it was all about Malcolm. He said, "You are right. You have to learn from your mistakes." I told him we had to revert to a Westminster system, letting ministers do their jobs, but not to speak outside their portfolios.'

Turnbull was not only listening, he was acting.

The first of several critical gatherings between Turnbull and core members of the group that was to meticulously plan the leadership coup was held at Turnbull's Kingston apartment on Thursday 13 August, two nights after the marathon meeting on same-sex marriage, and three days after the election of the new Speaker.

Mitch Fifield and Scott Ryan were invited to join Turnbull, James McGrath, and Simon Birmingham for supper. McGrath and Birmingham were already fully signed up, but the induction of two members of the right was a boost for Turnbull.

Casual discussions or encounters turned deadly serious that night. The common view was that Abbott's position was untenable. They discussed the impact of Tuesday's debate on the party, and they reviewed the effect the Bronwyn Bishop saga and the election of Tony Smith as speaker had had on the mood of their colleagues.

Smith, who had been in contact with almost every single Liberal member of the House of Representatives in his campaign for the Speakership, was invited over to the apartment for a late-night drink that same evening. Smith had also resigned from the Turnbull frontbench in 2009 when his leadership was in meltdown, and subsequently voted for Abbott, but there had been a rapprochement between him and Turnbull.

Smith did not take part in any of the planning, but he could provide valuable intelligence on what the colleagues were thinking as a result of his extensive discussions.

There was also discussion that night about the upcoming Canning by-election, and what effect that would have on the government and Abbott's standing.

Turnbull was hot to trot. Separately, he told Ian Macfarlane he wanted to pull it on then. Macfarlane counselled him to wait—it was too soon, and he did not think the numbers were there. Other supporters of Turnbull thought the debate had damaged him, that it had brought back memories of the old Malcolm. They, too, thought the time was not right.

Parliament sat for another week after the same-sex debate, then rose for two weeks. It gave MPs the opportunity to get feedback from their constituents.

Craig Laundy had taken a year off to campaign for the seat of Reid in 2013, during which he knocked on more than 40,000 doors. A lot of people told him in the vilest language possible that they wanted Gillard gone.

At the end, it was similar with Abbott. Whether it was on the street or in the pub, the message was the same everywhere. Abbott had to go. They kept telling Laundy that he had to do something, and that something, eventually, was to get rid of Abbott and replace him with Turnbull.

Laundy did not live in fear of losing his seat. He was independently wealthy, and he could go back to his pubs. But he didn't want to lose. He wanted to stay and do good things.

His friends, like Sukkar and Seselja, stuck with Abbott. While he respected their views, and respected them, Laundy could see only one way out.

CHAPTER EIGHT

ABBA (Anyone But Bloody Abbott)

If anything, the mood amongst many Liberals outside parliament in late August and early September was worse than the mood inside parliament. There had been a glimmer of hope for Abbott with Hockey's second budget, which had stabilised the government. The backbench had made its move in February. This time, there had to be a challenge from one of the big three—Malcolm Turnbull, Julie Bishop, or Scott Morrison. Turnbull was the only one actively taking soundings to see if there had been a shift in mood. It was circular.

The citizenship debate was being framed to make Turnbull look like a softie on national-security issues. He wasn't. Cabinet colleagues cited as proof his arguments in cabinet for Australia to take more Christian refugees from the Middle East, an argument he had been making for more than a year because he believed that, in any final solution to the Syrian civil war, the ones most likely to be unable to return would be the Christians. In Abbott's final week as prime minister, when he announced that Australia would take 12,000, predominantly Christian, Syrian refugees—given their persecution, an eminently defensible decision—one cabinet minister described it as a vindication of Turnbull's position.

To outsiders, it looked as if Liberal MPs were all sitting on the train waiting for it to crash. Friends were telling Turnbull that if Abbott stayed as leader, they would lose the election. Turnbull had already put in a lot of work to repair relationships with his colleagues, but after the debate on same-sex marriage, he picked up the pace. Time was running out.

Obviously, not everyone was privy to the planning that was going on inside. Outside, serving and former members of parliament, long-time Liberal supporters, business leaders, and donors were having panic attacks.

They did not know how well advanced Turnbull's plans were; many of them were ignorant of any plans at all. They were worried that soon it really would be too late for any change. When they were speaking frankly, some of them were dubious that Turnbull had either the ticker or the wherewithal to do it.

The weekend before the coup, word reached a couple in the Group of Eight that at least one Liberal leader was preparing to go public, urging Abbott to resign. They also heard that one party official, fearful of a wipe-out in his state (take your pick which one) was also getting ready to go public. 'There was a sense of potential madness coming through, with suggestions people were trying to stir up news stories,' one recalled. They didn't want that kind of messiness or bloodiness to hijack or derail their careful planning, but they also could not afford to alert anyone to what they were doing.

Separately, former MPs also began formulating their own plans. One option was for a delegation to appeal to the former prime minister John Howard to prevail on his former protégé to stand down. This was never going to happen.

First, Howard would never intervene in such a direct manner on such a sensitive issue, even though his concerns about the way his political love child was going about his business were mounting. Howard had already twice counselled Abbott — once before the spill, and then again after, on the operations of his office and on the friction that it was creating in the government. He had urged him to make changes to his office, and had told him that Hockey was not working as treasurer. Howard had told friends he believed Abbott had delegated too much of his authority as prime minister to his chief of staff. Abbott ignored Howard's advice on that, as he did everybody else's.

Second, how could Howard tell Abbott to do something he would not countenance himself — that is, step aside to allow a rival to have a go? Howard had counselled Turnbull to stay in parliament after he lost the leadership in 2009. So had his former chief of staff, Arthur Sinodinos. Why? Partly because, in politics, you just never know what might happen.

Another option was to get David Gillespie, now a serving National Party MP for the seat of Lyne, who had been best man at Abbott's wedding, to speak to Margie. They hoped Margie would then convince Abbott, for his own sake and for the sake of his family, to quit. Friends were saying she was beside herself.

A third option was for them to begin circulating a petition to like-minded folk, asking him to step down. That sounded like the most workable idea. It was actively being considered barely a week out from the coup, and, if it had eventuated, would have been devastating. It was the sort of thing, depending on which names were attached to it, that had the potential to trigger action. If Turnbull had not moved, they would have. They were not going to sit back and watch Bill Shorten become prime minister.

There was a lot of anger about Abbott's failure. Howard's former department head, Max Moore-Wilton, was watching in disbelief from Sydney. 'It's going pear-shaped,' he told business mates.

Another, who had known Abbott for twenty-five years, was appalled at his behaviour, trying to understand what had happened to his old friend, why he had sat back and allowed his colleagues, his staff, and his friends to be so badly treated — to have it all, and then to throw it all away.

'This is running the country,' he said when it was over. 'He had to make decisions about life and death, and peoples' futures. He couldn't run his own friggin' personal life and his office. It was diabolical. All in the space of twelve months, not two years.'

There were romantic notions that Peter Costello might be persuaded to return to politics. Back in the day, his colleagues — people like Nick Minchin and Chris Ellison — had tried to talk him out of going, particularly when it seemed inevitable that Brendan Nelson's leadership could not be sustained.

There was no staying for Costello, nor was there ever the prospect of a comeback by him, so when Abbott became leader by accident, it was a matter of everyone hanging in behind him, for better or for worse.

The doubts about Abbott were around from the early days of his leadership. Despite his near-victory in 2010, and his resounding win in 2013, he was not a beloved leader. He had a committed following in the party's conservative wing, although more mainstream liberals suspected, especially when they cranked up email campaigns to MPs offices, that they were religious-right remnants of the DLP/National Civic Council. Ultra-conservative commentators also remained true to him, which was curious, given his failure to deliver on issues dear to them, such as the repeal of section 18C of the Racial Discrimination Act, which makes it unlawful for someone to act in a way likely to 'offend, insult, humiliate or intimidate' people because of their race or ethnicity. Abbott's argument to the conservatives — and he put this explicitly to people such as Rod Kemp after he reneged on his pledge to repeal 18C—was that it was either him or Malcolm Turnbull. Turnbull was being held up as the bogeyman—which, as far as many conservatives are concerned, he is.

But Abbott's rougher style, combined with his lack of economic-policy depth, had not built up the respect in the broader church of the party or business community that Howard had commanded.

From the time he assumed the leadership in December 2009 until he left it, his messages—or slogans—remained largely the same. In opposition, his daily mantra was that he was going to scrap the carbon tax, scrap the mining tax, and stop the boats. Then, in government, when asked to list his achievements as prime minister, it was that he had scrapped the carbon tax, scrapped the mining tax, and stopped the boats. This was all well and good, but people needed to hear something new.

Not only was he not saying anything new, he was not wearing anything new. The blue tie remained. A few years ago, when I questioned one of his advisers about the reason for it, he said to me: 'Well, at least they're not talking about his budgie-smugglers any more.' Seriously. I would have thought the best way to stop people talking about his red bikini bottoms was to stop wearing them in public—but, hey, what do I know?

Senior Liberals, sick of hearing the same thing day in, day out, who had fought countless campaigns, and who paid close attention all the time to what was being said, could not work out the government's agenda. They had no idea what the government's story was on the economy, the environment, childcare, regional Australia, health, the deficit, debt, higher education, defence contracts, unemployment, or business and consumer confidence.

They would try to think of which words or what pictures they would want to see on the party bunting around polling stations on election day, and work their way back from there. In mid-2015, all they could see was a huge sheet of blank paper with a little sign in the corner saying *Don't risk it (with Bill)*.

Business confidence had plummeted. Business leaders were complaining to insiders that they had better access to and got a better hearing from the Gillard government.

Warwick Smith, a former Howard government minister, who had built a successful career outside politics, was worried early on about how the government was travelling. Around the middle of 2014, Abbott ministers were already so concerned about the operations of Abbott's office that one of them spoke to Smith, who had lost his lower-house Tasmanian seat in the 1998 GST election. As they discussed likely solutions, Smith offered to set aside his business interests and begin work in the prime minister's office. He wanted to help. His offer was never taken up.

Robert Webster, who as a National Party MP held senior ministerial portfolios in the Fahey government in New South Wales, had lived until recently in Abbott's electorate. Webster joined the Liberal Party in 1996. He served as the party's state treasurer for a few years.

Webster had known Abbott for more than twenty years. He recalled Abbott visiting him in the early 1990s, while Webster was still a New South Wales government minister, seeking guidance on a political career. Webster says Abbott had told him he wanted to run for the National Party in a New South Wales seat. Webster had told him it wouldn't work, explaining the difficulties of non-locals running for country seats.

After all those years, Webster was well plugged in to New South Wales politics, and he was becoming increasingly worried by the level of disdain for Abbott being expressed in his electorate—a disdain that Webster also noticed among professional women at

Korn Ferry International, the world's largest executive-search firm, where he is a director.

Not long before Abbott's demise, Webster passed on a message to the party hierarchy from one of its best donors. This donor had said that much as he liked Abbott, he believed he should vacate the prime ministership because he could not win the election. 'It wasn't personal, although I guess in a way it was personal, because the person wasn't performing. People felt he had to go. I never felt that about a Liberal leader since Billy McMahon. He was terribly divisive. And embarrassing,' Webster told me with unsparing frankness.

The McMahon analogy was taking firm hold amongst former Coalition MPs. While they would only say it privately, Webster was happy to put it on the record.

Webster went on: 'You only have to look at the way David Cameron operates, or the way Mike Baird operates. Tony didn't change his style from combat to collaboration. There was no ecumenical approach, which you need in government.

'There are obviously people who are deeply conservative, who are deeply suspicious of Malcolm Turnbull. They are very worried about Malcolm — they think he's a commie. The truth is, there is not much ideology left in politics; it's all about that middle ground.'

That middle ground had grown battle weary, exhausted by the prime minister's aggressive or inappropriate language.

'The people (in his electorate) who you would have expected to be his strongest supporters — people 60-plus, Catholic, where half the guys went to Riverview — I couldn't find one of them who had a good word to say about him. They couldn't understand where he was coming from,' Webster said.

Peter Charlton, a publisher, businessman, and Liberal

fundraiser, saw Abbott at a dinner in Sydney before Christmas 2013. He asked Abbott if he would participate in an event he was planning, probably around mid-March 2014. Abbott said he would. Charlton duly sent out a flyer to a few people on 24 January 2014, foreshadowing Abbott's appearance on 14 March.

Next thing he knew, a few days later, Credlin had fired off an angry email:

From: 'Credlin, Peta' <Peta.Credlin@pm.gov.au>
To: 'Charlton Info' <info@charlton.com.au>
Cc: 'Peter Charlton' <peter@charlton.com.au>, 'Iafrate, Gemma' <Gemma.Iafrate@pm.gov.au>
Subject: FW: Announcing The 2014 A Group Council—What it Does for you—Presented by The A Group Council [SEC=UNCLASSIFIED]

Dear Charlton Group / A Group Council

Please take the Prime Minister's name and image off this circular as the Prime Minister has not agreed to attend this event. It has been sent to our office by the media asking if we are attending but we have made it clear that this reference was made without any agreement from this office.

I expect the change to be immediate and any reference to the Prime Minister to be removed.

I am very disappointed that this is the second time that the Charlton Group has used the name of the PM to garner support for an event where he has previously declined the invitation.

We will not accept it happening again.

As a result, the Prime Minister has asked me to make it very clear that he will not accept any invitation to attend any events

under the auspices of the Charlton Group or the A Group
Council now or in the future.

Regards
Peta Credlin | chief of staff
OFFICE OF THE PRIME MINISTER

Charlton was particularly incensed by the final paragraph. He
had helped raise hundreds of thousands of dollars for the Liberal
Party. He was friends with everyone who mattered in the Liberal
Party, from John Howard down, and had considered himself a
friend of Abbott's. He never lifted a finger again to help Abbott.

When it became obvious after February that Abbott's leadership
would not endure, and even before that, with the inevitable
parlour games that go on about what might happen if he fell off
his bike and under a bus, there was the inevitable weighing-up
of alternatives. In the early days of the government, Joe Hockey
looked good, thanks to a strong performance in parliament. His
biographer, Madonna King, did two face-to-face interviews with
Peta Credlin, who told her that after Abbott, Hockey was 'first cab
off the rank'. Publication of Credlin's comments in July drew howls
from MPs that an unelected staffer had seen fit to insert herself into
leadership matters. The howls were published in *The Australian* by
Peter van Onselen, which triggered another outburst from Abbott
to Chris Mitchell, filled with expletives, about her treatment at the
hands of van Onselen and myself, days after Abbott had asked me
to stop criticising her.

Hockey soon fell to the bottom of the leadership pile, thanks to
the first budget and his own lack of empathy with poor folk.

Then it was like roulette. The ball would land on one number,
then on another. Malcolm Turnbull, Julie Bishop, and Scott

Morrison were the three everyone talked about.

Turnbull was the most popular electorally, but there were—still are—bad memories of him from the first time around. If he respected you even after a conflict, there would be a make-up. If he thought you were a fool, you were insufferable. So was he.

Until the cabinet citizenship dust-up, Turnbull had not been involved in any overtly disloyal activity—just a few pricks here and there. But Turnbull's intelligent exposition of the rights and wrongs of the issue, after the various leaks to the media, provided a welcome contrast to Abbott's sloganeering on national security.

Citing the problems caused by the leaking of the metadata-retention decision, which had been taken without reference to Turnbull, Abbott's supporters inside cabinet thought that Abbott and Credlin should have been smarter about the way they treated him.

'If Malcolm Turnbull had been brought in, if he [Abbott] had come to an accommodation with him, he would have been better able to manage the relationship in government,' one cabinet minister said.

'Malcolm wanted to be closer to the centre of government, and Abbott and Credlin didn't want him to be anywhere near the centre of the government. If Abbott had brought him into the leadership group, and worked very hard to get him on the team, if he had felt he wasn't on the periphery, I don't think he would have done the same as what he has.'

When MH17 was downed by Russian-backed rebels in the Ukraine on 17 July 2014, it gave Abbott an opportunity to shine, which he did, but it also allowed Bishop to show her mettle. Turnbull had yet to be rehabilitated. Morrison was marked as someone to watch.

Bishop shone in New York at the United Nations, held firm

in the Ukraine, stayed stoic in the Netherlands. After Abbott mis-stepped by threatening to shirtfront Vladimir Putin, she buttonholed the Russian president at the sidelines of a summit in Milan. It took some of the heat out of the expected meeting between Putin and Abbott at the G20 summit in Queensland.

When she wasn't overseas, she was in electorates with her colleagues. They liked her, because she worked hard and she wasn't precious. Warren Entsch tells a wonderful story about his flirty encounters with the foreign minister as he walked to Parliament House along Canberra's premier street, Mugga Way. Entsch reckoned that if he had his headphones on and didn't hear her as she was running past, she would give him a whack on the bum and keep going. He reckoned it was a real heart-starter early in the morning.

He also reckoned that if he didn't have his headphones on, he could hear her coming, and would turn around as she approached around the Carmelite nunnery, and return the favour by trying to grope her backside. There are those who say that Entsch has taken poetic licence with this story. Bishop goes with it.

Liberal MPs told me in September 2014 that if Abbott were to disappear, for whatever reason, at that time, Bishop probably would be elected leader. If Abbott was to disappear a year on from that, Liberals thought Morrison would be in strong contention. Publication of that column, effectively describing Bishop as an imminent threat, didn't help Bishop's relations with the prime minister's office. Paranoia levels soared about Bishop.

Turnbull had not seriously begun his rehab then; however, there was no doubt that by the time of the spill in February, Turnbull had the largest bloc of votes, even if he did not have a majority. His supporters described him as 'the most fully formed' of the alternatives. Bishop had at one point in February thought seriously about running, and then convinced herself not to. She was 'living the dream', as she kept saying to people, in the foreign affairs portfolio.

Morrison's performance in the immigration portfolio had been impressive. He wouldn't cop any nonsense from the media, he was tough, and he was effective. Under Labor, more than 800 asylum-seeker boats, carrying more than 50,000 people, attempted to make the journey from Indonesia to Australia. No one is sure how many people died while trying to get to Christmas Island—the known tally was more than 1,000. In 2014, one boat made it, with a significant saving to the budget. It was a staggering achievement.

When Abbott shifted Morrison to Social Services, after it seemed he might be installed in a new homeland-security-type portfolio, Morrison wasn't sure whether he was being punished or rewarded. He worked well with Abbott, but they could not be described as friends. However, the switch did give Morrison a toehold in the economic sphere. He was on the cabinet's expenditure review committee, and the switch gave him a chance to show a softer side. He had bromances with the male crossbenchers, and he won support from the Australian Council of Social Services for welfare changes.

Morrison's success was attributable to hard work, focus, and preparation, which backed his finely honed political instincts. His approach was the same, whether it was applied to turning back boats or cooking a Sri Lankan fish curry for Annabel Crabb's *Kitchen Cabinet* TV program. He practised the dish on his family first. When his wife, Jenny, pronounced it edible, it was on the menu.

As Hockey deflated, Morrison soared. Turnbull had been willing to make Morrison treasurer back in February, and Morrison was willing to serve. The option was there for Abbott to make the switch, but he wouldn't do it. Not till his final hours, that is—by which time it was way too late.

Back then, Morrison was the right's preferred candidate if Abbott fell over. However, there was no way he was ready to step up to the prime ministership in 2015—he needed a lot more time as a senior minister. People had watched what happened when Julia Gillard assumed the top job before she was ready. It was one reason why she crashed and burned.

It was obvious in August 2015, despite the view that he might have damaged himself in the same-sex marriage debate by being too strident, that Turnbull was the only viable option to replace Abbott.

CHAPTER NINE

G8 Plus One

After the marathon party meeting on same-sex marriage, and with the Canning by-election only weeks away, the immigration minister, Peter Dutton, decided to embark on what, for him, was a very delicate mission. He spoke first to his good friend Joe Hockey. He told Hockey that he had to get out of the Treasury portfolio. It wasn't working well for him, and it wasn't working well for the government. Hockey, not surprisingly, did not agree.

Undeterred, Dutton then went to see the prime minister. He told Abbott that he had to remove Hockey from Treasury. Credlin sat in on that meeting. Dutton had already previously, cautiously, broached the subject of Credlin with the prime minister, but hadn't pressed him hard on it because he had seen how defensive or antagonistic he became with others who raised it, so he saw little point in pursuing it. Like others, he believed that Abbott's dependence on her had become deeply psychological; like others, he had witnessed Abbott held in thrall by other strong women such as Jane Halton and Claire Kimball, and, also like many of his colleagues, he believed the prime minister's office was dysfunctional.

But on the matter of Hockey and the Treasury portfolio, Dutton put his case forcefully. He had no particular knowledge of a challenge; however, he could see it coming around the time of Canning, particularly if it was a bad result.

He told Abbott and Credlin that the government needed a credible economic narrative. He thought Hockey was too far damaged in that portfolio to recover, and considered that his best chance to rebuild his career was to do it elsewhere, perhaps in the communications portfolio.

Dutton's solution: Abbott should appoint Malcolm Turnbull as treasurer. Abbott hadn't wanted to hear this from Howard in the past, nor was he prepared to countenance it in August 2015 when Dutton proposed it.

Abbott was prepared to consider appointing Scott Morrison, but would not even think about appointing Turnbull. Dutton believed that Morrison did not have enough economic experience, whereas he believed Turnbull was ready-made for the job.

Dutton's solution was motivated by two factors. Well, three, actually. The first was that he believed it would give the government an immediate lift in economic credibility. The second was that it would also stymie any challenge. Turnbull would not have been able to refuse the offer; if he had, the story would no doubt have leaked, and Turnbull's standing in the party as well as the community would have taken a hit. He would have looked churlish, or cast as a wrecker. The third was that Dutton knew the Abbott government was in deep, deep trouble.

Abbott and Credlin were intransigent. Even when it was obvious that their own survival depended on them taking drastic action, even when their friends were warning them that their self-interest dictated they should promote Turnbull in order to defuse him, they refused. Dutton left, in an extremely pessimistic frame of mind.

Another cabinet colleague summed up Abbott's thinking this way: 'In his mind—and I am not saying he was right—he was under a lot of pressure to throw Joe and Peta under a bus, but he thought, after that, they would come after him anyway. A vote of no confidence in Joe was a vote of no confidence in him.'

The most surprising aspect of the challenge to Abbott when it came a few weeks after Dutton's intervention, on 14 September, was not that it happened, but that it happened in the week before the Canning by-election, set for 19 September. In fact, if Abbott had not flown to Port Moresby for the Pacific Islands Forum leaders meeting on Wednesday 9 September, it would have happened that day. Or the next. The numbers were there—somewhere around the mid-50s, they reckoned. The group was ready to launch its challenge that week, depending on what happened with Julie Bishop. She was critical, but she was uncommitted. There was a reason she had survived as deputy when a procession of leaders failed. She had an acute sense of the separation of powers between her own role and that of the leader. Equally importantly, she was no one's patsy.

Her survival was not dependent on Abbott's. Far from it. Nor had she had to rely on Malcolm Turnbull when he was elected leader the first time, or on Brendan Nelson before him, to be elected deputy. She hadn't been on their tickets, just as she wasn't on Abbott's, either, in 2009 or February 2015. Looked at clinically, Abbott needed her more than she needed him, which made the treatment of her by him and his office a protracted exercise in self-harm. It was both damaging and short-sighted, then they resorted to bitching about her when it was all over, when it was obvious to everyone that she couldn't save him even if she had wanted to.

Such was Bishop's standing inside the party that both sides needed her tacit endorsement, at the very least; yet only one courted her, while the other treated her with contempt.

The spill in February was a case of spontaneous combustion.

In September, the planning against the prime minister was held tightly within the G8—James McGrath, Simon Birmingham, Peter Hendy, Mitch Fifield, Scott Ryan, Arthur Sinodinos, Wyatt Roy, and Mal Brough—with Malcolm Turnbull in control. It was precise, it was discreet, it was swift, and it had every possible contingency covered.

There were multiple meetings, multiple phone calls, multiple phone hook-ups. Directing it all was Turnbull, sometimes with all members of the group, occasionally only with some. They did not operate in silos, nor was he playing one off against the other, because the G8 would then tell each other what was happening, but Turnbull dealt with each of them as needed, and depending on what it was they offered, or what he needed them to do, on any given day. As the saying goes, what that group did not know about politics was not worth knowing.

The core Group of Eight held a number of meetings in the week from Sunday 6 September. It was the day before the resumption of parliament after a two-week break. They still had not succeeded in locking Bishop in, nor in convincing her that they had the numbers and were therefore in a position to challenge.

The substance of the discussions at all those meetings seldom changed. What was Abbott doing, and how would he react if this or that happened? After all, Abbott was odd, he was eccentric, he could do anything. How were the numbers shaping up? Had anyone switched? They went through 101 names every single time, attaching comments to each, in an incredibly time-consuming process. Should they go before the Canning by-election or not, and what, if anything, would Julie Bishop do?

Hendy, who had worked for Bishop for three years from 2010 until he re-won Eden-Monaro for the Liberals at the 2013 election, talked numerous times to her in the lead-up to the challenge. So did Turnbull—he met and spoke with her countless times. Hendy was a vital conduit. Although he had been Brendan Nelson's chief of staff when Turnbull toppled him, their relationship was soon repaired. One of the first things Hendy did when he began working for Bishop was to re-establish contact with Turnbull.

When Hendy ran for the bellwether seat of Eden-Monaro in 2013, the New South Wales Liberal campaign team did not think he could win it. Scott Morrison and Joe Hockey were told not to bother visiting the electorate. Abbott did not visit Eden-Monaro during the campaign.

The two who did bother were Bishop and Turnbull. Bishop said she'd been told not to waste her time, but she had a habit of helping out wherever she was asked.

If things had turned out differently in February, if the leadership had been vacated, and if Bishop had run, Hendy would have voted for her. After the spill, she made it clear repeatedly to people that she would not challenge Abbott.

Only a few months before, at the end of the budget sittings, other backbenchers might have been feeling a little more hopeful, a little rosier about the future. Not Hendy. He had known Abbott for twenty-five years, and he had got to know Credlin well, too. He had no confidence in their ability to turn things around. He had also learned a bit about power plays from his old boss Peter Reith, so he visited Turnbull in his office as parliament prepared to rise in June for the winter recess.

Hendy told Turnbull that if the government was still behind in the polls when MPs returned in August, 'People like you, Malcolm, are going to have to make a decision about the leadership.' Malcolm did not say yes then. He told Hendy that he (Hendy) should talk to Bishop and Morrison. Hendy had already spoken to Bishop, and she had told Hendy she was not interested.

Hendy knew Bishop well, so he knew how to approach her, but Bishop had not survived this long by acting without thinking long and hard. His arguments to her in the weeks leading up to the challenge were multi-pronged—essentially harking back to her own words in February, emphasising that one of her duties as deputy was to look out for the wider interests of the party. He also had to try to convince her that they were serious, and that the numbers had shifted decisively to Turnbull. The group was not convinced she was convinced until the very morning of the challenge.

They had a contingency plan if she did not agree to go to the prime minister. That would have involved a petition of backbenchers calling for Abbott to go, with a delegation of MPs visiting the prime minister to tell him. Their spill motion, drafted along similar lines to the one initiated by Luke Simpkins in February, was to be moved by Hendy, but it would open up one position only—the leader's.

In some ways, in view of the result, it is a statement of the bleeding obvious that Abbott's defence in the face of Turnbull's highly skilled operation was incredibly inept. Despite the warnings, Abbott was pathetically ill-prepared. The older members of his Praetorian Guard, more like a platoon out of *Life of Brian* than *Julius Caesar*, lacked vital intelligence about the numbers, leaving younger conservatives who volunteered to help or chose this time to watch from the sidelines, shaking their heads in disbelief.

Abbott and those around him had convinced themselves that Turnbull either didn't have the guts or didn't have the numbers to challenge, and even if he thought he had, he would not dare do anything until after the by-election for the Western Australian seat of Canning, precipitated by the sudden death of the extremely popular local member, Don Randall.

Published polls had consistently shown that the government faced a likely swing of 10 per cent against it in the by-election. This was much larger than the 2 to 3 per cent normally registered in a by-election after the death of a sitting member. Randall had built up his margin to an impressive 11.8 per cent. No one really thought the Liberals would lose the seat; what mattered was the size of the swing.

Later, the former prime minister would claim that internal polling showed there would have been a swing of only 5 to 6 per cent in Canning, so the reason the plotters moved in advance of the vote was because a swing of that limited magnitude would have robbed them of the momentum they needed to launch the challenge after the by-election.

There is an element of truth in this; however, there were other factors in play in the by-election itself, or which stemmed from the timing, that influenced the thinking of the G8.

First, the Liberals had selected a former SAS commando, Andrew Hastie, as their candidate. He proved to be an extremely capable campaigner. There was hardly any campaign material for the Liberals that featured Tony Abbott. Labor's bunting for polling booths was all about Abbott. After the leadership coup, it had to be spliced. When Turnbull ascended, the Liberals didn't have to change a thing.

The Liberals' state director, Ben Morton, one of the party's best campaigners, worked his socks off to keep the campaign strictly local. Abbott visited briefly a few times, with every effort made to ensure that the focus was on local issues.

Western Australia was renowned as a stronghold for the Liberals; however, it had also turned sour. Abbott was as on the nose in the west as he was elsewhere. The day before Hastie's endorsement as the candidate by the party's state conference, on

Saturday 22 August, Abbott had arrived in Perth. Knowing in advance he would visit, the party had tried to organise a private fundraiser. They wanted ten people to pay $20,000 a head for the privilege of meeting privately with Abbott. There were only four takers, two of whom were prepared to pay but not attend, so reluctant were they to be in the same room as Abbott—one because he was so disappointed with Abbott for not delivering the stability and confidence he had promised, and the other equally disappointed that Abbott had broken his promise of no new taxes by introducing the high-income deficit levy.

Organisers decided to halve the price to fill the table. When those who had paid the full amount found out, they were furious. They demanded their money back. Abbott left Perth for Broome immediately after the state conference (without visiting Canning), where he dined that night with media mogul Kerry Stokes. There had been suggestions that the prime minister and his party would stay with Stokes at his house there; however, plans were changed just days out, and they stayed at a nearby hotel. It would not have been a good look if Abbott as well as members of his travelling party had stayed with Stokes.

There was no denying Abbott's unpopularity in the west. Whether that made a difference or not is, for some, debatable. The professional campaigners disagree on the interpretation of the result. According to one, a major factor in the eventual lower-than-expected swing was that everything possible was done to keep the campaign local, to keep the focus off Abbott, and on Hastie and the people of Canning.

All true, according to another key Liberal strategist; however, his argument was that the Canning by-election could have shown MPs that it might have been possible, with the right campaign, and focussing on the right issues, to win a general election with Abbott as leader. According to this campaigner: 'The most unpopular person in Australian politics was Bill Shorten. I was happy to have Tony Abbott visit; I was more than happy to have Bill Shorten visit.'

This is strongly discounted by other professional campaigners. Keeping it local in a by-election with the benefit of an outstanding candidate is both desirable and possible. Doing this in a federal election, when national issues feature daily, is impossible. Trying to play hide-the-leader while focussing on issues that the local mayor or premier would handle would not only be impractical, it would be counterproductive — because that in itself would become a major story.

Labor's national secretary, George Wright, believes Labor was in with a chance pre-Turnbull, although he concedes that getting the final 1 per cent needed to win would have been difficult.

'Nine days out from Canning, our polling had us at 49 per cent,' Wright told me later. 'We hadn't yet started our main television advertising campaign. We were hopeful that we could get an extra point, then get home.

'They spent most of their campaign on print; we were going to fight on TV. I reckon we could have got there. The deeper into a swing, the harder it gets. Ten per cent into a swing, they are pretty hard-core Liberal people. The idea that it was a 4 or 5 per cent swing is just crap.'

As for playing hide-the-leader, Wright knows about that, too.

'I was a humble campaign booth-worker in 2004. We got our little kit for the campaign,' he recalls. 'Our kit had one picture of Mark Latham. All our bunting was Medicare Gold. I arrived at the polling station, and the Liberal bunting had Latham all over it.

'Our bunting for Canning was Abbott's head and our candidate's head, saying reject Abbott, vote Keogh. We had to cut

10 kilometres of bunting in half to get rid of Abbott's head [after Turnbull deposed Abbott].'

Labor had also picked up on what the Liberals also knew. Abbott was unpopular with women. Women, according to one strategist, thought he was 'creepy'. If Labor didn't know this from their own research, they recognised it in the attempts by the Liberals in the 2013 campaign to mitigate it. When Abbott wasn't with Margie, he was with his daughters.

Ultimately, the swing in Canning was 6 per cent. According to some locals, it might have been lower still, although not by that much, if it had not been for the leadership change, but this is highly questionable. Morton maintained that the challenge reminded people of the games politicians played in Canberra.

Morton told Bishop and Turnbull, as he did everyone at the beginning of the campaign, that the combination of Randall's absent personal vote and normal by-election effects could see the swing reach double digits. But the week before, he was confident it would go well, that the strategy was working. 'The last thing we need is crap in Canberra,' he told people. Little did he know, little did anyone know, there would soon be an avalanche of crap in Canberra.

The members of the G8 who coalesced around Turnbull, who meticulously planned the mechanics of the coup as well as sounding out colleagues, were a disparate bunch. A few of them had had serious problems with Turnbull in the past. McGrath, Hendy, Sinodinos, Roy, Birmingham, and Brough signed up early. Mitch Fifield and Scott Ryan joined later. Each was critical to the success of the coup. The induction of Fifield and Ryan was vital both because of their early history with Turnbull, and also because of their standing within the right—at least the sensible part of it. Their involvement sent a message that Turnbull was inclusive and that he could repair relationships.

For slightly different reasons, they had all reached the same conclusion: if Abbott stayed leader, the Coalition would lose the election. Therefore, they all shared the same objective: to remove Abbott, and to do it as quickly and as cleanly as possible. Nothing personal, as Turnbull was to say after it was over—just business.

Fifield was one of the most under-rated ministers in the Abbott government. As the minister charged with delivering the National Disability Insurance Scheme (NDIS), he had hundreds of stakeholders.

Labor was itching for a fight over the scheme, looking for any chink to exploit, hoping the sector would rise up against the government. The reason it never happened was because the sector, by and large, trusted Fifield to deliver on what he and the government had promised. His last act in the portfolio was to sign the agreement setting up the scheme with the premiers of New South Wales and Victoria.

Fifield had a long history in the Liberal Party. In 1990, when he was a young staffer for the then New South Wales transport minister, Bruce Baird, he was dispatched to an inner-Sydney suburb to schmooze a punter who had written on behalf of his neighbours to object to the number of trucks and heavy vehicles using their narrow street.

It was an incredibly polite gathering of about a dozen people. They put on a morning tea, and Fifield undertook to get the department to look into their complaint. As he was leaving, the organiser, the punter who had written the letter, reached out to shake hands, saying: 'Ah, mate, here's my business card. If you want to know anything else, give me a call.' Fifield froze, fearing a set-up, when he saw that his affable host worked for *The Australian*, but then he relaxed when he read down and saw that Tony Abbott was the paper's editorial writer, and not its transport roundsman.

About a week later, Abbott rang Fifield to tell him he had resigned from *The Australian* to become press secretary to the then opposition leader, John Hewson. Fifield also moved to Canberra soon after, to work for star National Party MP John Anderson. No one could have guessed then that Fifield would help trigger the events that secured the Liberal leadership for Abbott in 2009, and would then go on to become the assistant minister for social services in his government, with responsibility for delivering the NDIS — another great Labor idea left with no structure and no money, destined to go the way of other multi-billion-dollar projects, but which Fifield pledged to deliver, come hell or high water.

As it happened, Fifield was to play key roles in both removing Turnbull and in reinstating him. In 2009, he was one of three parliamentary secretaries — the other two being Brett Mason and Mathias Cormann — who precipitated the spill against then opposition leader Turnbull because he was determined to vote for Kevin Rudd's Carbon Pollution Reduction Scheme. One by one, in the space of an hour on 25 November, they each rang Turnbull to tell him they were quitting his frontbench.

Fifield was either the second or the third to ring Turnbull, by which time he had well and truly got the drift. 'OK, good, thanks,' Turnbull said, and hung up.

Turnbull now says, ruefully, that he was amazed he lasted as long as he did as opposition leader. He thought he was a goner when Godwin Grech set him up with fake emails. His rush of blood in calling for the resignations of Kevin Rudd and Wayne Swan saw his poll ratings plummet, and raised serious questions about his judgement.

After he resigned as a shadow, Fifield did a very tough interview with ABC radio, telling Turnbull publicly that he had forfeited his right to lead the party, and that, for his own sake as well as theirs, he should quit. Abbott, who had been alerted to Fifield's remarks by a friendly newspaper columnist, stopped him in the corridor to register his approval.

Fifield and his colleagues resigned from the frontbench because, as Fifield was to say later: 'If we didn't change the leader we couldn't change the policy, and if we didn't change the policy we were buggered.'

They didn't have a candidate to replace Turnbull. What's more, they didn't care. They thought Hockey might emerge. If you had told them that day that Abbott would win the leadership a week later, they would have scoffed—just like almost everybody did when Abbott won by one vote.

Mason, who rapidly became disillusioned with the prime minister's office and with Credlin, was announced as ambassador to the Netherlands in April 2015, and left the parliament. Cormann went straight into cabinet as finance minister in 2013. After carefully weighing up the pros and cons of switching camps in the lead-up to the challenge, the Belgian Bulldozer, or the Mussels from Brussels, as he is also known, stuck by Abbott. He thought Abbott had always been underestimated, and would come good.

Fifield always maintains that what happened in 2009 was driven by policy differences, and not by personal animosity towards Turnbull. The two later reconnected through their portfolios. If there were problems surrounding the NDIS when Turnbull was doing media, he would ring Fifield directly to get briefed, rather than leaving it to his staff. Whoever in the prime minister's office had the brainwave of appointing Fifield to represent Turnbull on communications in the Senate could not have made a worse choice. There was no obvious fit between the two portfolios, but it led to even more contact between the two ministers. When Fifield needed briefing for Senate estimates, Turnbull would personally sit in on the meetings. The two would have regular chats.

Fifield stuck with Abbott in February 2015, believing he was honour-bound as a minister to vote against the spill motion, although his disillusion was growing.

Scott Ryan was not a main player in the plan to dump Turnbull in 2009, but his conversion in 2015 to Turnbull had a deep impact on Julie Bishop, who was obviously central to Abbott's demise.

At the Coalition Christmas Party in 2009, held before Abbott deposed him, she witnessed Turnbull unload on Ryan as they discussed Rudd's emissions trading scheme. It became a standing joke between Bishop and Ryan at every Christmas Party thereafter. In the years that followed, Ryan barely spoke with Turnbull; they might have exchanged greetings two or three times, mainly when their paths crossed in the parliamentary corridors.

Then Victoria's new Liberal leader, Mathew Guy, who had had some dealings with Turnbull, suggested he should reach out to Ryan. Ryan shared a house in Canberra with James McGrath, whom he had met during university days when both were involved, albeit in different factions, with the Australian Liberal Students Federation. Simon Birmingham was also in the ALSF at the same time. They all knew one another only vaguely back then, but those early tenuous connections helped build the trust necessary to execute a momentous task.

McGrath was involved in the planning from the outset, but Ryan was not privy to it until the final few weeks.

Ryan's discontent had also grown steadily. He was angry that the Liberals had lost office in Victoria in late November 2014. While the Napthine government had problems, there was no doubt there was an Abbott factor in the campaign, which Labor played up heavily in its advertising as well as at its launch, especially after

Abbott deliberately hugged Napthine at a doorstop, providing Labor with invaluable footage to demonstrate a close connection.

Abbott was sensitive to criticism that he was in any way responsible for Napthine's defeat. After a column in the lead-up to the state election, in which I canvassed the possibility of Napthine becoming a one-termer, with some of the blame being laid at Abbott's door, as well as pondering whether Abbott himself could become a one-termer, there came the obligatory text from Hirst: 'PM was so unpopular in Victoria we picked up three seats last year. Good logic Niki.' And lost two (Sophie Mirabella's seat of Indi, plus missing out on a third Senate seat for the second election in a row), but, hey, who's counting? Actually, lots of people were. Especially when opinion polls were showing Labor at 59 per cent two-party-preferred in Victoria, while the Coalition hovered around 41 per cent—an outcome that the new state president, Michael Kroger, was telling party members could see the Liberals lose between six and eight seats if replicated at an election.

(The Victorian polling stayed dire. There were two state by-elections scheduled for 31 October 2015, and before the coup there was a real risk they could be lost. Tracking polling had them both in negative territory, minus five. On the polling, the Liberals were even at risk of losing the safe federal seat of Wannon, held by Dan Tehan. The Liberals retained the state seats after the federal leadership change.)

Ryan, along with others, had also been infuriated by a story in the first edition of the *Telegraph* on 15 December 2014, which asserted that a group of malcontents was briefing against Credlin. It conjured up positively Nixonian overtones of enemies' lists:

Despite pledging public support for Ms Credlin, Foreign Affairs Minister Julie Bishop is said to be among those undermining her. Others include Communications Minister Malcolm Turnbull and Queensland backbenchers Jane Prentice and Teresa Gambaro. Victorian backbenchers Kelly O'Dwyer and Scott Ryan were also outed as part of the group, along with Ms Bishop's West Australian colleague, Ken Wyatt.

Again, those named believed that either Credlin, or sources close to her, were responsible for the story.

Then there was the Prince Philip decision — bad in itself, but its announcement so close to the Queensland election didn't help Campbell Newman. Nevertheless, when the spill motion was moved in February, Ryan stuck with Abbott, partly out of a sense of duty as a parliamentary secretary, partly because there was no challenger, and partly because he hoped that, in the six months Abbott had asked for, there would be an improvement. Unlike Craig Laundy and others, who told Abbott directly in January he should sack both Credlin and Hockey, Ryan told Abbott the night before the ballot that the situation for the government was dire; the situation for the party was dire. He criticised the operations of his office.

McGrath, the son of sugar-cane farmers from Bli Bli on the sunshine coast, ran his first political campaign when he was a student at Toowomba State High School. The principal had been sacked, and McGrath organised protests to get him reinstated. He couldn't save the principal, but the sitting state member lost his seat at the next election.

Politics was in McGrath's blood. He studied law, completed university, did his articles with a suburban law firm, and along the way decided that the last thing he wanted to do was practise law. He worked one day a week for Bruce Laming, the father of federal MP Andrew, who served as a Liberal MP in the state parliament.

According to Bruce, McGrath walked into his office one day in 1994, saying: 'I want to get rid of Labor. Can I have a job, please?'

He worked for the South Australian Liberals, then headed off to the UK, where he worked for the conservatives. It was Mark Textor who put him in touch with Malcolm Turnbull. McGrath finished a campaign in the Maldives, flew back to Australia, met with Turnbull at his Point Piper home, and was offered a job.

He became deputy to Brian Loughnane at the federal Liberal Party secretariat in Canberra. The two got along very well to begin with, but then Loughnane sacked him one Friday afternoon, without warning. Liberal MPs went into meltdown. Don Randall, blunt as ever, rang McGrath to ask him if he had been caught fiddling—either party money or his own private parts—and when reassured that he hadn't been, Randall became Loughnane's implacable enemy.

As deputy federal director with responsibility for Queensland, McGrath was credited with securing a net gain of nine seats in the 2010 federal election, which helped destroy Julia Gillard and consolidated Abbott's leadership. Later, as the Queensland LNP's campaign director, he helped engineer Campbell Newman's historic win in Queensland in March 2012—the biggest electoral victory in Australian history and possibly the Commonwealth—then watched in horror as a senator when it all disappeared in 2015. McGrath was not blind to Newman's faults, but he was furious with Abbott over the intrusion of federal issues into the campaign, which he thought sealed Newman's fate.

Unlike Mal Brough and Wyatt Roy, whose agitation precipitated the February spill against Abbott, McGrath stayed out of those leadership machinations. But he made sure that Abbott knew back then that he held him at least partially responsible for Newman's loss. McGrath remained traumatised by it.

He did not agitate for the spill; however, when it came, he voted for it. Nor did he want to be part of a challenge to Abbott's leadership. He would have preferred it if a delegation had approached Abbott to ask him to step aside for the sake of the party and the country. McGrath was conscious of the damage that a spill could inflict on the fabric of the party.

However, like the others, he believed that if Abbott stayed, Shorten would become prime minister, and there was no way he was going to sit back and allow that to happen. McGrath is both highly eccentric and highly effective. His 2015 Christmas card said it all. The top half of the card was a photo of the Mother of Good Counsel Catholic Church in Innisfail built in 1928, then restored by the local community after Cyclone Larry struck in 2006. The bottom featured three cartoon characters from The Minions. It was incredibly serious and incredibly funny.

If the insurgents had waited, the question for observers is whether Abbott would have survived. It is possible. But for the G8, the question was not really why they should wait until after Canning. Rather, it was what would be the point in waiting until after it?

They worried that word would seep out. No matter how careful they were, staff and other MPs must have noted the G8's irregular office visits, changes to their schedules that had them arriving earlier or leaving later than usual. They were committed to changing the leadership, so what was the point of delaying? They knew they had the numbers. A cardinal rule of politics is, when you have the numbers, use them. He who hesitates is lost, and all that. If the numbers had not been there, they would have had no choice but to wait. Canning might or might not have provided momentum for a tilt. They knew in their bones that, sooner or later, something else would go wrong, another political problem would arise, and, given the nature of the warrior beasts, that too would be mishandled. The more time there was between a change and the election, the better, because it would give Turnbull more time to turn things around.

They also knew that Abbott would not sit still, waiting for them to come for him after the by-election. There had been chatter about a reshuffle. In fact, Abbott had publicly flagged it. There had been a subtle but perceptible change in his language in support of Hockey. If he dumped Hockey to put Morrison in the job, that might stymie them. They worried that Abbott would then race off to an early double-dissolution election to thwart any prospect of a challenge. One cabinet minister told me before the coup that he was certain Abbott would rather be defeated in a general election than face the humiliation of being removed by his own colleagues. He would prefer, fighter that he was, to go down with all guns blazing, rather than be sliced up in a party-room coup.

When a story appeared in the *Daily Telegraph* on Friday 11 September, headlined 'Abbott planning purge of cabinet', it only confirmed the view of the G8 that there was no time to waste. They hoped that the transaction cost of an immediate switch would be less than if it happened after news of their own plans leaked, causing days of upheaval, bloody infighting, and damaging headlines.

The *Telegraph* piece said Abbott was planning to axe up to six ministers in a wholesale reshuffle, but would keep the treasurer, Joe Hockey. Those in danger were said to be Kevin Andrews, Eric Abetz, Ian Macfarlane, Andrew Robb, Nigel Scullion, Michael Ronaldson, Jamie Briggs, and Bob Baldwin.

Bishop texted Abbott at 6.00 am on the day the report appeared, to say they needed to speak. When she did not hear from him, she called him. In the interim, she had received calls from ministers expressing concern about the piece. She told Abbott the story was highly damaging, and that MPs believed it had either come from the prime minister's office or that it had his imprimatur.

She also told him that, given how volatile things were, with speculation of a challenge by Turnbull surfacing, the article 'could bring things to a head'.

He told her it had not come from him, and asked her who she thought was responsible. She told him it didn't matter what she thought; it was what his colleagues thought that mattered, and they thought it was the prime minister's office. Abbott agreed it was unhelpful, but reiterated that he had not had anything to do with it.

They exchanged texts during the day. Bishop was seeking a meeting with him the following Monday to discuss diplomatic appointments, so he agreed to meet with her then. There was a missed call from him on Saturday, but he left no message and did not try to call back. She tried to call him back on Sunday.

One of the most popular games in Canberra is 'Spot the leaker.' No one can ever say for sure who sourced what. However, given the close relationship between the author of the *Telegraph* article and the prime minister's office, from Abbott down and particularly Credlin, Turnbull supporters were convinced that the prime minister's chief of staff was responsible — or, if not her, then Abbott himself.

The article had been presented, along with an editorial, as a means to enable the prime minister to reset his agenda. He had to seize the agenda. It read like it was meant to help him. In fact, it helped kill him.

A different version of the origins of the story was circulating among Abbott's supporters. According to one version put about by Abbott's friends and Turnbull's enemies, the *Telegraph* had been planning to run a piece saying there would be another challenge that would precipitate a major reshuffle, leading to the promotion of a lot of young people. The prime minister's office had got wind of it, and had then intervened to try to manage it. If true, this would have been another triumph of media management that succeeded in turning one bad story into an even more damaging one.

Abbott, while denying that he or his office had anything to do with it, was pointing the finger at Turnbull. Turnbull scoffs at this suggestion—as if the *Telegraph* would have taken his word on anything at that point. However it came about, the appearance of the article raised anxiety levels sky-high in both camps.

Up until then, Abbott had been having a good week after announcing that the government would accept a greater-than-expected intake of 12,000 Syrian refugees. It had taken Abbott a few days to appreciate the impact that the plight of refugees swarming into Europe was having on Australians—particularly the effect of photos of a drowned toddler—and then only after Mike Baird, Barnaby Joyce, Craig Laundy, and others went public, saying Australia should increase its intake. Having come round, he was looking and sounding more like a prime minister. Could he finally be getting the hang of it?

The G8 did not think so. McGrath, Fifield, Ryan, and Birmingham had made their threshold decision at the meeting at Turnbull's apartment on 13 August that Abbott had to go, that his track record showed it would only be a matter of time before he or his office launched another disaster, and that the Coalition would lose the election. There was no turning back for them.

On the eve of the resumption of parliament on Sunday 6 September, after another two-week break, there was a further meeting at Turnbull's Kingston apartment. The G8 was going through the numbers again, following the rule laid down that two of them had to be able to verify each vote. 'You have to be certain they will vote for you, even with your pants down,' Ryan emphasised. Laundy, who was also there that night, burst out laughing. They could be flippant then, while it was still abstract. Not later.

They thought that the votes for Turnbull were in the mid-50s.

Turnbull said that he had decided to do it—the only question was when. 'I can tell you I am definitely going to challenge before Christmas,' he told them.

He wanted, if he got it, a full year in the job. He thought if they waited until after Canning, that could push the challenge out another five weeks. 'That would mean we would lose one-tenth of the time we would need,' he said.

Of course, there was also the worry that if they went before Canning and the vote turned sour, it would be a terrible beginning to his leadership. Also, he did not want to upset the Western Australian MPs. He needed their votes. Again, they discussed Bishop; again, Hendy was urged to speak to her.

On the evening of Tuesday 8 September, Hendy and Turnbull met with Bishop. Turnbull left that meeting muttering. He was completely clueless about her intentions. They reported back to another meeting of the group at Turnbull's apartment that night, and decided on a different tack.

In February, despite toying with the idea of making a run herself, and despite being part of the discussions with Turnbull, Bishop had ultimately sat pat. She rightly deduced that the spill motion would fail. This time, they had to find the means to convince her that the numbers had shifted decisively against Abbott. They needed Bishop onside, but they were far from confident they had her. There was what one of them described as a 'strong disposition' to pull it on the next day, but this was complicated because they had been told Abbott would be flying to Port Moresby. None of them knew what time he was scheduled to leave.

Ryan contacted Bishop that night, seeking an appointment with her the next day, 9 September, a Wednesday. It was set for 7.30 am. At this stage, they still thought there was a possibility they could mount the challenge that week. The group also pencilled in another meeting in Birmingham's office, immediately after the Bishop meeting, to recap. Fifield spoke to the Western Australian senator and fellow minister Michaelia Cash, who was a good friend of his, inviting her to accompany them to the meeting. Cash, also from the right, had also crossed over.

Among other things, Cash had been dismayed by a decision in May to cancel the planned announcement of a $100 million package to tackle domestic violence. As the minister assisting the prime minister for women, Cash had formulated the package, then secured Abbott's agreement for it to be included in the budget. However, at the last minute, Credlin decided it would not be announced. No explanation was given. Cash assumes concern about it being swamped by other budget measures might have been a factor, but believes that was a mistake, because it would have given hard-pressed backbenchers something else that they could go out and sell. Also, governments have been known to leak bits of their own budgets in advance to create interest and also to ensure worthwhile measures don't get overlooked.

The domestic-violence package remained under wraps until the leadership switch. With a couple of tweaks, Turnbull announced it less than two weeks after he became prime minister — with the Australian of the year, Rosie Batty, and Cash, as a cabinet minister, standing beside him — setting an early theme of respect for women as one of his motifs.

Cash also got along well with Bishop. Her presence at that early-morning meeting, to signal her abandonment of Abbott, underlined the message they'd been giving to Bishop about the fragility of his numbers. They were slipping away, from the right and from within the ministry.

Bishop kept a poker face, but she was, to say the least, surprised by what they told her, which was that they could no longer support Abbott. She was especially surprised by Ryan, given his history with Turnbull. And she was even more surprised by Cash. Nevertheless, her immediate reaction was low key. She had even more thinking to do. They did not discuss with her the timing of any challenge against the prime minister.

In any case, Fifield, Ryan, and Cash believed they were speaking to the deputy leader in confidence, as they were entitled to do, and that she would not dob them in. Turnbull spoke to her again, this time to gauge her reaction to the meeting with the right-wing trio, but she was still not on board.

Her view was that if she raced off to tell Abbott whenever colleagues registered their unhappiness with his leadership, she would have had to take up residence in his office.

Of course, the other objective of the meeting was to reassure Bishop that her position was not under threat. All of them were incensed by Credlin's habitual ill-treatment of Bishop.

'Julie has incredible goodwill in the party,' one of the G8 said later. 'She will do a fundraiser for anyone, anywhere. It was also an indication people were looking after her interests. She had been mistreated by Credlin on a number of occasions, and she is elected deputy leader by the party room. She has an independent mandate.' And they wanted that preserved.

Fifield, who was also manager of government business in the Senate, left Bishop's office to attend the regular leadership group meeting in the prime minister's office. The rest of the group was gathering in Birmingham's office to review the discussions with Bishop.

Birmingham was paranoid that people, including his own staff, would get suspicious if they saw such a disparate group assembling in his office so early, for no apparent reason. So he despatched a staffer to buy a cake. They put a candle on top, lit it, then sat around his office, singing happy birthday to Peter Hendy. Of course, it wasn't Hendy's birthday. (He was born on 10 January.) The carrot cake became cover for a coup.

At that meeting, Hendy was charged with drafting the letter for the spill. They were as certain as they could be that they had the numbers to defeat Abbott that day. Like so many others, they did not have access to the prime minister's diary, so they did not know exactly when he would be flying to Port Moresby. Wednesday was still a live option, until Fifield reported back from the leadership group meeting that the prime minister would indeed be leaving the country shortly. In fact, Abbott did not make it to question time that day. Turnbull had also spoken again to Bishop, and reported back on his discussion with her about her talks with the trio. He told them he would be talking to her again on the weekend. So it looked as if nothing was going to happen that week.

Hendy began gathering signatures for the petition calling for the spill, just in case Abbott refused to call a party meeting on the day when confronted by the challenge. Hendy also spoke again to Bishop, once again to underline her obligation to the party.

Turnbull also met that Wednesday afternoon with Luke Simpkins, the man who had moved the spill motion against Abbott in February. Simpkins had been told by a colleague a couple of weeks before that 'Malcolm's going to run—Malcolm's going to step up.'

'I was a bit surprised by that,' Simpkins told me subsequently. Simpkins' meeting with Turnbull that day was to discuss communications issues in his electorate of Cowan. When that conversation ended, Turnbull asked the advisers to leave. Once they were alone, Turnbull asked him how he thought things were going.

'Not very well,' Simpkins replied. He had been dismayed by the handling of the Bronwyn Bishop saga. Turnbull told him that if their colleagues wanted him to, he was prepared to step up. Once again, Simpkins had come to the conclusion that there had to be a change. Only this time, for the first time ever, he was prepared to back Turnbull. 'I have always been clear-cut with people every leadership change,' Simpkins told me. 'I have never said one thing to anybody, then done another.'

Simpkins left the meeting thinking that Turnbull would make a move early the next week, before the by-election. He says he got that impression because Turnbull was asking him about Canning. 'He was worried about whether that would hurt us or help us,' Simpkins said. 'But, really, with the number of people that I talked to who said they had a problem with Tony, I thought it was better to do it and give ourselves a better chance of winning, rather than risk losing it.' He told me later he felt vindicated in his view by the number of people who approached him after the by-election to say that if Abbott had not been deposed, they would not have voted Liberal.

Ian Macfarlane recalls Turnbull showing him the numbers on his computer that Thursday. Turnbull, being the tech head that he is, kept the tally on Google Sheets. Only a select few could access the spreadsheet. Obviously, Turnbull was one, McGrath another, and the third was Turnbull's closest, most trusted, adviser, Sally Cray.

Macfarlane remembers it as a traffic-light system. Red marked the no-go zone, for those who would not vote for him under any circumstances; green was for those good to go; and amber marked the possibles.

Others, however, confirm that it was divided into five voting blocs: hard no; soft no; hard yes; soft yes; and unknown/undecided. It looked to Macfarlane as if they could be over the line, but he was still uncertain about the timing. He and Turnbull spoke again over that weekend.

Hendy, meanwhile, kept talking to Bishop, going over the same arguments that her principal loyalty was to the Liberal Party. She had been elected leader multiple times in her own right. At no time had she been on a ticket with any of the leaders. She had her own separate mandate, and a large chunk of her duties involved the protection of the party.

There were also other meetings taking place. On that same Wednesday 9 September, Jamie Briggs met with Peta Credlin and her deputy, Andrew Hirst. Briggs was good friends with both McGrath and Birmingham. Birmingham had been a groomsman at Briggs's wedding, and was godfather to one of his children. Birmingham had not sounded out Briggs, believing he would not shift, but Briggs later told people he had been sounded out by Turnbull. Briggs had also overheard Pyne say that the only hope they had of holding seats in South Australia was to build the submarines there, destroy Nick Xenophon, and remove Abbott.

Briggs told Credlin and Hirst that night that things were moving.

Their first response was dismissive—arrogant, even. They said that Turnbull didn't have the numbers, so if he tried it on, he would be the one destroyed. Briggs told them: 'They are coming, they are organised. I think it's going to be very difficult to hold them back.'

He had their attention, but they were convinced that Morrison would stick, that Morrison would swing his people behind Abbott, and that Turnbull did not have the numbers and that the party would not move to him. Briggs was convinced otherwise. He had put it much more bluntly to his good friend and housemate, Joe Hockey, the night before, after he had heard what Pyne said.

'We are fucked,' Briggs told Hockey when he got home.

The point was that everyone knew Turnbull and Abbott were heading for a showdown. What they—including the G8—did not know was precisely which day it would happen. Everyone had assumed it would be after the Canning by-election. The timing of the by-election was no accident. It had been scheduled at the end of a sitting fortnight, with a three-week break to follow after the vote. Dispersal of MPs to their electorates would militate against a revolt.

Briggs's instincts, backed by the intelligence he had garnered, were spot-on. He would not change his position, mainly because of his loyalty to Hockey, but he knew that others, including Pyne and Brandis, had moved.

Abbott flew to South Australia on Sunday 13 September. That afternoon, he met with Pyne at the Adelaide Club. Over a few drinks, at Abbott's request, Pyne went through the areas where he thought the government was going wrong, and what he thought needed to change.

Pyne told the prime minister there should be personnel changes (code for shifting Credlin); there was no economic narrative, which he regarded as a fiasco; and he believed the handling of the same-sex marriage debate was a disaster. He told Abbott that MPs were coming to the conclusion they had a responsibility to stop Bill Shorten and the CFMEU from getting hold of the reins of power, which was on the cards if Abbott stayed as leader.

He also told Abbott he did not believe there would be a challenge in the next week, but he warned him that a challenge was coming. Abbott rebutted every point Pyne made. The whole thing was very amicable—so much so that Pyne left for the airport to fly to Canberra thinking he had made no impression whatsoever on the prime minister.

Pyne was deliberately left out of the loop on the detailed planning of the coup. They all knew Pyne had dropped off Abbott long before, and they also knew he would vote for Turnbull whenever the ballot was held, but that he had been dubious about whether Turnbull would be able to muster the numbers.

In published reports afterwards, there were suggestions that Pyne had had early, inside knowledge that the coup was imminent because he had texted Credlin a few days before to recommend that Andrew Robb have a few days off, after the trade minister had lost his cool in the parliament. This was presented as evidence that Pyne was trying to remove Robb from the action because Pyne knew the challenge would be on the following week.

In fact, Pyne texted Credlin after Labor's Gary Gray had expressed concern to him over Robb's outburst in parliament before the coup. Gray confirmed later that he had spoken to Pyne. Gray said he was concerned on two counts. First, as a longstanding friend of Robb's, he was worried that the trade minister was overwrought and might not have fully recovered from a bout of shingles. Second, he feared that Robb's approach in the house could be counterproductive, because it would drive Labor away from acceptance of the China Free Trade Agreement, rather than towards it.

The next morning, Monday, Abbott made a major roads announcement with Briggs in Adelaide. Briggs had spent months fighting with the deputy prime minister, Warren Truss, to get this up, because it involved shifting unspent money from Queensland to South Australia. Abbott would tell Briggs he had his support, then melt in front of Truss's intransigence, then follow up by yelling at Briggs for not managing to get the money. It was not until Cormann told Truss the money would go back into the budget that he relented. So Briggs had been hamstrung by Truss, then stung by the story in the *Daily Telegraph* on Friday saying he faced dumping in a planned Abbott reshuffle later in the year.

He raised this with Abbott that morning. Abbott told him he was not responsible for it. Briggs put it down to payback from the *Tele* for him not handing over stories on the second airport at Badgery's Creek.

That Monday morning, Briggs told Abbott, in Credlin's presence, that the prime minister had a 'big problem'. In spite of everything he had heard directly from Pyne the previous afternoon, Abbott told Briggs he thought Pyne would be 'OK'.

'No, mate,' Briggs said.

Briggs said to him: 'Pyne thinks he is going to lose his seat. He is a survivor.' Briggs believes it finally sunk in then, so they should have been on their guard. There had also been another warning the previous night, Sunday. Laurie Oakes, still the best of the best, went to air on the Nine Network, saying that Turnbull had rejected a request from Abbott supporter Andrew Nikolic (perhaps momentarily forgetting he was no longer an army brigadier, but a junior backbencher elected in 2013) to rule out a challenge, and that a move against Abbott was possible before Canning. Oakes is often first, and seldom, if ever, wrong.

Briggs spoke to Turnbull again on Monday, and told him he would let him know later in the night what he would do in the event of a spill. He rang him back to tell him he would be voting for Abbott. Briggs couldn't bring himself to do it to his friend Joe, nor to Abbott either, really.

Polling in his electorate of Mayo, just as the Bronnie helicopter crashed, showed a swing against Briggs of 10 per cent. His margin was 7.7 per cent. If nothing changed, he was certainly a goner.

Briggs knew it was only a matter of time before the challenge was launched, although he could not be sure when—partly because even the protagonists were not sure themselves.

Ewen Jones, one of the funniest, best-natured MPs in the parliament, was oblivious to all of it, even though he and Wyatt Roy shared a house in Canberra. He spoke to both Briggs and Pyne on the Sunday (after Pyne had spoken to Abbott) about portfolio matters, and neither let on.

Jones ended up voting for Abbott, because he has a thing, like many MPs, about always voting for the leader, and he did so in spite of his irritation at getting the Credlin treatment in the final four months of her reign. Before that, he had had instant access, either for a few minutes or twenty minutes, whenever he sought it. Then he said something—he can't remember what, exactly, although it was not anything personal about Credlin—that resulted in her putting him in the freezer. Now he experienced what others had been saying about their treatment by the prime minister's office: no phone calls returned, no emails, nothing.

The G8 had their final meeting on the night of Sunday 13 September at the Queanbeyan home of Peter Hendy. It wasn't actually in Hendy's house—it was a large shed about the size of a small house, or what one later described as a man-cave complete with pool table, dartboard, and books, out the back of his bush block. Birmingham could not make it to the meeting, but rang in for a briefing. A few others were there that night. Outspoken marginal-seat holder Craig Laundy was one. Turnbull's most senior political adviser, Sally Cray—the woman Credlin had vetoed as Turnbull's chief of staff after the 2013 election — was another.

To the surprise of some of the group, Murray Hansen, chief of staff to Julie Bishop, was also there. He had been invited by Hendy, who had worked with Hansen in Bishop's office. Hansen did not say much; his was more a watching brief, to report back to Bishop.

Laundy had decided long before that Abbott had to go, but wavered about who should replace him. Like other MPs, at one stage he had been weighing up whether it could be Morrison or Bishop.

Months before, when Shorten was in a momentary spot of bother after his appearance at the royal commission into trade unions, Brough had told me that whoever changed leaders first would win the next election. Brough, like the others, was convinced there was no time to waste.

So that night of 13 September, Hendy had savoury mince, tuna mornay, and rice ready for his guests. Some arrived in time to watch Oakes's report that the challenge could be on before Canning. They were relieved that Oakes did not have more detail.

For the best part of three hours, they talked, took calls, or made calls, just like they would any other Sunday night. They did not want to arouse suspicion. They also spoke to their colleagues, firming up the numbers.

If Turnbull was the general in charge of the entire operation, McGrath was the keeper of the numbers.

McGrath was the point of contact at critical times for the other members of the group, unless Turnbull contacted them directly for different reasons. All of them reached deep into the party. Whatever information was gathered was fed back to McGrath so he could update the Google Sheet.

That night at Hendy's, McGrath appointed himself chairman,

bringing them all to order when they started talking over one another or getting off track. There was a lot of nervous energy in the room. When Turnbull went outside to make a call, Cray told them all to chill. Turnbull knew what he had to do, she told them.

Turnbull told the group he was deeply worried about the potential consequences of not acting—further damage to the government, the Liberal Party, and the economy, because of the failure of leadership—and ultimately the consequences for the country if Bill Shorten became prime minister.

McGrath produced his spreadsheet so they could go over the numbers again. They compared notes. Had anyone switched or shifted? While they were confident about their range of numbers, there would always be crossover. There were always people who you expected to vote for you who didn't, or people who said they wouldn't and then did. But the group had done their work well. Their count that night was pretty close; it was out by only a few votes. They had it at 57. In the event, there turned out to be two absentees—Michael Ronaldson and Dean Smith—who were down as yeses for Turnbull.

Again, they discussed whether they should wait or not. They had seen Rupert Murdoch's tweets, saying Abbott should call a snap poll. Was Rupert reflecting something that Abbott had already told him?

At previous meetings, there had been jokes and a bit of laughter in between the planning and the serious discussions. Not that night. They were all conscious of the gravity of what was being planned—they were about to launch a coup against a first-term prime minister.

At one point, Fifield observed that it was human nature to look for reasons not to do something, even more so with party-room ballots. He told them that the Canning by-election was just another rationalisation for putting off a decision, and that there would always be a reason to delay. If a change of leader was the right thing to do, 'it was the right thing to do now', he told them.

They were preparing, as one said later, to do something 'momentous'. Summing up the mood, another described it as 'apprehensive but committed'. Another said: 'No one was flippant that Sunday night. There was no one there who had not decided. Everyone had crossed their own little bridge.'

Still another said: 'It was a bit bi-polar. It was very serious, but everyone would try and speak over everyone else.'

There was a lot of talk about the tactics for the next day. They tossed around the option of forming a delegation to the then prime minister to tell him it was over. Roy thought that if Bishop did decide to front Abbott to tell him his numbers had deserted him, it might be better if she had some support. Fifield said he was prepared to be part of a delegation.

They were undecided about which was the best way to go. They agreed that, as deputy leader in the Senate, George Brandis (who was not at the meeting) should speak to Bishop the next morning, firstly to ensure she was prepared to visit the prime minister, and, secondly, to let her know that if she wanted him and Turnbull to accompany her, they would. They discussed the possibility of Pyne and Macfarlane going as well.

Turnbull, who had already spoken to Bishop on Saturday night, when they both attended the same function in Sydney, also spoke to Brandis that Sunday night. Brandis had flown to Canberra that afternoon on the same flight as Hansen; however, while they briefly discussed 'the troubles', Hansen did not tell him he was heading to Hendy's.

Hendy said it would be best if Turnbull just took the decision to proceed, because that would force Bishop to act. Brough agreed.

They discussed tactics for the next day down to the minutest detail. Turnbull said he had decided to approach Abbott after question time.

Then, as they were preparing to leave, after most of them thought everything had been covered off, Sinodinos said to Turnbull: 'You should sleep on it.' At that point, a couple of the others could have happily throttled their great friend Arthur.

'Of course I reserve the right to think it over,' Turnbull replied. Except that there wasn't much that they hadn't thought about already.

The meeting at Hendy's ended at 8.40 pm, again with full agreement that it had to be done. They were still not absolutely certain it would happen the next day, nor were they certain exactly how. That would depend on Brandis's conversation with Bishop the next morning. As one of them said later, they were confident but not certain she would confront the prime minister.

'She could just have easily said, "No way, Jose,"' one of them said. When the meeting finished, Hansen texted his boss to see if she wanted to talk about what happened. She told him to save it till the morning.

Turnbull, usually restless, always pacing and texting, a bundle of activity, seemed absolutely composed. There was something about his body language that night which convinced them of his utter determination. 'He just was stock still,' one of them said. Ultimately, of course, the decision was his alone. Not that he had much choice, really. He was either up or out. He either challenged or he quit. He could not continue to serve in a government that was dysfunctional, where cabinet process was ignored, where decisions were leaked—sometimes before they were even made—directly from the prime minister's office, he believed.

None of his troops got much sleep that night; they got even

less the next. In contrast, Turnbull felt calm, and slept very well. It was a trait. When something terrifying was happening, he would fall asleep instantly, while the most trivial things kept him awake all night.

CHAPTER TEN

Execution

James McGrath took up residence in Malcolm Turnbull's ministerial office from around seven o'clock on the morning of Monday 14 September. Counting as harshly as he could, he gave Turnbull 52 votes.

In a sign of the depth of planning undertaken to ensure it went as smoothly and as cleanly as such an inevitably bloody project possibly could, McGrath had instructed the group the previous night to make sure their mobile phones were charged and that they carried portable power packs. If and when the story broke, they would need to move quickly.

They had all been delegated MPs to look after, as well as journalists to brief. They knew the prime minister was in Adelaide, but they were not sure what time he would be arriving back in Canberra.

At 6.00 am, Turnbull rang Ian Macfarlane to tell him the spill motion was scheduled to be brought on that day. Macfarlane was on standby in case it was decided to send a delegation to see Abbott, but he was still unsure about the wisdom of going before Canning.

Turnbull told him to ring McGrath, which he did. Macfarlane

wanted reassurance on the numbers. McGrath said they were sure they had them, but who could know what would happen in a month, after Canning, after the three-week break in the sitting? Macfarlane rang Turnbull back and told him it was time to go.

McGrath also went round to the attorney-general's office to brief Brandis.

The group then waited for Brandis to speak to Julie Bishop. Brandis met with Bishop in her office around 9.10 am for between thirty and forty minutes. Brandis was convinced the numbers were there. His job was to impress upon her that Turnbull had them, that he was committed to using them, and to encourage her to go and see Abbott that day. If she did not, they would have to switch to plan B, where they would present the petition and the motion for a spill, or even perhaps postpone it for another day.

Brandis also told Bishop if she thought a delegation to the prime minister was the best way to go, he was prepared to accompany her. Turnbull had also rung to tell her he would accompany her if she wanted.

The conversation with Brandis ended with Bishop resolved to go and see Abbott on her own—a decision that Brandis endorsed.

Brandis later dismissed suggestions that Bishop had either been complicit or had in any way acted improperly. 'When the leadership is in meltdown, the deputy leader has to be the trustee of the interests of the party,' he told me.

This was also what he sought to impress on Bishop that morning, as well as to convince her that the prime minister had lost the majority support of his party room.

Birmingham also defended Bishop. 'I think she did conduct herself in a careful and cautious manner throughout,' he said.

'Those who want to believe that she should have been loyal to Tony at all cost to herself and the party would never be satisfied with the role she played. If you accepted that her loyalty is to the party that elected her as deputy leader, she played a careful and cautious role.'

After her meeting with Brandis, Bishop also wanted to speak directly with Pyne. She wanted to hear from his own lips that he would not be voting for Abbott and that he no longer supported him as prime minister. She also knew that Pyne was very good at taking the pulse of the backbench through his role as leader of the house, so they would be able to compare notes. Pyne went up to her office around 10.00 am. He confirmed directly his abandonment of Abbott, and she told him what she was about to do. She told him about her meeting with Fifield, Ryan, and Cash, and her belief that the prime minister no longer had the majority support of his backbench or cabinet.

Pyne did not favour sending a delegation to the prime minister. Bishop said she was prepared to do it on her own because she was the only one, as deputy leader, he could not sack. Pyne went back to his office and locked himself in. If, after the debate on same-sex marriage, MPs did not know where he stood, they never would.

Bishop sat alone in her office, thinking about what she would say. She preferred to do it on her own, in her own way. It was only now, when she was convinced the numbers were there, when she was convinced that Turnbull was indeed committed to challenging, when she was convinced it was her duty as deputy to look out for the interests of the party, that she felt compelled to tell the prime minister.

She knew it would not be an easy thing to do, but that it would be best if she did it on her own. She texted Abbott, saying she wanted to see him. He texted back almost immediately to arrange the meeting within minutes of his return from Adelaide. The swiftness of his response made her think he knew or suspected what it was she was going to tell him.

Just before midday, she walked into the prime minister's suite to tell him she believed that he had not only lost the support of a majority of his backbench, but that he had also lost the support of a majority of his frontbench. He wanted to know which of his ministers had shifted, but she refused to tell him.

She told him there were now three courses of action open to him. The first was to sit pat, do nothing, and take a punt that Turnbull would not challenge. The second was to wait for Turnbull to declare a challenge, then call a party-room meeting. The third was to pre-empt a declaration from Turnbull, call a party meeting, then dare him or anyone else to bring it on.

Bishop was trying to offer him options. But whatever she said, however she tried to dress it up, she was in effect telling him his leadership was terminal. Bishop has since been criticised by conservatives, inside as well as outside the party, for not warning him sooner; however, what she did that day took courage. Abbott and his supporters later accused her of disloyalty, but in fact Bishop treated Abbott much better than she had been treated herself by him and by his chief of staff.

Abbott seemed distracted, acting as though he wanted their meeting brought to an end. He told one of his supporters later that she kissed him as she left, although she has no memory of this. He did not ask her whether she was going to stick with him. It was curious that the leader would not, even as a matter of formality, ask his deputy at this critical point whether she was going to stand by him. Then, again, this was reflective of their relationship—her views or her station were seldom taken into account. If he had asked her then, she probably would have said she would vote for him, because she believed that was what deputies did. 'He despised her,' was the view of one of her colleagues.

After she left, Abbott called in Credlin. They were joined soon after by Credlin's husband, Brian Loughnane; the party's federal president, Richard Alston; Kevin Andrews; Eric Abetz; and Kate Raggatt. They were the most loyal of the inner circle, but when it came to precision planning, think *F Troop* rather than *Saving Private Ryan*.

Abbott and Bishop did not speak to each other again, neither that day, nor—at the time of writing of this book—since. They did subsequently exchange texts. She texted him first, seeking a rapprochement, but his response left her in no doubt that he wasn't interested.

He did not contact her to tell her he would be calling the party meeting that Monday evening. The next thing she knew, from seeing it on television, was that Abbott had decided to spill both the leadership and deputy leadership. This meant her job was up for grabs. This also meant she was no longer under any obligation to vote for him.

After the leadership vote in 2009 in which Abbott deposed Turnbull, Abbott had sent two colleagues to the whip's office to check over the ballot papers to see if they could spot Bishop's paper (she had a distinctive pen), to determine which way she had voted. (Liberal Party ballot papers are kept, and MPs are entitled to inspect them.) Bishop believes that Abbott told Turnbull at the time that she had voted for Abbott. In fact, Bishop had used a pencil, not her pen, in the ballot. Also, the ballot papers were numbered, so she made a note of hers. This meant she was able to cite her ballot paper after Turnbull expressed his doubts that she had voted for him. She proved to him that she had done what she always did, and voted for the leader. There would be no need for such a forensic investigation this time.

Around 12.40 pm, not long after Bishop had finished seeing

Abbott, Scott Ryan received a text from his friend, former long-time Liberal adviser David Wawn, who had worked for Abbott in opposition, to ask him if he thought there might be a challenge 'this week'. Ryan was one of the few who knew that Bishop had just gone to see Abbott.

Ryan responded truthfully, without giving the game away: 'Anything is possible here at the moment mate.'

Most MPs were oblivious to what was going on. The G8 was going about business as usual, doing their best not to speak to journalists until they were told it was safe to do so.

Dan Tehan saw Malcolm Turnbull approach Tony Abbott after question time, but thought nothing of it until after it was all over. Tehan, a Liberal MP from rural Victoria, and a firm supporter of Abbott's, went to a meeting of the agriculture committee when question time concluded. During the meeting, the agriculture minister, Barnaby Joyce, received a text to tell him that Turnbull was challenging, but he did not advise the others. As he was leaving the meeting, Tehan heard from a staffer that it was on. He had constituents in town, so he spent the next hour listening to their representations before he could tune into what was happening.

Turnbull had approached Abbott at the end of question time as he was preparing to leave the chamber, saying he wanted to have a chat about a very important matter. Abbott said OK, and they walked back to his office in silence.

Peter Dutton walked out of the chamber with Turnbull and Abbott. He had not been told about the meeting between Bishop and Abbott, and did not have a clue what was happening, but as the three of them headed towards the executive wing he could tell by the body language of the other two that something was up.

When Turnbull left the chamber with Abbott, McGrath had people strategically positioned to report back once they saw both men walk into the prime minister's suite of offices. They had to be sure the meeting was taking place. When they walked in, McGrath was alerted, then he told the rest. They fanned out to let the 'uber loyal' know what was happening. Then they began to 'shepherd' their people, to make sure they were not picked off.

The 'chat' between the two rivals was described later by those familiar with what occurred as 'brutal'.

'It was on between young and old,' they said.

Turnbull told Abbott he was going to resign from his communications portfolio to challenge him for the leadership. Abbott was at first incredulous, then very angry. He told Turnbull it was madness. How could he do this in the week of the Canning by-election? Turnbull told him the vote in Canning would improve as a result of the change. Abbott told him he would wreck the government.

It was as if he refused to believe what he was being told. It was as if it had come as a huge shock—as if the conversation with Julie Bishop that morning had not taken place, or the conversation with Jamie Briggs the previous week had not happened, or as if the previous month he had not listened to what Barnaby Joyce had told him.

Again, it seemed to confirm what they had long suspected. Abbott lived in a bubble built for two.

Turnbull basically told Abbott what he was to tell the media only minutes later: the government had been behind for thirty Newspolls; if Abbott stayed on in the job, Bill Shorten would be elected prime minister; cabinet government did not exist; and the country lacked economic leadership.

The whole thing took less than twenty minutes. As Turnbull prepared to leave, Abbott finished by saying: 'I will assume you are going back to your office and going back to work.'

Turnbull replied: 'No. That would be a rash assumption. I am going to make a statement to the media.' And minutes later, after going through his notes, and speaking again to Sinodinos about his key point on the need for economic leadership, Turnbull fronted the media to announce he was challenging Abbott for the prime ministership.

Turnbull's spiel announcing his challenge impressed even those who were not prepared to vote for him. He nailed it. Even people who supported Abbott conceded that Turnbull had zeroed in on Abbott's main weakness. It was not only that Abbott had been behind for so long in the polls, but the fact that he didn't get it on the economy. There was no narrative, there was no coherent policy approach, there was no consistency.

Within minutes, they all hit the phones, either to media or to colleagues who they thought might swing across.

Turnbull called the environment minister, Greg Hunt. Hunt had stood by Turnbull in 2009, telling Abbott that he would do so before the challenge. After Abbott won the leadership, he explained to Hunt where he saw the climate-change issue going, with the emphasis on direct action, and if Hunt felt he could do it, the job was his. Hunt listed a few conditions of his own, as noted earlier.

When Turnbull called him that afternoon in September 2015, Hunt told him: 'When you were down to your last ten (in 2009), I stood behind you. It wouldn't be right for me to jump from Tony now, whatever the consequences might be.' Turnbull told him that if he won, he looked forward to working with him in cabinet. Hunt knew that Turnbull had the numbers. When he and his good friend Scott Morrison sat in their usual two-seater couch at the front of the party room looking back across at their colleagues, Hunt estimated the vote at 54–45. When it came time to vote for the deputy leadership, he reckoned it would be 70–30. Hunt knew before Turnbull called him that it was over for Abbott.

Turnbull also called Mathias Cormann. Cormann did not budge from Abbott. He also knew it was over. So did Andrew Robb.

The precision planning of the Turnbull group stood in stark contrast to the chaos of the Abbott camp.

Turnbull supporters believe the Abbott camp made a number of fundamental errors that day. The first was in pulling on the vote that night; the second was in Abbott declaring both leadership positions vacant. They believe he should have waited a couple of days, at least, to let the shock-jocks do their worst, then he should have called for the spill.

Ministers and MPs said later that, only a few hours before the vote, Abbott was convinced he had the numbers. He should have known that Turnbull would not have moved unless he was certain he had them.

Abbott was advised by both Cormann and Robb to bring on the vote that night. They did not believe he would benefit from delaying. They did not believe that if he waited, his numbers would improve; in fact, they were worried they could worsen. They deduced that the bloodletting would not help Abbott; it would only encourage more of his colleagues to decide it had to be brought to an end. They were also concerned about the damage that days of anarchy would inflict on the party and the country. Neither was blind to his faults; however, they were being loyal to Abbott while trying to be loyal to their party and their country. Both had an obligation to Abbott. Abbott had been especially kind to Robb after his depression was diagnosed, giving him space and time to undergo treatment. Cormann had been promoted straight into the cabinet after the election.

Zed Seselja questioned the wisdom of bringing it on that night,

268 THE ROAD TO RUIN

but didn't go in hard to argue against it.

In any case, parliament was sitting. How could Abbott front up for question time the next day? It was untenable. They knew in their heart of hearts that it was over.

As one of Abbott's diehard supporters later conceded: 'There was conjecture that he should have dug in. Anyone who thinks our position was going to improve with the chaos … essentially the view was that the best chance lay in doing it quickly, the damage to the country, our reputation overseas, and the way it would play out domestically — all on the downside.

'My view was that the situation was only going to get worse; it wasn't good for the country and for the party. To have the authority of the prime minister in doubt for any longer than is necessary is just not tenable.

'Even if you lose, you have to make judgements about the broader interest of the government and the people.'

When Abbott rang Connie Fierravanti-Wells that night, she told him that if he managed to survive, he needed to make major changes, including removing Credlin from her job. She thought, even at this late stage, that if he had delayed the vote until the next morning, and let it be known that Credlin was leaving his office, he might have been able to hold on.

After Turnbull officially declared his challenge, Abetz contacted Fierravanti-Wells to see if she knew what Scott Morrison was going to do. She texted Morrison, asking him to contact her. He did not respond. She also believes that if Morrison had insisted on his people — probably half a dozen — voting for Abbott, they would have, and Abbott probably would have survived.

Alex Hawke, the young conservative MP from New South Wales, who is close to Morrison, was one of those taken aback when he heard that Abbott had called on the ballot that night.

'That was the biggest tactical error of the entire episode. Whoever advised him made a major error,' he told people.

Hawke and his friends assumed the ballot would be delayed until Tuesday or Wednesday. In February, the conservative broadcaster Alan Jones had swung into action on Abbott's behalf, ringing marginal-seat holders to convince them to stick with his friend the PM.

Hawke spoke to Morrison once that night. Morrison told him Abbott had offered him the deputy leadership, and he had rejected it. This was one sign to Hawke of how much trouble the prime minister was in. The clincher came when Abbott himself—following up calls from Credlin and Kate Raggatt—rang Hawke to offer him a ministry if he won the ballot. At that point, Hawke was certain Abbott did not have the numbers.

Although he advised Abbott on what he should do, Robb had not gone out to publicly state his support for him. In February, Robb thought it was 'madness' to move against the prime minister. He threatened to run against anyone who ran against Abbott, even though he could understand why MPs were upset. Decisions were being made then reversed, leaving them looking like dills in their electorates after they had been despatched to argue for them. There was no economic narrative; there was no story of hope or optimism.

In February, Robb was troubled by the fact that the prime minister did not have any close confidantes (other than Credlin) who could influence his decision-making, but he was more troubled by the Liberals looking as if they were following Labor's example in making disposable prime ministers.

He believed that if the prime minister had to be replaced, the public would have to see it coming, they would have to be prepared for it, they would have to see the logic of it, and they would have to know that due process had been followed.

Looking back, he believes the spill move became part of that conditioning process, but it could not be allowed to succeed in February. It would have looked too much like what Labor had done to Kevin Rudd — an overnight assassination that stunned many Australians.

Robb made it clear to Abbott in February that if it happened again, he would not be able to save him. He also advised Abbott to do whatever he needed to do in the six months he had bought himself to make sure it did not happen again.

Another key figure who did not venture out in support of Abbott that night was Morrison. Clear-eyed, Morrison was looking to the future, not the past. Those who did go out for Abbott were Kevin Andrews, Eric Abetz, Peter Dutton, Josh Frydenberg, Mathias Cormann, and Joe Hockey.

Cormann, with help from Frydenberg, ran the numbers for Abbott in February, but not in September.

Frydenberg was another colleague who had delivered a warning that the challenge was imminent. He told Credlin more than a week before that it could come before Canning, or if not, after. He reckoned he could feel it seeping through the walls of the building. The response, as Frydenberg was to tell associates later, was 'more than a sense of complacency'. He described Abbott's reaction to colleagues as wilful blindness. Abbott and those around him simply refused to see that the numbers had shifted, and could not accept that MPs were prepared to countenance Turnbull's return.

Turnbull had also spent the Friday before the challenge in Frydenberg's electorate. They did not discuss the leadership, but they did discuss the article in that morning's *Telegraph* on the reshuffle. Frydenberg could not believe the prime minister's office was behind it because it was so damaging. Surely they were not that silly. He also could not believe Turnbull was behind it, simply because the *Tele* would not have run it based on Turnbull's say-so—unless it was to say that Turnbull had said it.

The other thing that struck Frydenberg was the almost complete lack of preparation by Team Abbott in the face of Turnbull's challenge. He had worked for Howard, and knew that Howard would have known down to the last backbencher where they would stand in any ballot.

In February, he had been highly active in the media and in the talks with colleagues. This Monday evening, he appeared on Sky to pledge his support for Abbott, but that was about the extent of his involvement. Team Abbott had no battle plan.

Cormann was feeding intelligence into the defence team, which was being run out of Abbott's office. The main numbers sheet, such as it was, was held by Abetz.

Ensconced in Abbott's office for the duration were Loughnane, Credlin, and senior adviser Kate Raggatt. Others, including Robb, Cormann, Andrews, and Abetz, would drift in and out.

The two next-generation conservatives, Michael Sukkar from Victoria and Zed Seselja from the ACT, volunteered their services to help with the count, reporting back to Abetz.

Sukkar, with Abbott staying on as leader, stood to lose his marginal Victorian seat of Deakin, but put his philosophical interests as well as loyalty to the prime minister above his own survival.

Seselja had been leader of the ACT Liberals. Abbott had done as much as he could, above and beyond the normal remarks by a leader in support of an incumbent, to prevent Seselja knocking off Gary Humphries for the ACT Senate spot. Nevertheless, Seselja forgave him, because they were factional allies. Sukkar and Seselja were also best mates with Laundy, who was helping the other side.

Sukkar was housemates with Mitch Fifield, but was completely unaware that the man he shared a quiet beer with at the end of long sitting nights had switched, and was deeply involved in the Abbott coup. Only on the day did Sukkar get suspicious when Fifield didn't return his call.

Just politics—not personal.

Sukkar and Seselja had only been in the federal parliament less than two years. Never in their wildest dreams did they imagine they would be called on to try to help save Abbott's leadership. Neither of them could believe how ill-prepared Abbott, and those around him, seemed to be.

They had also read the *Telegraph* story on the Friday about the reshuffle. They spoke about it over the weekend. They agreed something was up, thinking the anti-Abbott forces were behind the story, simply because they could not see how Abbott could have benefitted from it in any way. Seselja got a few calls from journalists asking if he had heard anything to suggest a challenge might be on. He had not. He rang a few colleagues, who also professed not to know anything, although he was later convinced that at least one MP he had spoken to did know.

Just to be on the safe side, Sukkar and Seselja agreed over the weekend that they would dust off the list they had used at the time of the same-sex marriage debate, because it might come in handy.

They had begun working on that list since at least May, knowing the same-sex issue would blow up. The list, which they compiled meticulously, and used on 11 August to make sure that those who opposed same-sex marriage and opposed a free vote—particularly marginal-seat holders—spoke first, helped engineer a victory on the day for the prime minister.

This was a whole different ballgame.

On the morning of the challenge, armed with their list, Sukkar and Seselja had coffee. Seselja put out feelers to the prime minister's office: did the office want them to do some quiet counting? The office said 'Yes', with an emphasis on 'quiet'. They remembered what had happened in 2010 when Julia Gillard found out that Kevin Rudd as prime minister had asked his chief of staff, Alister Jordan, to take soundings of MPs. When news leaked, it gave Gillard the excuse to launch her assault on Rudd. Abbott's office did not want to do anything that would provoke Turnbull. Too late, she cried.

After question time, Seselja was sitting in the office of a senior staffer to the prime minister when Credlin walked in and announced, somewhat flustered, that Turnbull had just told Abbott he was going to challenge him. Using their list, he and Sukkar immediately began ringing around. They were not then, or later, aware of any detailed, comprehensive, or remotely reliable list of likely votes held by the prime minister. It was also strange that the pair had not been alerted and asked to help earlier, particularly after Bishop had been to see Abbott, given that they had already volunteered their services.

By the time the same-sex debate was brought on in August, they had been preparing for months. On this much more crucial confrontation, they only had a few hours. As it unfolded, they learned one of the most valuable lessons in a leadership stoush—the only people you can believe when you ask for their vote are the ones with the guts to tell you they won't be voting for you.

They soon realised that the prime minister's count, such as it was, was hopelessly out. No wonder the office had been dismissive of Turnbull's prospects. The two young conservatives found people in the wrong columns—for and against—so have no truck with suggestions by others that the prime minister's office had been on a war footing for a long time. One former Abbott supporter claimed:

'The prime minister himself and all of his staff knew there was going to be another problem. They were planning for it every day of the week. It was like they were at war with their own side.'

Not true, say Sukkar and Seselja. Or, if they were, their battle plans were hopeless. 'We were sucker-punched, hopelessly unprepared,' Sukkar said. They were fighting a rearguard action.

Twenty minutes before the party meeting was due to begin, Abbott was still making calls to shore up his support. One of the MPs he rang was Andrew Southcott. Southcott, who had voted for the spill in February, had already been sounded out by fellow South Australian Simon Birmingham. He was firmly in Turnbull's 'Yes' column. Abbott told Southcott he did not know why Turnbull was challenging, he did not know what had come over him, why he was trying to blow up the government in the lead-up to the Canning by-election. This was not the Labor Party, he told Southcott. Southcott told Abbott he was voting for Turnbull. He advised Abbott not to waste what little time he had left before the vote in talking to him.

By the time they walked into the party room, Sukkar and Seselja thought they might have had 52 votes for Abbott—a slim majority—but they were not confident. 'We applied a discount of between 10 and 15 per cent,' Sukkar said later. Even if Abbott had won so narrowly, they knew it would not be enough to end the insurgency.

It wasn't just the philosophical affinity that motivated Sukkar. He swears that if Turnbull were to come under challenge as prime minister, he would defend him, too, whether his seat depended on it or not. 'I would never, ever work against a prime minister,' he vows.

On Monday afternoon, after having resisted for more than a year the entreaties from his colleagues to remove Hockey, Abbott sent an emissary around to Morrison's office to ask him if he would run as his deputy in the ballot.

A lot of fire was directed at Morrison — including from Abbott himself — after it was over for not having done more to save Abbott or for not warning him the challenge was coming. As it happens, even if he had wanted to compel his supporters to vote for Abbott, it is doubtful that Morrison could have forced them — although there are several in the right who, so far, cannot forgive him for not trying. They believe he could have compelled them if he had wanted to. That is unlikely. Most of them knew by then that Abbott was a goner. Morrison could not have saved him, because Abbott had not done what he should have done to save himself.

It was also not true to say, as Abbott was to later allege and then retract, that Morrison had not delivered a warning to him.

On the Friday before the challenge, Morrison spoke with Credlin after he had attended a media conference with Abbott and Dutton. Referring to the leadership, Credlin asked him if he was aware of anything happening. He told her he did not know anything. However, he told her what the whole world knew, that things were 'pretty febrile'.

'I would be on high alert,' he warned her. It was intuition that made Morrison say this, rather than any particular knowledge that a move was imminent. That night, Abbott called Morrison as he was on his way to attend a function. Abbott thanked him for helping work out the policy on the 12,000 Syrian refugees when Morrison was co-opted on to the national security committee to help with the policy's formulation. Abbott did not mention anything else, including Morrison's conversation with Credlin, so Morrison didn't raise it either. It was a brief conversation. On the Sunday, when others were preparing for meetings or talking leadership, Morrison went to watch the Cronulla Sharks play the

South Sydney Rabbitohs. There, he ran into Labor's Anthony Albanese. They talked football, not politics.

Morrison's next conversation with Abbott on the leadership question was on Monday. Abbott's offer to Morrison to run on a ticket as his deputy would have bolstered Abbott's prospects, and maybe Morrison could have saved Abbott that night. But even if he had, it would have been a short-term thing, given the rampant dysfunction of Abbott's office, which was not about to change.

Morrison was seeking counsel from people he trusted, including Peter Costello and former Costello adviser David Gazard, with whom he had been friends for a long time, and who was with him in his office that afternoon. Along with a few others, such as Shane Stone, Lynton Crosby, and Mark Textor, he regarded Costello as a mentor. The bottom line in their advice to him was that if he accepted the offer, it would not be a long-term proposition. Obviously, he should stay true to his word and vote for Abbott, but he should not tie himself in too tightly: this ship was going down. It was inevitable.

Morrison appeared to his friends that night to be self-assured. After discussing Abbott's offer of the deputy leadership with Costello, Gazard, and others, he went round to see Abbott in his office. He wanted Abbott to spell it out—that as deputy leader, Morrison would have a choice of portfolios, and that Abbott therefore wanted him as his treasurer. Yes, Abbott said, that was what he wanted. Morrison asked Abbott if he had spoken to Hockey about this. He had not. Morrison, who has a habit of thinking a few steps ahead, asked the prime minister—assuming he accepted his offer—what the story would be the next day about what had happened to Hockey. There was no real answer. Morrison told Abbott he would think about it.

Morrison left Abbott's office. Within minutes, as he was heading to the house for a division, a couple of his colleagues asked him if it was true he was running for deputy. Morrison was staggered that this had been put about so quickly. He was also angry. He had already told Abbott's emissary that if word of the offer leaked out, that would be it—forget it.

Morrison spoke to Bishop, asking her if she was on a ticket with Turnbull. She said she wasn't. Morrison did not want to set himself up against Bishop. He also did not want to be deputy, with everything else that entailed. Although he had wanted to be treasurer, he did not want to dud Hockey like that, particularly as Abbott had given Hockey repeated assurances that his job was safe.

In any case, he knew that if Turnbull won, the job would be his.

Morrison went back to Abbott's office. He told Abbott the offer made no sense to him. He said he would not run for deputy. He said he did not want to throw Hockey under a bus. He told Abbott he would vote for him as he had promised, but he would not tell his supporters what they should do. This was a massive blow to Abbott. Morrison's view was that this was not a contest between him and Bishop, nor a contest between him and Hockey. It was a contest between Abbott and Turnbull.

Morrison left the prime minister's office and went straight to Hockey's office. Hockey was with his friend Andrew Burnes, the Liberal Party's federal treasurer. Morrison told Hockey what had happened. Hockey had only just found out himself that his job had been offered to someone else, behind his back. He was not a happy man. For what it was worth, Morrison told him he was not taking up Abbott's offer.

Morrison went back to his office and contacted David Speers at Sky News to tell him he was voting for Abbott, so that Speers could put it to air. Then he and Gazard sat watching it all on television while they ate a leftover curry that Morrison had made the weekend before.

This left Abbott without a running mate. Greg Hunt was sounded out — not by Abbott, but by someone close to him from the Praetorian Guard, in a rushed conversation to say that if Abbott won the ballot, they should talk, overnight, about Hunt running probably the next day for the deputy leadership, because Hunt would be well placed to go for it. Hunt did not know if Abbott had authorised the approach, or whether there was some freelancing going on. The mechanics of how the ballots would work under that scenario were also unclear to Hunt, but he thought it was irrelevant anyway, because he was sure Turnbull would win.

It was a wild night. If anything, it got wilder.

At 6.18 pm, after Morrison had conveyed his decision to Abbott, Abbott announced that the party meeting would be held in less than three hours. As Turnbull headed off to the party room, accompanied by his G8, Hendy said to Malcolm's wife, Lucy, 'Everything is on track. We are confident.'

Usually cool and collected, Lucy replied: 'I am glad that someone is.'

She wasn't the only one apprehensive. Inside the room, a nervous Scott Buccholz called for nominations for the leadership by asking candidates to 'please stand in your chairs'. Turnbull rose instantly; Abbott, a fraction of a second later.

There were no speeches.

The G8 had its contingency plans. If Abbott had called the meeting but not declared the leadership vacant, Hendy would have moved the spill motion.

Their numbers had all been predicated on a spill motion, knowing that if it got that up, there was no doubt the leadership vote would go their way. Within half an hour, Turnbull was elected leader, by 54 votes to 44.

Unlike in February, when then whip Philip Ruddock had handed Abbott the ballot paper, this time his replacement, Scott Buccholz, read out the result. MPs did not see the two men shake hands afterwards.

Turnbull spoke briefly, paying tribute to Abbott, saying he had been a great Liberal leader.

In his speech, Abbott began graciously, then soon descended into recriminations, confirming for many that they had done the right thing. Abbott said how disappointed he was to have been 'torn down' in such a way, such a short time into his tenure. Barely containing his anger, he did not admit to any mistakes, nor did he accept any responsibility for what happened. Instead, he blamed his own dire position and the government's on disloyalty and white-anting.

In the same way that he convinced himself he had not broken any election promises, and therefore was not lying when he said he hadn't, he also convinced himself that his downfall was all the fault of others. He never wavered from that view.

Twice, he told the room he had been 'torn down'. MPs believed he was directing those remarks to Bishop, who sat listening, stony-faced.

Turning his attention to the victor, he said that Turnbull had wanted the job for years, but now he had it, he would find out how difficult it was. 'This is a job for a steady hand,' he said, warning that someone with a more 'febrile personality' might find it difficult. He then made pointed remarks to the man who deposed him, saying: *Malcolm, you are wrong when you say I did not run a cabinet government; Malcolm you are wrong to criticise Hockey for his economic management.*

Whether out of shock, relief, guilt, or sympathy, MPs slowly stood and applauded when he had finished. Bishop, clearly offended, remained sitting for the longest time before standing and clapping.

The whip reminded Turnbull that the question of the deputy leadership also needed to be resolved. Turnbull turned to the room, hands outstretched, palms upward, asking what they wanted to do. A few voices called out it that should be done by acclamation, and leave it at that.

There was a very loud, very firm '*No*' to this suggestion. That came from Joe Hockey. Others called out 'Spill, spill.' More seconds passed after nominations were called for the deputy's slot. Turnbullites expected Peter Dutton would stand, but he didn't. Abbott had not asked him to run as his deputy. Other colleagues had sounded out Dutton, but he felt he had been damaged during his term as health minister because of the Medicare co-payment debacle. Dutton was aware even then that he had work to do to rebuild his standing inside the Liberal Party, including with the conservative wing. This was one thing he sought to remedy later, with mixed success, given his problems with things mechanical.

Turnbull was about to declare it a no-contest when Kevin Andrews stood up to declare he would run. Even though he got only 30 votes, the right was happy with that. They saw it as their base number, something they could build on.

When it was over, Roy hugged and kissed Bishop, thanking her for having had the guts to do what she did. McGrath, who had told Turnbull after he lost the leadership in 2009 that he should quit politics, visited her in her office on Thursday to personally thank her.

A small group, including Bishop, walked back with Turnbull to his office. Along the way, he stopped to officially tell the National

Party leader, Warren Truss, that he had been elected. They ran into Michaelia Cash, who also hugged Bishop. People peeled off. Hendy continued walking with Turnbull, who had been joined by four beefy blokes. 'Who are you guys?' Malcolm asked. 'We are your security detail,' they informed him. He shook their hands, then introduced them to Hendy.

People drifted in and out of Turnbull's ministerial office. Every now and again they would get shooed out of the inner sanctum and out to the staff offices, but they would gravitate back in. Michael Thawley had a quiet chat in one corner with the prime minister-elect. At one stage, Mal Brough opened the heavy timber door from inside the office, looked down the corridor, and called out to the others, with a meaningful inflection: 'Brian's here, everybody.'

All conversation stopped. They knew what had been going on. Loughnane walked in with the party president, Richard Alston. They congratulated Turnbull, then left soon after.

McGrath, Fifield, and Ryan pulled in to McDonalds at Manuka close to eleven o'clock that night after the vote. They ordered fries, Macs, nuggets, and Coke, and went to the Ryan-McGrath apartment. McGrath felt sick, couldn't drink, and didn't eat much. They were drained, strung out.

Birmingham stayed in Turnbull's office until close to midnight. He left Morrison and Bishop to their private conversations with him. Lucy was still there, wondering how she would get home. Birmingham gave her a lift in his car. Lucy was once again calm, taking everything in her stride. Birmingham was flat. He had listened to Abbott's speech in the party room, feeling sad that it had come to this. He drank probably half a glass of wine all night.

After the vote, Abbott walked back into his office, where his loyal staff were waiting for him in the foyer. He gave what one described as a remarkable speech about public service. He did not want them to lose faith. It stood in stark contrast to the one he had just given in the party room, and also the one he gave soon after in the cabinet anteroom where he, his staff, and supporters drank till almost dawn. One person who attended later described it as 'debauched'. Male MPs had their shirts off, dancing. Abbott stripped off his white business shirt to his white singlet.

His chief of staff gave a bitter speech to the assembled faithful, accusing his colleagues of treachery and undermining, saying it had been going on for six years, laying the blame at the feet of Turnbull and Bishop. Staff later described the speech as vicious. They remember that, as she vented separately to people at the wake, Credlin repeatedly called Bishop 'Lady Macbeth'.

Abbott followed Credlin with an equally bitter speech about the undermining and treachery that he said had brought him down, specifically naming both Turnbull and Bishop as perpetrators. He spotted his national-security adviser, Andrew Shearer, and finished by commiserating with him. He said Shearer would now not be going to Washington as ambassador to the United States. Staff had been hearing the rumours that Abbott was going to award him the plum post, and now this was confirmation of his plans. As it turned out, Turnbull plucked Hockey from under the bus and sent him to Washington.

Abbott's speech in the anteroom, unlike the one in the foyer of his office, revealed to staff that the enormity of what happened had sunk in.

Different people jumped onto an expensive marble-topped Italian table to speak or dance, but when Joe Hockey hopped onto it, the marble cracked. Hockey fell straight through the middle. People were initially shocked, worried that he might be hurt. They rushed to help, as did Abbott, sustaining a cut in the process that needed to be bandaged. The office medical kit was found, in amongst the detritus, the next day. Reassured that Hockey was OK, staff scooped up broken bits of marble to keep as souvenirs. (Abbott subsequently paid for the damage.) Jamie Briggs injured his knee when he tried to crash-tackle Abbott. He left before the marble cracked, but turned up to a party-room meeting the following morning in a wheelchair, so he looked like the chief suspect.

Was it any wonder that Abbott's advancer, Richard Dowdy, called out to Turnbull that he was a 'c—' as he saw the prime minister-elect approach down the corridor that night with his wife, Lucy, and Julie Bishop after their press conference? Dowdy then walked around the anteroom, telling people what he had done. They laughed about it. When he got back, Turnbull told people in his office what Dowdy had said. They were shocked. Weeks later, taking the advice of wiser heads, Dowdy wrote a letter of apology to Turnbull.

Others who had not voted for Turnbull behaved with dignity. Dutton had never had any problems with Turnbull, barely exchanging a cross word with him. He was bitter about Bishop's role, refusing to believe she had not been involved in the planning, but he thought Turnbull had behaved as well as any challenger could in the circumstances. No coup was pretty, but Dutton could see why it had been done; he could see the problems going all the way back to the SBS interview the night before the 2013 election, which had ended up saddling him with the impossible task of trying to sell the co-payment/Medical Research Fund.

At 10.38 that night, Dutton sent Turnbull a text. 'Mate congratulations on becoming prime minister. As [sic] amazing honour. I obviously offer my resignation and will do so formally tomorrow. I was loyal to Abbott as leader but sincerely offer you every success.' Turnbull rang him, basically to tell him not to be silly. Dutton kept his cabinet portfolio, but was dropped from the national security committee, which Turnbull's opponents later used against him.

Another key figure the day of the challenge was Brian Loughnane, later described as a member of Abbott's Praetorian Guard, who was feeding in intelligence on who he thought fitted where.

Turnbull supporters were incensed when they heard that the federal director of the Liberal Party was essentially trying to shore up support for the prime minister. They considered it highly inappropriate for a party official to become involved in what was essentially a matter for the politicians to sort out. He should have remained completely aloof. No other federal directors would have done it—they would have retreated to the federal secretariat, leaving the politicians to it.

However, Loughnane was 'family' in the way that no other federal director had been, because of his marriage to Credlin. Lines that had been blurred were now crossed. The conflict that people had warned about was manifest.

Hence the silence when Loughnane turned up in Turnbull's office the night of the vote. Talk about awkward. Normally, the party's federal director would be close by, ready to brief the new leader on messages for his victory press conference. But to go to the victor's office after spending the day doing what he could to ensure he did not win was bizarre. Loughnane's days were numbered. Julian Sheezel, Loughnane's deputy, was one option to replace him; however, he soon accepted Kelly O'Dwyer's offer to become her chief of staff. Sheezel had had every right, after the 2013 election, given the number of successful campaigns he had helped run, to expect that Loughnane would leave after a decent interval so he would finally be given a chance at the top job. In fact, Loughnane had wanted to leave and hand over to Sheezel, but Abbott had other ideas. Perhaps he was worried that Loughnane's departure might precipitate Credlin's departure, or he felt that he had to do whatever he could to preserve his shrinking inner circle.

When Abbott called Loughnane and Sheezel to his office in late 2014, it was not to organise a succession plan, which would have been a sensible exercise, and which had happened previously when Tony Eggleton made way for Andrew Robb, Robb made way for Lynton Crosby, and Crosby made way for Brian Loughnane. The meeting was to tell everyone he wanted them to stay where they were. He wanted Loughnane to stay as director and Sheezel to stay as his deputy. Loughnane acquiesced. It was telling that it was the prime minister, and not the federal president or the federal executive of the party, who was determining the leadership of the organisational wing of the Liberal Party.

Abbott's formal resignation as prime minister did not happen until late the next day.

Ever on the lookout for leverage, the Nationals presented the prime minister-designate with a new Coalition agreement. They could see the change coming, and had prepared secretly at a meeting weeks out, then finalised their demands at another meeting of all National MPs on the day of the challenge. They had a list of ten conditions. They wanted — among other things — to assume responsibility for water. They did not want the carbon tax back. They wanted a plebiscite on gay marriage. And they wanted more help for stay-at-home mums.

Truss spoke to Turnbull on the night, and they met again the next day. There was an unmistakeable message from the Nationals, not expressed by Truss in his discussions, but which was made clear via tom-toms to Turnbull, that if they did not get the lot, Turnbull would have no agreement. They had done their numbers, too, and they knew that without them, Turnbull could not form government. At 7.00 the next morning, Turnbull rang the former president of the Queensland LNP, Bruce McIver, seeking advice on how to deal with it. McIver had texted both Abbott and Turnbull on the Monday night, offering commiserations to one, and congratulations to the other. Abbott texted him back at 4.16 am.

McIver, who got along well with both men, advised Turnbull to 'be flexible'. Turnbull signed. It was not till after the agreement was signed that Abbott faxed his resignation to the governor-general. That, and the Nationals playing hardball, held up Turnbull's swearing-in for a few hours.

When he finally appeared in the prime minister's courtyard for the last time to deliver his statement, Abbott looked terrible—hollow and hungover. Staff say he had been throwing up in his office. Abbott did not blubber like Rudd had, but it was not a graceful exit. He did not mention Turnbull's name once. He claimed not to have leaked or backgrounded against anyone, which drew sharp intakes of breath from those who remembered otherwise. He promised there would be 'no wrecking, no undermining, and no sniping'.

He recapped his achievements, deplored the poll-driven panic that had produced a revolving door prime-ministership, and the sour, bitter, character assassination of media commentary.

He thanked his wife, Margie, for her grace and dignity throughout his public life, before thanking his staff, 'especially my chief of staff, who has been unfairly maligned by people who should have known better'.

His office played silly buggers. His staff spent three-and-a-half days shredding whatever documents they could lay their hands on, including all the files on the opposition. 'Six years of research just disappeared,' one despondent insider said. The password for the internal communications system was disabled. They were not asked to hurry up and vacate the office. Abbott left for the last time from the prime ministerial courtyard on Friday afternoon to fly home to Sydney, where Margie had stayed to pack up their possessions at Kirribilli House.

Those who knew him well, who had worked as closely with him as he allowed over his years in the leadership, who stuck to the end, for whatever reason, conceded privately later that, as outstanding as he was as opposition leader, Abbott simply wasn't up to the job as prime minister.

One cabinet minister who had voted for him said: 'As opposition leader he had purpose, he had conviction, he had stamina, he was consistent. He slaughtered them.

'He was very unlucky not to win in 2010—which was probably just as well, because we weren't ready in 2010.

'He never got comfortable with being prime minister; he never looked on top of the job.

'There was a lack of confidence. If he was presented with the information and the arguments, he invariably made the right decision. When there was little or no advice or alternative views, he made shithouse decisions. The captain's calls were a disaster.

'Every policy we took from opposition to government was a success. Except for the captain's call paid parental-leave scheme.'

Five weeks after the coup, Turnbull, with wife Lucy, got up early to go for a walk in Canberra. Turnbull pulled on a Wallabies jersey. As happened many mornings, their daughter, Daisy, still in bed with her husband, James, and their son, Jack, called her parents on the mobile for face time. When she saw him in the footy jumper, Daisy yelped that he really was prime minister. Turnbull had morphed into John Howard. It could have been worse. A lot worse.

His six years out of the leadership—as many as Howard, before he reclaimed the title—taught him a lot of things. One was to curb his temper. Another was to listen. Another was to consult.

Another was the pain of defeat that comes from massive public humiliation. Turnbull can be disarmingly frank, such as when he admitted he had lasted longer as leader the first time around than he thought he would, after the way he had stuffed up. He knows that one day what befell his predecessors could just as easily befall him. He had a taste of it as opposition leader. Painful as that was, it would not compare to losing the prime ministership.

Only a couple of weeks after he ascended to the top job, as he expressed empathy for Abbott's plight, he confided: 'It will probably happen to me one day.'

CHAPTER ELEVEN

Death before Dishonour

A week or so after the challenge, Ian Macfarlane spoke to Tony Abbott. Abbott had moved into his new digs, a backbencher's office, awkwardly located next to Bronwyn Bishop's. Bishop's revenge against Abbott was to vote for Turnbull in the leadership ballot, so two victims of a single helicopter crash shared a small slice of real estate reserved for those enduring an exquisitely agonising political purgatory. Even though she was kicking herself with her immaculate, sky-high stilettos, Bishop was handling her demise a whole lot better than her neighbour, telling people 'I just have to suck it up' as she declared to her constituents she wanted to stay on to fight terrorism.

Macfarlane later described his conversation with Abbott as 'very uncomfortable'. He was upfront, telling Abbott he had not voted for him. This came as no surprise to Abbott.

'Macca, I knew you would always vote for Turnbull,' Abbott said. Abbott was very angry, very hurt. The chief target of his anger was Turnbull, whom he believed had white-anted him. Julie Bishop was right up there, too, in that conversation. He was claiming she hadn't delivered the message she had told others, and that the first he knew there would be a challenge was when

Turnbull confronted him in his office.

Macfarlane was also feeling mightily aggrieved, although initially he did a pretty good job of hiding it. He had been one of Turnbull's staunchest supporters. Macfarlane's wife, Karen, had their bags packed ready to fly to Canberra for the swearing-in of Turnbull's first ministry when the new prime minister rang him on the weekend after the challenge to say he had some 'unhappy news'. Macfarlane had been dumped from cabinet, and from the frontbench altogether. He was gutted. He told me with considerable grace only a matter of days after he got that call, not long after he had spoken to Abbott, and well before his decision to defect to the Nationals became public, that he believed Turnbull would make a great prime minister. Above all else, he said he wanted the Coalition to win the next election. Macfarlane was clear in his own mind that this would best be achieved by his return to the cabinet, and that the best way to accomplish that would be for him to switch to the Nationals. His rationale for making the switch, apart from his restoration to the frontbench, was that it would provide stability for the Nationals after the departure of Warren Truss and what he expected would be the elevation of his deputy, Barnaby Joyce.

Macfarlane had driven to Maryborough to express his unhappiness to Truss the weekend after he received the 'unhappy news'. The two discussed it again before briefing Queensland's LNP president, Gary Spence, the Nationals president, Larry Anthony, then Joyce. Turnbull was told the day before it was announced on 3 December, the last parliamentary sitting day of the year. After the LNP executive aborted the defection, when he spoke to Turnbull, the typically blunt-speaking Macfarlane told his old friend: 'You've got more problems than I have.' Completely unrepentant about what he had done, satisfied that he had given it a 'red-hot go', he was alluding to the much more assertive approach many people were expecting from Joyce, which Macfarlane was arguing he could mitigate by his shift to the Nationals into a prominent position. Funnily enough, a lot of his Liberal colleagues, including Turnbull—despite his exterior calm—didn't agree with him.

So, in that other awkward early encounter, during which, Macfarlane swears, he did not tell Abbott he was contemplating defection, Macfarlane tried to explain to a battered former prime minister that his colleagues had removed him because they were worried that if he had stayed at the helm, they would lose government. Abbott rejected this absolutely. He believed—a view encouraged by Brian Loughnane—that when the time came to mark the ballot paper, Australians would not have voted for Bill Shorten to be prime minister. They would have voted for him.

They went back and forth a bit, neither conceding, until Abbott said: 'Macca, in the end, death before dishonour.'

Macfarlane was taken aback. 'What would John Howard say to that, Tony?'

Abbott replied: 'I don't care what John Howard would say to that—that's my view.'

Abbott was already furious with Howard for having called a press conference, the day after Turnbull's ascension, to appeal for unity. At his press conference, Howard, who would seldom complain about his treatment at the hands of media, even though there was more hostility across the board to him than there ever was to Abbott, rejected Abbott's claim that the media was in part responsible for bringing him down.

Abbott subsequently unloaded on Howard over a meal, where he repeatedly complained that the former prime minister's press conference had gone on for thirty-eight minutes—although it is unlikely he would have been any happier if it had only been for eight minutes. Howard had done as much as he could to help Abbott, from the beginning of his leadership to the end. He had given advice, much of which had been ignored, but he nonetheless felt Abbott's pain, describing him later as 'bruised'. He does not apologise for what he said the day after the coup. Reporters had arrived at his house early in the morning as he set off for his ritual walk, so he told them he would say something later in the day.

Like so many others, Howard had not wanted Abbott to fail. He was more than disappointed that he had. But the Liberal party room had spoken, and its decisions were sacrosanct. He could not criticise that. Nor did he criticise either man, except that he did take the opportunity to remind Turnbull that the Liberal Party was a broad church.

It was true that Howard had talked Turnbull out of resigning when he lost the opposition leadership in 2009. Turnbull rang him soon after he made his formal announcement that he was retiring from parliament, to say he thought he had made a mistake. They arranged to meet soon after. Howard told him all he had to do was reverse the decision. Turnbull worried about the embarrassment he would suffer if he did so. Howard assured him that the ridicule might last for forty-eight hours, then it would pass.

'You've got enough money. You don't need to go out and make any more,' Howard told him. He also remembers that, at that time, there was concern that without Turnbull the Liberals might lose his seat of Wentworth. He always thought that Turnbull was a talent, and felt he could continue to make a contribution to public life. Was there a part of Howard that also thought, *You never know what might happen*? Well, yes, of course there was, but that was not the prime motivation behind his effort to convince Turnbull to change his mind. He wanted Abbott to succeed. He thought Turnbull would have helped Abbott do that as treasurer, and that

Abbott would be the ultimate beneficiary as a result. But either out of loyalty to Hockey, or fear of Turnbull, Abbott wouldn't do it.

Howard had benefitted mightily from Peter Costello's work as treasurer, which guaranteed in every opinion poll that the government was way ahead on the question of which side was best equipped to manage the economy. Howard wasn't blind to Costello's talents, nor to his ambition. He was smart enough to use the former while thwarting the latter.

Howard also knows better than anyone that all leaders serve at the pleasure of their party rooms, and that his or her security of tenure depends on the support of their MPs. That was but one reason why he made sure his colleagues were always well-looked-after by himself as well as his staff.

Macfarlane took Abbott's 'death before dishonour' remark to mean that regardless of which of them was right, the honourable course for the party would have been to stick with him, rather than trash the Westminster system by discarding a first-term prime minister.

There had been a lot of tosh said and written about how the system was broken, that reform was now nigh-impossible, that the revolving door of prime ministers—with Abbott making it five in six years—was proof that something was profoundly wrong. Well, there was something profoundly wrong with the system: the quality of the people in it. Abbott himself acknowledged this point when he launched Paul Kelly's *Triumph and Demise* in August 2014, little more than a year before he was deposed:

> The system that produced the Rudd/Gillard government is the same system that produced the Hawke government, the same system that produced the Howard government. The Hawke government was undoubtedly the best Labor government in our

history, and along with the Menzies government, the Howard government can lay claim to being the best conservative government in our history.

If this system could produce, in the recent past, two outstanding governments, there is no reason why it can't, in the near future, produce other outstanding governments.

It's not the system which is the problem; it is the people who, from time to time, inhabit it.

Our challenge, at every level, is to be our best selves. The challenge for all of us and everyone in this room today as part of the system, is to lift ourselves so that we see the system at its best, not the system at its worst.

The mission, if I may say so, of the current government, is to demonstrate, through its action, ultimately through its record, that the last six years — the six years between 2007 and 2013 — is not the new normal; that it was in fact just a passing phase.

Our challenge — the challenge of the current government — is to show that the age of reform has not ended, it was merely interrupted. I believe it is absolutely critical for our country that we succeed in this task.

Clearly, Abbott had not risen to the challenge, yet his solution for the Liberal Party, when it was obvious a majority of his MPs had decided he had failed, was that they persist with him, even if it meant that he would lead them to glorious defeat after just one term. His solution was not a solution at all; it amounted to a suicide pact. Nothing about Westminster traditions implies that electors or parties are bound to stick with people who are clearly not up to the job. Or that people who are damaging the institutions they are meant to serve or protect — the parliament, the cabinet, their own parties — should be permitted to stay in the job until even more damage is done.

The most profound shock to 'the system' occurred on 11 November 1975, when the governor-general, Sir John Kerr, sacked the elected prime minister, Gough Whitlam. Walking along the corridors of old Parliament House that day and in the days that followed, I remarked to people that if this had happened in Greece or Cyprus, there would have been blood on the streets.

It was described then as a constitutional coup d'état. So it was. But it did not spark revolution nor terrorism, although if there was ever a time the system was going to go bust, it would have been that day.

The events of 11 November 1975 gutted millions of Australians. But they liberated or exhilarated millions more. Malcolm Fraser went on to serve as prime minister for seven years, winning in two landslide elections, before Bob Hawke toppled him to become Labor's most successful leader of all time, serving almost ten years. Paul Keating followed Hawke to win another election, giving Labor thirteen years in office. John Howard defeated Keating to rule for almost twelve.

Debates about the propriety of what Kerr did — the legality, the constitutionality, of his actions — have raged in the decades since. They will no doubt continue for decades to come. That's it. We talked about it. Lots. Many of us maintained our rage. Then we just got on with it.

Between late 2007 and 2013, the 'system' threw up three deeply flawed and deficient individuals who became prime minister, then the system rose up to eject them. The fact that this could happen is proof that it works well, that it does the job it was designed to do. The alternative would be to persevere with leaders to the point where structural damage is inflicted, where faith in the body politic is completely, utterly lost. There has been loss of faith in the body politic, already—no doubt about it. But to say that the removal of Kevin Rudd, Julia Gillard, and Tony Abbott was evidence that the system had become unworkable, or that it meant reform was no longer possible, was plainly ridiculous.

Less than two weeks after the Abbott coup, while the angry white male conservative commentariat that had nurtured Abbott still mourned, continuing to lash out at those they felt were responsible—everybody except the man himself, his divisive chief of staff, and the deficient cabinet he selected—there was a much more pragmatic view expressed by most voters. Anything but shocked, they either accepted that it had to be done, or were relieved that it had been. They could see it coming better than Abbott could.

Initially, there was not a massive bounce in the polls in the party vote, although Turnbull trounced Shorten as preferred prime minister. People were waiting to see what the new government would do. They had been taken in before by newbies, so they held back. However, in an early sign of what was to come, research conducted almost immediately after Turnbull's victory in the western suburbs seat of Lindsay, held by Fiona Scott with a margin of 1.2 per cent, showed a big bounce in support for the Liberals.

Gradually, the Coalition was restored to an election-winning position. Subsequent analysis of the first three months of Newspoll under Turnbull showed that he had lifted the Coalition's vote in the regions, in the cities, among women, and across age groups. It was a comprehensive endorsement of Turnbull, and a vindication of the decision to replace Abbott. This may or may not last, but one thing was obvious and indisputable: most people were overwhelmingly glad that Abbott was gone.

The professionals also had a much more realistic view, painful as the whole thing was for some of them. Ben Morton bravely spoke for them when he said: 'When the prime minister loses the support of their party room, regardless of how people remove him, or how unpalatable the measures are, there is only one person responsible. That's the leader.'

Liberal MPs reported a couple of branch resignations, although not of a magnitude to unsettle them.

Within days of the coup, George Brandis visited Longreach and Toowomba. Brandis, branded a moderate, expected to be monstered. It didn't happen. Conservative voters did not complain to him about what had occurred. They took a pragmatic, business-like approach. What they wanted most was for everyone to get behind Turnbull, and get on with the job.

In the immediate aftermath of the change, a couple of hundred people threatened to resign from the Liberal National Party in Queensland. Eventually, between thirty and forty people quit, but the ledger was more than balanced when hundreds joined. Ten weeks later, the *Courier Mail* ran a Galaxy opinion poll showing the Coalition on 58 per cent and Labor on 42 per cent, which—if repeated in an election—would garner the Turnbull government an extra two seats. In its online edition, the paper headlined a preview of a comment piece by its Canberra bureau chief, Dennis Atkins, with: 'Poll Proves Queenslanders Hated Abbott.' Ouch. Atkins, one of the most astute political commentators, had not said that. However, the Galaxy poll showed what the improved membership was already telling the party: people were very happy with the change.

Jamie Briggs—who soon came to grief as a Turnbull minister because of more silly late-night behaviour—found in the immediate aftermath of the coup that friends who previously could not find time to help with fundraising suddenly became available.

Whether they stick remains to be seen. Briggs will have to work even harder to hold on to his seat.

My pals from the Howard days, many of whom had vowed not to vote for the Coalition so long as Abbott led it, who were in despair over his conduct, were back in the fold. Before the challenge, I was taken aback by the vehemence of some of them. These were people who had devoted years to working for the Liberal Party. A few, through their new jobs, had dealt with the Abbott regime. They had found it a deeply unpleasant experience.

The footy finals season also followed soon after the coup. Those who had been prominent in the coup were stopped in the stands or in the boxes to be commended for what they had done. Others who had a lower profile, from more conservative areas, stayed quiet, not certain what the reaction would be.

Mitch Fifield was clear both before and after about what had needed to be done and why he had acted.

'In the first two years of government, we consistently failed in terms of our tone,' he told me later when I asked him why.

'We often sounded shrill, and looked like we were picking fights for the sake of it. It was almost as though the mark of a good minister was one who offended their stakeholders. Compounding this, the leaders of both major parties had vacated the centre ground.

'The public wanted change. They wanted a centrist government with a new leader and a civil tone. Malcolm Turnbull was the people's choice of leader. He has provided what they wanted in tone and approach to governing.'

Most of Abbott's principal supporters knew that the die had been cast in February 2015. Abbott was done for, from that day on. In retrospect, Turnbull was right not to put his hand up then, although it did not seem so at the time. It looked as if it might all pass him by, that he would get overtaken. However, the timing was all wrong in February. Even though mortal wounds were inflicted on Abbott, it was too soon to strike him down. Andrew Robb was right. People—the public, the party—needed time to get used to the idea.

They did very quickly, adding further to Abbott's hurt and humiliation.

Connie Fierravanti-Wells, appointed assistant minister (the new term for parliamentary secretaries) for multicultural affairs by Turnbull, said that although there had not been mass resignations, she feared that the switch to Turnbull would induce many party members to down tools and refuse to help out on election day.

Connie, who is as tough as they come in politics, also knew about disappointments after Abbott denied her a spot in the ministry by making her a parliamentary secretary. Some months after that, she and Abbott had a chat about it. Abbott complimented her on the way she had gotten on with her job, despite her disappointment. He told her that the character of people was forged by the way they dealt with disappointment, rather than on how they dealt with success.

After the coup, Connie relayed the same advice to Abbott. It was obvious that he wasn't taking it.

Barnaby Joyce also visited Abbott in his backbencher's office soon after he moved in. Joyce found it surreal. There were bodyguards still at the door. Prime ministerial memorabilia was displayed around the rooms. *Like last year's Christmas presents*, Joyce thought to himself. Abbott was still in shock. Joyce reminded Abbott of their conversation in August when he had tried to warn him they were coming after him. He wanted Abbott to appreciate that he had tried to do the right thing by him, even though he was convinced that Abbott's office, and Peta Credlin in particular, were instrumental in pressing Truss to stay in order to block him from the leadership for as long as they could. Joyce had asked Abbott at the time the reports surfaced if there was any truth to the suggestions that his office didn't want him as leader. Abbott said it was a 'complete fantasy'.

Others, claiming inside knowledge to the contrary, disputed that to Joyce. He believed them.

Joyce's conservative constituents were not happy with the way the Liberals had disposed of Abbott. Nor was Joyce. But after Abbott was gone, they also made it clear to Joyce that they just wanted everyone to get on with it. Later still, despite some lingering suspicion about Turnbull's social policies, they were more open in their opinions of Abbott as prime minister. He did not look comfortable in the job, or sound it, so consequently he made them feel uncomfortable, too.

Unlike some of his associates, Joyce remained confident that a Turnbull–Joyce combination would work well, so long as Turnbull didn't get fixated on issues that the Nationals believed were inimical to their interests. Like climate change, for instance. Joyce believed Turnbull's urbanity would be well complemented by his own — shall we say — more unconventional approach. Joyce was also smart enough, self-aware enough, to know that if he got there — and Truss strung out his retirement to see if either Michael McCormack or Luke Hartsuyker might emerge as rivals to Joyce — he needed to keep people like Matt Canavan around who were not afraid to tell him when he had gone over the top. He knew that, in order for him to succeed, Joyce would have to take their advice. The same observation pertains to Joyce as the one I made years ago about Abbott. He has the potential, as a leader, to be bad, or brilliant, or both. It's up to him.

Longstanding friendships were shattered by the leadership

battle. Christopher Pyne had known Abbott for many years. He was as close to Abbott as anyone could be, although it is possible, as he says, to have 'friends' but still be classed a loner, as others had observed about Abbott. They would have dinner at least once a week at Portia's at Kingston during sitting weeks in the Howard years.

Pyne made no secret of the fact that he had always voted for Turnbull. Even so, he had done as much as he could to ensure the success of the Abbott government. He described the events in September as traumatic, but concluded there was no other way out. Days after the coup. he texted Abbott, then wrote him a long letter. As this book went to press, Abbott had not responded.

Weeks after the coup, another long-time associate of Abbott's spent forty-five minutes with him. If anything, Abbott's state of mind had worsened. Abbott had moved out of his Spartan room in police headquarters and into the nearby apartment of Peta Credlin and Brian Loughnane. Loughnane told people he was the one who had invited the former prime minister to stay with them while he was in Canberra, because they were so worried about him.

Abbott's friend found him angry, bitter, and vengeful—particularly towards Bishop and Morrison. When his friend dared to criticise Credlin, Abbott gave him a silent death-stare that seemed to stretch for minutes, but actually lasted around ten seconds.

In a conversation with him, one cabinet minister who had stayed true asked Abbott if he was OK, warning him he would have red days and black days—days of anger as well as days of depression.

He would say he was OK, even though he didn't look it, but he was in no hurry to make a decision about what to do next. Some of them counselled him to go quietly for his own sake as well as the party's, gently warning him that if he tried to spoil or wreck Turnbull's government, history would judge him harshly.

Others reported that he was 'in a dark place'. Margie, according to people close to her, had behaved stoically. She stayed in Sydney while he remained in Canberra until the afternoon of Friday 18 September. She texted friends that what didn't kill you made you stronger, but she had, according to people close to the family, made clear to him that it was time he gave it away.

Weeks after his dismissal, over a meal with Loughnane and Credlin, Abbott was still focussed on the so-called treachery, wondering who, which staff, had leaked against him. He bitterly accused former staff or particular journalists of having run a jihad against him.

In subsequent interviews during which he defended his legacy, Abbott described as 'complete fantasy' reports of untoward behaviour by him or his office during his prime ministership. He staunchly defended Credlin, saying any complaints about her properly belonged to him. He was ultimately responsible for it. Which, indeed, he was. He rang former staff to plead with them not to speak to me for this book, or at least not to say anything that would diminish their achievements. Having tolerated their poor treatment for years, he now sought to convince them to keep it quiet.

In an interview with Peter Hartcher, in which he also tried to deny having sought my dismissal from *The Australian*, he continued to blame 'well-organised white-anting' from inside his government for his demise.

He was in a world of pain and delusion, unable to admit his own mistakes nor to concede that Credlin was culpable in any way. His internal support-base had largely disintegrated. Those philosophically in tune felt for him, but many of them had told him what he needed to do to save his leadership, and they had been ignored. They were looking forwards, not backwards.

They were sorry for him, but there are few pity votes in politics, and, a few months later, whatever public comments they were making, most of them were ready to move on. They wanted to resuscitate or rebuild their own careers, not continue to mourn his or, indeed, seek to resurrect it. Except Eric Abetz, who, despite everything, thought Abbott should be returned to the frontbench.

After his overthrow, Abbott's three regular defenders were Eric Abetz, Kevin Andrews—whose underwhelming performance as a frontbencher stretched across several regimes in a variety of portfolios—and Andrew Nikolic. Even Cory Bernardi grew weary.

Abbott called Bernardi to ask him to go out in defence of his government in early December 2015, following the publication of a series in Fairfax Media on his downfall. Bernardi told visitors to his office he was sick of being asked to go out to publicly defend the former regime. He says he told Abbott he should get someone else. 'Who?' Abbott asked.

In the early stages of his grief, word seeped out that he was promising the second Abbott government would be better than the first. Abbott told one businessman—someone who had quite liked Abbott—that he knew what he had done wrong, and when he became prime minister again, he would be better.

Obviously, it was a painful adjustment for Abbott and Credlin.

When Kevin Rudd was sacked by the party, his young press secretary, Lachlan Harris, told the prime minister's office staff to keep working. He advised them that if they made themselves useful, perhaps they would be kept on. Many of them were.

Credlin did the exact opposite, in a crystal-clear address to Abbott's staff at a meeting the day after the coup. Tony Nutt, who was handling the transition, had relayed a request from Turnbull to address the staff. Actually, Turnbull's staff had made contact with Credlin to try to arrange it, but she was not responding well. Credlin gathered staff inside the prime minister's office and told them she had rejected Turnbull's offer, even though he was seeking to reassure them there would be jobs for them if they wanted to remain. She told Abbott's staff she would help them find new jobs.

'No one is to work for the other side,' Credlin told the staff.

'If he [Turnbull] wants to be a good prime minister, he's going to have to learn to do it on his own.

'I've worked for him before and I am a hard worker, but working for him almost gave me a nervous breakdown.'

The next day, she had a screaming match with Nutt, where she also broke down and cried.

Turnbull ensured that the staff received generous payouts. He also agreed to additional benefits for Abbott. He didn't want to do anything that would increase the pain they were all suffering. Nor, obviously, did he want to provoke public outbursts or background briefings claiming they were being ill-treated.

Abbott made at least one significant job request towards the end of the year. It was not for himself; it was for Brian Loughnane, who had resigned as federal director to be replaced by Tony Nutt. Abbott wanted the new regime to appoint Loughnane as ambassador to the Vatican. He was deadly serious.

Even though there were those who thought it would be a good idea for Loughnane to be sent to the Vatican (or even better if Abbott himself were interested in it, which he would not have been, given his earlier rejection of the high commissioner's job in the UK), there was considerable resistance inside the new government to the idea of appointing the former federal director to a cushy diplomatic post.

His request was wisely denied by Turnbull. Opponents had feared a backlash, both from the Loughnane–Credlin enemies inside the Liberal Party, as well as outside from the community. 'Can you imagine how ridiculous that would look?' one incredulous senior government figure asked. Well, yes.

Abbott also sought assurances that there would be no recriminations against Credlin, that if she was seeking or was approached for a private-sector job in Australia, she would not be 'blackballed' or 'blacklisted' as a result of interventions by members of the new government.

Credlin's edicts to staff not to work for Turnbull stood in stark contrast to her public comments a few days later at the *Australian Womens Weekly* event where she said that she wanted the new government to do well. They also stood in stark contrast to what had happened in 2009, when Turnbull allowed Abbott to speak to his staff (which included Credlin), so they could be reassured about their futures. They had welcomed that at the time.

Abbott's appeal for there to be no recriminations against Credlin also stood in stark contrast to his own behaviour towards those of his former staff who went to work for the new administration, and also his own words in the prime minister's courtyard the day after he lost the leadership, where he pledged to make the change as easy as he could, declaring that: 'I want our government and our country to succeed. I always have and I always will.'

Abbott's former finance adviser, Kathryn Lees, who, in spite of everything, still spoke well of Abbott, also went to call on him in his new office, only for him to close his door in her face. Lees, pregnant with her first child, had accepted a job in the office of the new cabinet secretary, Arthur Sinodinos.

Abbott behaved very badly when he rang one former female staffer — not a policy adviser — who had joined Turnbull's office.

She could hear another voice, male, prompting Abbott as he asked her what she was doing. When she told him, he told her he was 'disappointed' she had crossed over, because 'they' had done bad things 'to us'. Later, Abbott got an attack of the guilts, and texted his former staffer, who had been extremely distressed by his call, to say that, although he was disappointed, he was glad she was doing something she loved because she was good at it.

Early on, when Credlin heard of people who were approached to stay on with Turnbull, she would either tell them 'you can't work for Malcolm' or, if they had agreed to do so, she would engage in textual harassment of them.

She texted one woman, who was employed in a junior role in the Turnbull office, that if there was anything she could do to help her find a job she would, adding ominously that she had read that some support staff had joined the Turnbull team. Then came the crunch line, or the punch line, with its unmistakeable intent. She said she had assured the PM [Abbott] 'that wasn't you, because I am sure you would take the payout, and the PM [Abbott] was pleased.' Here were shades of the filled-with-darker-meaning text to Senate president Stephen Parry. Other advisers who signed up were also repeatedly texted.

They had mortgages and families to support. Or they were committed to the cause. They did not want Bill Shorten to become prime minister. Plus, they were sick of being pushed around. Abbott and Credlin's behaviour was inexcusable.

Good people were brought back to work for the new government. Phil Gaetjens, Costello's former chief of staff, who went on to become head of the New South Wales Treasury, a man with a wealth of experience, signed up as Morrison's chief of staff. Nigel Bailey, who did more than anyone else to get Costello through the 1998 election fault-free on tax, who also helped with the design of the 2007 Howard–Costello tax cuts, and who had also worked with Gaetjens in the New South Wales Treasury, became chief of staff to Arthur Sinodinos.

Tony O'Leary was brought in part time to help with media and communications. Yes, my husband, Vincent Woolcock, was also taken on part time to help with advancing.

Silly rules that had made life harder than it needed to be were reversed. Areas of the executive wing where staff had been forbidden from walking, which they assumed was for security reasons, but which were actually due to the command-and-control approach of the former prime minister's office, were suddenly opened up — as was the entrance foyer to the prime minister's office that separated one suite of offices from another.

Abbott embarked on a series of interviews, including one less than a week after he was dumped as he was coming out of the surf, to dump on Morrison, denying that Morrison had warned him or his office.

He had to recant when Ray Hadley questioned him about it a few days later. Yes, there had been a conversation, Abbott admitted, but his office [Credlin] had put a different 'construction' on it than had Morrison. Of course. It was just like his dismissal of Scott Buccholz's warning to the office about Hockey as a 'complete invention', or his other admonition to me not to accept the word of his ministers because they lied, or his refusal to admit he had broken any promises.

Lots of lies were told in those two years, no doubt about it.

In private conversations with his old allies, Abbott continued to rail against both Scott Morrison and Julie Bishop, blaming them both for his downfall. Right-wing MPs remained disappointed with Morrison; but while it is possible they will forgive him, in time, they are not prepared to forgive Bishop. They are building for an assault on her position as deputy after the 2016 election. The thirty votes against her is the base for the disgruntled. If they can build on it, they will have a go. Early on, it looked like Peter Dutton would be their candidate, although he stalled his rehab in late 2015 by accidentally sending a text to Sam Maiden, instead of to Jamie Briggs, calling her a 'mad fucking witch'.

Dutton should not have been providing succour to Briggs, who had been forced to resign over an incident in a bar with a young female diplomat; he should have been counselling him.

Bishop knows that her biggest defence against their challenge will be her performance. If she continues to shine as foreign minister, if she remains the second most-popular figure in the government, if she continues to help her colleagues whenever or wherever they ask her — requests spurred by constituents who admire Bishop — she will remain in the job. If she falters, they will go for her.

Abetz was roundly abused by Credlin on more than one occasion. Despite this, when questioned about her behaviour, he defended her, he counted Abbott's numbers, and he rallied round when he was dumped. Yet news that Bishop's chief of staff, Murray Hansen, was present at Peter Hendy's the night before the coup was enough to propel Abetz in front of the cameras to complain about inappropriate behaviour of staff. Again, he was demonstrating his loyalty to conservatism, this time above consistency.

Luke Simpkins, for one, does not think that Bishop could have saved Abbott.

'I don't see how anybody could say that Tony was ambushed, or not warned, or deceived — apart from people who said they would vote for him and didn't,' he told me later.

'He had the chance to get it right [after February]. It is completely unreasonable for people who are not really connected to the views of the real world to say we were somehow going to win under Tony.'

Abbott was desperate to reconnect, but his private behaviour continued to puzzle colleagues, while his public behaviour infuriated or disappointed them, particularly in view of his pledge not to snipe or undermine or wreck. A few weeks after the vote, one backbencher who had voted for Abbott told me if there was another ballot that day, Turnbull would win by 80 votes to 20.

Before he flew out for London to deliver the Margaret Thatcher lecture, an excited Abbott told a friend: 'I am being taken to the south of France. I don't know where — it's a surprise.'

News broke that a villa had been rented. He was going to spend time there with Credlin and a couple of other former staff. His wife, Margie, who had accompanied him to London for the Thatcher lecture on 27 October, flew back home on her own. He flew to Paris.

He spent his 58th birthday in France with Credlin, the c-bomber Richard Dowdy, and former media aides Nicole Chant and Adrian Barrett. At least two people who voted against him contacted him to wish him well. Macfarlane rang to sing him a gravelly happy birthday. Warren Entsch texted his best wishes. For many of his colleagues, the whole thing was as bizarre as some of the events they had witnessed during the Abbott–Credlin tenure. It sent the rumour mill into overdrive.

Abbott's speech in London, urging Europeans to follow Australia's lead in turning back boats, was his first clarion call to conservatives. Using national security, he was desperate to consolidate his capital-C conservative base.

Abbott was reactivated again after the co-ordinated attacks on Paris by IS terrorists, arguing there should be at least SAS troops on the ground in Syria. He and former defence minister Kevin

Andrews launched regular multi-frontal assaults on Turnbull, once again designed to convey the impression the new prime minister was weak on terrorism.

Abbott also wrote a highly charged opinion piece for the *Daily Telegraph*, in which he urged a reformation of Islam and claimed cultural superiority for the West. He knew exactly the impact his words would have. Once again, he propelled himself into the spotlight, despite his repeated claims that none of it was about him. This was as disingenuous as his claim that by speaking out on what he regarded as falsehoods, he was actually helping Turnbull, because it protected his record, and his record was the foundation of Turnbull's record.

Abbott demanded bipartisanship from Labor on national security, which he received, despite continual prodding to see if he could open up a wedge. Yet he had no compunction, as a former prime minister who knew the weight his words would carry, in separating himself from Turnbull on national-security issues. He was playing a dangerous game in a volatile sphere; but, then again, subtlety was never his strong suit. There is a fine line between legitimate, open debate to foster constructive change, and providing succour to ultra-conservatives, or positioning to embarrass your successor. Abbott was dangerously close to crossing it.

Of course, as a former prime minister he has every right to speak out. But he also has a duty to ensure he does not say or do anything that would foment community unrest. He was fostering the impression that, having used national security to gain advantage while in office, he was prepared to use it to claw back some standing now that he was out of office.

The dissemination of sensitive material pertaining to national security, which had become a feature of Abbott's tenure and which was privately deplored by the country's most senior national-security advisers, continued with a leak to *The Australian*'s Greg Sheridan that the director-general of ASIO, Duncan Lewis, had counselled MPs to watch their language on Islam and Muslims in the wake of Abbott's opinion piece.

In fact, Lewis had not stomped all over free speech. MPs had not been told to stop speaking out, as the Abbottophiles tried to make out—only that they should choose their words carefully.

Lewis had spoken to two MPs, Andrew Hastie and Dan Tehan, the chair of the parliamentary joint intelligence committee. They, with Lewis's encouragement, spoke to other colleagues, and before too long the Abbottophiles, who had not spoken to Lewis, were briefing journalists about their version of events.

It was made to look as if Turnbull was using ASIO as a political weapon to get back at his opponents or to silence them.

Lewis had not behaved improperly. Turnbull later made it clear that he was happy for Lewis to continue talking to people, while admitting to the *Sunday Telegraph*'s Samantha Maiden that he had given Hastie's number to Lewis.

Hastie, who had been commanded in the SAS by Lewis, later said: 'At no point did I feel my ability to speak my mind was affected.' Tehan also dismissed suggestions that Lewis had in any way sought to exert improper pressure.

While Lewis was in effect conveying the widely held view of security analysts that Abbott's choice of language, even while prime minister, was inappropriate, he had been following the previous practice of his predecessors by speaking to politicians. Former colleagues believe he might have erred by referring to 'blasphemy' in an interview with the *Sunday Telegraph*'s Samantha Maiden, but they defended his discussions with MPs.

'People who were figures of substance on both sides, I tried to keep in the loop,' one former ASIO chief told me. 'I would talk to significant figures on both sides, regularly.' He rejected outright suggestions that Lewis had behaved inappropriately.

'Directors-general don't play games of that kind. People who run the system have to do their job as effectively as they can. It's not a game for them, it's not a joke — they see all the evidence.'

For some, positioning on the issue of national security had strong politically strategic motivations; for others, it was profoundly personal.

In an interview on Sky on 29 November, cabinet minister Josh Frydenberg went public with strident criticisms of Australia's grand mufti, Ibrahim Abu Mohamed, for initially failing to go in hard enough against the Paris attacks. Frydenberg, who is Jewish and who was in Paris soon after the attacks took place, also called for reform of Islam, echoing the words of his former leader.

At the following cabinet meeting, Frydenberg broke down during a general discussion on national security when he was talking about the need for armed guards at Jewish schools and other institutions. He was arguing for federal money to be made available to help pay for them.

Frydenberg began crying as he tried to speak of the potential dangers for Jewish families, including his own. He was so overcome he could not continue. He was, according to several sources, sobbing uncontrollably. Frydenberg's startled colleagues began asking if he was OK. Turnbull told the health minister, Sussan Ley, who was sitting next to Frydenberg, to give him a hug. She patted his hand, trying to soothe him until he regained his composure.

Frydenberg's emotional outbreak inside the cabinet room, and his unapologetic attack on the grand mufti, combined with Abbott's pushing and prodding and the right's opportunistic assault over the Lewis briefings, showed just how fraught the issue was for the government—and how careful Turnbull needs to be in his handling of this, as well as so many other tricky issues where right and left divide.

However, the suggestions by some that Turnbull was lacking a sure touch in this area—as if Abbott's warning about the death cult coming to get us, his threat to shirtfront the Russian president, his proposal to send 1,000 troops into the Ukraine after the downing of MH17, and the constant flow of information from the national security committee to the tabloids showed some deep affinity for the area that Turnbull lacked—stretched credulity.

Gareth Evans had a name for Abbott's affliction. He once called it Relevance Deprivation Syndrome. Abbott was in part battling to burnish his legacy, and in part trying to make his case for restitution, at least into cabinet. He would have to undergo his own version of the enlightenment, admitting his culpability and that of those around him, before there could be any hope at all of this. There was no sign whatsoever that such a transformation was happening as Abbott searched for meaning in his new life, considering then rejecting an offer for a new think tank to be created especially for him, as well as dismissing the job of Australian High Commissioner in London. Abetz led the charge again, after Jamie Briggs resigned and Mal Brough stood aside for Abbott to come back into the cabinet. Turnbull rightly dismissed it.

It is difficult enough for former prime ministers to construct a life outside parliament; even more difficult for them to resurrect their careers or rebuild their lives inside parliament. History is littered with examples of those who stayed and failed: John Gorton, Billy McMahon, Gough Whitlam. As diligent as Abbott is in glossing over his failures, his acolytes are right when they say he is no Kevin Rudd—at least in a couple of important respects. Rudd's midnight assassination came as such a shock, at a time when it was still possible for him to go to an election and win, that there was still residual regard for him in the electorate. Plus Labor had no one else to turn to after Julia Gillard's leadership collapsed. In Abbott's case, a majority of Australians wanted him gone more than his party did, if that was possible. And if Turnbull fails, the party has plenty of other candidates: Julie Bishop; Scott Morrison, more immediately; later on, Christian Porter; later still, Angus Taylor, if he works harder on the whole humility thing.

Undaunted, almost exactly a year after he signed his own death warrant as prime minister with the announcement of a knighthood for Prince Philip, Abbott announced he would recontest his seat. Whatever motivated him — a mixture of pride, ego, a desire for retribution, absolute conviction that the conservative cause could only be entrusted to his safekeeping, an inability to find a single other occupation that could satisfy him, or the belief that he could one day regain the leadership — Abbott decided to stay. There was not a scintilla of evidence to indicate he would be happy as the humble backbencher from Warringah. There were no signs in the weeks leading up to his decision, or after, that his preoccupation was how best to be a team player, or that he had reflected honestly on the causes of his removal. In fact, the opposite was the case.

After his announcement, he delivered his second clarion call to conservatives in a speech to a right-wing Christian group in the US, the Alliance Defending Freedom, on the virtues of marriage. He blamed his political career for his absences from home, which he acknowledged had placed a great burden on his wife, Margie, and, intriguingly, according to an extract published in *The Australian*, argued rather elaborately that the job of policy-makers was 'less to be role models as spouses and parents than to build the best possible conditions for families to flourish'. As a rationalisation for any perceived personal failings, it was positively Jesuitical.

His opposition to same-sex marriage was more straightforward; however, unlike some of his colleagues, he said later that if the plebiscite passed, the parliament should reflect the will of the people.

Turnbull kept his cool, defending Abbott's right to speak, but the former prime minister's ADD provided daily distractions from the government's agenda, and gold for the media.

Turnbull made a brilliant beginning. He used the sunny side of his personality as a policy tool to boost confidence, but by the end of the year and the beginning of the next, with factional brawls over preselections, combined with Abbott's decision to stay in parliament and to search for the spotlight, it was obvious Turnbull was going to need a lot more than that to succeed. Another early sign that he was learning to sidestep landmines was his dismissal of the untimely calls to push ahead for a republic.

His first ministry had sent a message of inclusion and regeneration. Abetz and Andrews were dumped. The country got its first female defence minister, Marise Payne, without a murmur of complaint from the military establishment, or barely a word of regret over Andrews' removal, except from Andrews himself. Payne, Michaelia Cash, and Kelly O'Dwyer joined Julie Bishop and Sussan Ley in cabinet.

Those who had helped get him there were kept close. They remained his policy and political confidantes. Arthur Sinodinos was appointed cabinet secretary. Peter Hendy, James McGrath, and Scott Ryan were made assistant ministers in roles connected to his portfolio. Mitch Fifield took over Turnbull's previous portfolio of communications, with the arts attached. Wyatt Roy became an assistant minister.

There was also no retribution against those who had not voted for him, such as Andrew Robb, Mathias Cormann, Greg Hunt,

Peter Dutton, Josh Frydenberg, and Christian Porter. This did not stop the old, angry, white male conservatives from claiming there had been a purge of the right. They were doing their best to create friction. However, the young new right—people like Fifield, Ryan, Mathias Cormann, Peter Dutton, Zed Seselja, Michael Sukkar, and Taylor—will help set the course for conservatives, if Abbott steps back and gives them a chance to get on with it. That did not seem likely, at least in the short to medium term.

Brough's prior involvement in the James Ashby–Peter Slipper affair came back to haunt him and to plague Turnbull. Brough had to stand aside as special minister of state in late December, the same day that Briggs quit over his most recent late-night indiscretion. Macfarlane's aborted defection turned out to be messy; the national-security debate, disorderly. Even though the economy was doing better—confidence was up, and unemployment down—the budget was still in dire straits, with deficits stretching way beyond the horizon.

With the election looming, Turnbull and his key ministers were trying to formulate both a tax policy and a budget. It was like a new government starting from scratch, facing more pointed barbs from within its own ranks than from Labor and having, at the most, less than a year to fix it.

The findings of the royal commission into trade union corruption vindicated Abbott's decision to call it. It was a damning indictment of sections of the labor movement, but elicited a pathetic response from Bill Shorten and other serving Labor MPs, who somehow managed to sound angrier about commissioner Heydon than the malfeasance he exposed. Labor needs to do much much better than that—not just on this issue, but on many others—to regain public trust. They can't sit back and expect that Abbott and his remaining acolytes will do it all for them, although they have been doing their best.

Days, weeks, or mere months after Abbott had pledged not to snipe or undermine or wreck, his words sounded even more hollow than they had on the day he delivered them. Then again, he had always been at his most effective as opposition leader. Slipping back into that role was easy for him — except this time he stepped into the job, without benefit of a vote, from inside the government and against his own party. Obviously he could hurt Turnbull, but the greater damage could ultimately be to himself. Disappointed Liberals who compared his prime ministership to Billy McMahon's will now be tempted to draw comparisons with the ratty side of Billy Hughes and Rudd, too, after he stalked Gillard.

The more bloody-minded of the capital-C conservatives relished the contest. They would like nothing better than a schism within the broad church of the Liberal Party, even if that risked Bill Shorten becoming prime minister: bad luck for the country, but an essential part of the cleansing process for the Liberal Party, because it would purge Turnbull.

Former long-serving Queensland Liberal MP Alex Somlyay scoffs at Abbott's claims that he had never undermined colleagues, dismisses his assertions that he was brought down by white-anting, and continues to bemoan his lack of discipline during the early opposition years.

Somlyay was chief whip during the leaderships of Brendan Nelson, Malcolm Turnbull, and then Tony Abbott till the 2010 election, after which Abbott dumped him. Abbott gave Somlyay a bottle of Blue Label whiskey to apologise for going back on his word to keep him as whip, but also for going back on his word to back him for the deputy speaker's role.

Somlyay was not mollified. 'Tony, you are a pathological liar. That's your problem, you are a pathological liar,' he says he told him. Somlyay saved the whiskey to drink at the time of Abbott's demise.

He always remembered the note from Abbott that accompanied the bottle, saying that one day he would probably feel the way Somlyay did, acknowledging that his turn would come, too.

Somlyay recalls that when Abbott was leader he insisted on everyone being part of the team and playing a team game, but his own behaviour fell well short of what was required when he was an opposition frontbencher.

'He missed more divisions than anybody else. We were always chasing him to come into the house to handle bills. He wouldn't turn up. We had to get people like Louise Markus to do it,' Somlyay told me.

Somlyay recalled one critical night in opposition when Abbott goofed off. Abbott had gone to the dining room to have dinner with Peter Costello, Kevin Andrews, and Peter Dutton on the night in February 2009 when parliament was debating Rudd's second stimulus package.

Somlyay sent the whip's clerk, Nathan Winn, to get the group down to listen to Turnbull's speech. They said no, but they would be down for the divisions, which Somlyay thought was fair enough. Somlyay says the staffer noticed six empty wine bottles on the table.

Come the first division, the other three arrived in the chamber and duly voted. Abbott did not appear. Somlyay rang from the chamber to tell Winn to find Abbott and get him into the chamber to vote. Winn took along another staffer, James Newbury—whose employment in government was subsequently blocked by Credlin after a screaming match with Abbott that could be heard by other staff—because he was a bit frightened of what he might find. Newbury was the one who walked into Abbott's office and found him stretched out on his couch. He shook him a number of times, but there was no response.

'He was asleep. They couldn't wake him,' Somlyay recalled. 'He was so drunk. The next morning, Abbott rang me to say, "Mate, I am so sorry I missed that division. I fell asleep. I spent the whole weekend with the fire brigade."'

Somlyay wrote to him, upbraiding him for his repeated absences, counselling him to show more loyalty to the leader. He says Abbott never replied. He gave Abbott another piece of advice when he was chairman of the backbench health committee and Abbott was health minister — a good minister, Somlyay thought, although, as his parliamentary secretary in the first year, Trish Worth carried a lot of the load.

Somlyay told Abbott it was goal-kickers who won games, not head-kickers. 'Yeah, mate, but I love kicking heads,' Abbott replied. Therein lay the problem.

Others recalled Abbott's actions when Turnbull's leadership was under extreme pressure. As Turnbull's deputy, and with his permission, Bishop began taking soundings from backbenchers to assess their views on his support for Kevin Rudd's Carbon Pollution Reduction Scheme. They were deeply divided. She told Turnbull he was in trouble, but he was loathe to believe it. Talk about déjà vu all over again. Bishop sought Turnbull's permission to brief shadow cabinet on her findings. Again, he agreed, so she did.

The one person who later contacted Bishop to elicit more detail about the backbenchers' complaints was ... Tony Abbott. Talk about déjà vu all over again, again. Bishop had made up a list divided into columns, with backbenchers placed according to whether they supported or opposed Rudd's scheme, or supported some action being taken or none at all. Abbott asked for the names of MPs and where they lined up. She did not think anything of it at the time, other than that it was the first time in opposition that Abbott had shown any real interest in an issue.

Back then, she had also attended meetings with Abbott, as well as Hockey, where they discussed her position and their intention to challenge Turnbull. As she was to do with Abbott six years later, she warned Turnbull that they were coming to get him.

Abbott began the 2009 parliamentary year comatose on his office couch, and ended it by winning the Liberal leadership by one vote. Four years later, he was prime minister. Little more than six years later, he was back where he started. All of it wrought by his own hand. Is it any wonder he had trouble coming to terms with it?

In one way, his ascendancy made Credlin's role in enforcing discipline on Abbott all the more remarkable. However, the way it was enforced, the manipulation, the focus — on the fighting, the campaigning, the exclusion or alienation of almost everybody else who truly mattered — was lopsided, antithetical to good government, and ultimately destructive.

The legendary former federal director of the Liberal Party, Tony Eggleton, who has been witness to so much of modern Australian political history, once said that Abbott's focus and tenacity made him one of the best opposition leaders he had ever encountered. This was high praise from a man who had worked with Malcolm Fraser and Maggie Thatcher.

For seven years, Eggleton would frequently ran into Abbott early in the morning on Red Hill, a long spit from Parliament House. Eggleton walked; Abbott cycled. Abbott would peddle slowly and stop for a chat. Credlin was never mentioned. Nonetheless, by the end, Eggleton concluded that Credlin's role as chief of staff, and the extent of her influence, put Ainsley Gotto in the shade.

Eggleton was discomfited by the removal of a first-term prime minister, but he too could understand why it had happened.

A few devoted readers (only seeking to be helpful, of course) have harked back to my assessment of Abbott in *So Greek,* completed two days after his ascension to the opposition leadership by one vote. While paying tribute to him for having ticker, and looking forward to seeing him rattle Rudd's cage, I expressed doubts that he would ever be elected prime minister unless he moved to the centre, widened his circle of advice, and didn't allow his religion to infect his politics.

The real point always — even then — was whether Abbott was up to the job.

Turnbull is only too familiar with the dictum that all political careers end in tears. He alluded to it soon after he became prime minister, when he said he would probably go the same way as Abbott went. Those who doubted his courage, who thought he didn't have the guts to challenge, were proved wrong. Those who questioned his judgement might also be proved wrong, particularly if he listens to the wise heads around him in his office, in his ministry, and in the wider party, including Howard. We shall see.

Turnbull not only had to learn how to be prime minister, but he also had to learn how to be the leader of that hybrid beast called the Liberal Party. He has to succeed in both roles if he is to last longer than his three predecessors. Those who know him best, those who deal with him daily, swear that he has changed, swear it is true that he not only listens, but that he encourages people to tell him where he has erred and how he can do better, that he seldom if ever raises his voice, and only then if it is warranted.

He knows all the things that went wrong with his own leadership the first time around. He watched while Abbott and Credlin travelled down their road to ruin, even as they had watched Kevin Rudd and Julia Gillard travel down theirs.

It is all, now, entirely in Turnbull's hands. He does not have to follow the same road.

Acknowledgements

Just before the publication of my first book, *So Greek: confessions of a conservative leftie*, I sent a fax of the cover to my brother, Steve, so he could show our mother, Elpiniki. The cover featured a photo of me taken many years before, standing on a cliff top in Cyprus.

My publisher, Henry Rosenbloom, was reluctant to use that photo, but I told him not to worry, as the only person who would recognise that it was me was my mother.

Anyway, when Steve showed it to her, she looked at it a long time before she asked: 'She looks familiar, who is she?' I thought at the time, if I ever wrote another book, and I never thought I would—to paraphrase Peter Costello when he said he only had one more budget in him, I reckoned I only ever had one book in me—that that would make a good title.

I certainly never thought I would write a book about Tony Abbott's brief prime ministership. First, I confess I doubted there ever would be one. Second, when he got there, I thought his career would outlast mine. Ten months into his tenure, after he tackled me at *The Australian*'s dinner, I got fired up. It was also apparent to me that the whole thing was untenable, that sooner rather than later his colleagues would rebel. I sent an email to Henry suggesting another venture. He responded positively, asking me to provide a structure for the book, and so on. I began to make notes, storing accounts of conversations, just in case, but then I went stone cold. The thought of all the work was daunting.

However, when dear Henry emailed me after the coup to say how bout it, I took a couple of days to think about it. One of the first people I called was the then editor-in-chief of *The Australian*, Chris Mitchell. Mitchell did not hesitate to say he would support me, so I thank him for that and for standing by me. For their backing and guidance, I also thank the former editor, Clive Mathieson, my first op-ed editor, Rebecca Weisser, and then Matthew Spencer, and also Nick Cater, who, as editor of *The Weekend Australian*, was critical to my rehabilitation as a columnist after the publication of *So Greek*. All the crews at Sky and the ABC, in front of camera or behind it, deserve a special mention for their professionalism, hard work, and good humor.

I thank my dear husband Vincent for his help — emotional, physical, logistical — with all my ventures. I am blessed to have such a wonderful, supportive family in my brother, Steve; his wife, Dana; my nephews, Andrew and Peter; and their partners, Laura and Maria. Hugs and kisses either volunteered or provided on request from the twins, Thomas and Christian, have been invaluable. Without all of them, I would be nowhere.

Elpiniki's frequent pleas to God to take her were eventually heeded, although when it happened in August 2013, she wasn't all that happy about it. Needless to say, nor were we. She was exceptional. The life lessons that my mother, my father, Andreas, and my sister, Christina, taught me guide me every day. I only wish I was a more devout follower of them.

Elpiniki's ill-health over a couple of years, then her death, plus a combination of work commitments meant that a few other things got neglected. The last time I presented home-made muesli muffins to my young friend Jack Kunkel, he said he was unable to tell me if they were still his favourite school treat because it had been so long since he had tasted them, he had forgotten what they were like. That hurt, and that was a long time ago, too.

Once again, I thank my friends for their forbearance, their encouragement, and other things, too. Laurie Oakes has been a rock for me for more than forty years. Likewise Elissa, who hates being mentioned, but there you go. Pushing me along was another friend, Sue O'Leary, who also took pity on me when I told her I wasn't able to make my traditional Christmas cakes because of deadline pressures. Sue, an excellent cook as well as an acute observer of politics, made me one of her own that her husband Tony hand-delivered.

The Pages, Hunters, and Maillers remain great friends, excellent company, and wonderful sources of advice and support, as do Lajla and Beat Sidhu. Laura Grande had an altercation with a car. For a while it looked like she had come off second best; however, her recovery has been both remarkable and very welcome.

Madeline, Julie, and Jess at my local café, Beess, provided a welcome refuge as well as good coffee, while Matt Peacock again assisted superbly with the technical expertise necessary for someone raised on typewriters to write a book on a computer. I am in awe of people who wrote volumes by hand pre-internet.

Above all, I thank the many, many people who agreed to speak to me, on or off the record, for this book, as well as for my weekly columns for *The Australian*, which enabled me to record early on the fatal flaws that eventually brought down Tony Abbott and Peta Credlin. Many of them were too frightened to speak out publicly, but they were, almost from the beginning, deeply troubled by what was happening. I was happy to be their voice. They had a lot more to lose than I did. I also hoped that by making things public, it would force change. It never happened.

Finally, my gratitude to Henry Rosenbloom, and thanks to all at Scribe for their faith in me and for their altogether marvellous work.